ASSESSMENT ACCOMMODATIONS FOR DIVERSE LEARNERS

DAVID S. GOH

*Queens College of the
City University of New York*

PEARSON

Boston ■ New York ■ San Francisco
Mexico City ■ Montreal ■ Toronto ■ London ■ Madrid ■ Munich
Paris ■ Hong Kong ■ Singapore ■ Tokyo ■ Cape Town ■ Sydney

Executive Editor: *Virginia Lanigan*
Editorial Assistant: *Robert Champagne*
Executive Marketing Manager: *Amy Cronin Jordan*
Editorial-Production Service: *Omegatype Typography, Inc.*
Manufacturing Buyer: *Andrew Turso*
Composition and Prepress Buyer: *Linda Cox*
Cover Administrator: *Kristina Mose-Libon*
Electronic Composition: *Omegatype Typography, Inc.*

For related titles and support materials, visit our online catalog at www.ablongman.com.

Between the time Website information is gathered and then published, some sites may have closed. Also, the transcription of URLs can result in typographical errors. The publisher would appreciate notification where these occur so that they may be corrected in subsequent editions.

Library of Congress Cataloging-in-Publication Data

Goh, David S.
    Assessment accommodations for diverse learners / David S. Goh.
      p. cm.
    Includes bibliographical references (p.) and index.
    ISBN 0-205-33529-2 (alk. paper)
    1. Educational tests and measurements. 2. Learning disabled children—Ability testing. 3. Children of minorities—Ability testing. 4. Linguistic minorities—Ability testing. I. Title.
LB3051.G347 2004
371.26—dc21

2003050295

Printed in the United States of America

10 9 8 7 6 5 4 3 2 1   08 07 06 05 04 03

CONTENTS

Preface   vii

CHAPTER ONE

An Introduction to Contemporary School Testing and Assessment   1

TESTING AND ASSESSMENT   2

USES OF TESTS IN EDUCATION   3

CONTEMPORARY DEVELOPMENTS AFFECTING
ASSESSMENT IN EDUCATION   5

INCLUDING DIVERSE LEARNERS IN
LARGE-SCALE ASSESSMENT   12

RECENT TRENDS IN SCHOOL ASSESSMENT   13

SUMMARY   17

CHAPTER TWO

Diverse Learners, Standardized Tests, and Testing Accommodations   19

DIVERSE LEARNERS DEFINED   19

GENERAL REQUIREMENTS OF ASSESSMENT   23

CHARACTERISTICS OF STANDARDIZED TESTS   24

TYPES OF STANDARDIZED TESTS   25

USING TESTING ACCOMMODATIONS
FOR DIVERSE LEARNERS   27

LEGAL BASES FOR TESTING ACCOMMODATIONS   30

SUMMARY   34

CHAPTER THREE

Professional Uses of Testing Accommodations   37

PURPOSE OF USING ACCOMMODATIONS IN TESTING   37

BASIC CONSIDERATIONS IN USING
TESTING ACCOMMODATIONS   39

TYPES OF TESTING ACCOMMODATIONS   40

SELECTING TESTING ACCOMMODATIONS   44

REQUESTING AND GRANTING ACCOMMODATIONS   46

INTERPRETING RESULTS FROM ACCOMMODATED TESTING   49

REPORTING ASSESSMENT DATA FROM DIVERSE LEARNERS   51

RESEARCH ON THE USE OF TESTING ACCOMMODATIONS
IN VARIOUS SCHOOL ASSESSMENTS   52

SUMMARY   59

CHAPTER FOUR

**Psychometric Issues in the Use
of Testing Accommodations   61**

TESTING ACCOMMODATIONS AND PSYCHOMETRIC
SOUNDNESS   61

STANDARDIZATION   62

RELIABILITY   63

VALIDITY   64

TYPES OF VALIDITY EVIDENCE   65

EFFECTS OF ACCOMMODATIONS ON RELIABILITY
AND VALIDITY   69

EFFECTS OF ACCOMMODATIONS ON TEST PERFORMANCE   71

FLAGGING OF SCORES ON ACCOMMODATED TESTS   78

SUMMARY   79

CHAPTER FIVE

Using Accommodations for Students with Sensory and/or Physical Disabilities *by Laura Menikoff*   **81**

BLIND AND VISUAL IMPAIRMENT   **81**

DEAF AND HARD OF HEARING   **86**

PHYSICAL DISABILITIES   **89**

EMPIRICAL RESEARCH ON THE EFFECTS OF TESTING ACCOMMODATIONS   **93**

SOME CONCLUDING REMARKS AND RECOMMENDATIONS   **94**

SUMMARY   **95**

CHAPTER SIX

Using Accommodations for Students with Learning, Cognitive, and Behavioral Disabilities *by Laura Menikoff*   **97**

LEARNING DISABILITIES   **98**

MENTAL RETARDATION   **102**

ATTENTION-DEFICIT/HYPERACTIVITY DISORDER   **105**

BEHAVIORAL AND EMOTIONAL DISTURBANCE   **109**

EMPIRICAL RESEARCH ON THE EFFECTS OF TESTING ACCOMMODATIONS   **112**

SOME CONCLUDING REMARKS AND RECOMMENDATIONS   **115**

SUMMARY   **116**

CHAPTER SEVEN

Using Accommodations for English Language Learners   **119**

ELLS IN THE PUBLIC SCHOOLS   **119**

NEED FOR TESTING ACCOMMODATIONS FOR ELLS   **122**

STEPS IN ASSESSING ELLS WITH ACCOMMODATIONS   124

ASSESSING ENGLISH LANGUAGE PROFICIENCY   125

EXEMPTING OR DEFERRING ELLS FROM TESTING   127

MODIFYING STANDARD TEST ADMINISTRATION   128

USING TRANSLATED OR ADAPTED TESTS   132

USING BILINGUAL INTERPRETERS IN TESTING   135

COMMON GUIDELINES ARE NEEDED FOR PROVIDING
ACCOMMODATIONS TO ELLS   137

SOME CONCLUDING REMARKS AND RECOMMENDATIONS   139

SUMMARY   140

CHAPTER EIGHT

Alternative Assessment   143

WHAT IS ALTERNATIVE ASSESSMENT?   143

ALTERNATIVE ASSESSMENT AND DIVERSE LEARNERS   146

TYPES OF ALTERNATIVE ASSESSMENT   147

SPECIFIC ALTERNATIVE ASSESSMENT STRATEGIES   151

SCORING AND INTERPRETATION   156

TECHNICAL CONSIDERATIONS   158

MERITS AND LIMITATIONS   160

SUMMARY   162

References   165

Index   179

PREFACE

The recent years have witnessed an increasing use of accommodations in school assessment, especially in large-scale achievement testing. An examination of the professional literature reveals that most research on assessment accommodations is on students with disabilities, while a relatively small amount of research is devoted to English language learning students, or English language learners (ELLs). This book is intended to present a systematic discussion of the use of assessment accommodations with these two broad types of students—students with disabilities and ELLs. Together, these students are referred to as diverse learners in this book. The reason that students with disabilities and ELLs are addressed in the same volume is that many issues involving the use of assessment accommodations are common to both types of students. This can be seen from the organization of the chapters.

The eight chapters in the book can be generally organized into two parts. Chapters 1 through 4, are entitled "An Introduction to Contemporary School Testing and Assessment," "Diverse Learners, Standardized Testing, and Testing Accommodations," "Professional Uses of Testing Accommodations," and "Psychometric Issues in the Use of Testing Accommodations," respectively. The knowledge contained in these four chapters is important in assessing both students with disabilities and ELLs and is essential to understanding the second half of the book, which focuses on applications of testing accommodations to specific groups of students. Chapters 5 through 7 discuss the use of testing accommodations for "students with sensory and/or physical disabilities," "students with learning, cognitive, and behavioral disabilities," and "English language learners," respectively. Finally, Chapter 8 covers the use of alternative assessment for diverse learners.

The book has been written with several major considerations in mind. First, reasonable use of testing accommodations is an issue not only in large-scale standardized testing but also in individual standardized testing as well as classroom testing. Therefore, attempts are made throughout this book to discuss accommodations applicable to various school testing and assessment situations. Second, most current discussion on the use of testing accommodations has focused primarily on achievement tests. The present book expands this focus to include other tests as well, such as measures of cognitive abilities, language, or other skills. The third consideration is to maintain a balanced discussion between the practical and research aspects of assessment accommodations. To this end, a review of the empirical research on the use of assessment accommodations as well as the effects of accommodations on test properties and test performance are included in several relevant chapters. It is hoped that the book will serve as a useful guide to the proper use of assessment accommodations in all school settings for a variety of purposes.

This book is suitable for use by students in upper-undergraduate- and graduate-level assessment courses focusing on the evaluation of students with various types of school-related disabilities or of students with limited use of English. The book can also serve as a resource reference on the use of assessment accommodations for all school professionals who are involved in testing and assessment, including general and special educators, bilingual educators, administrators, psychologists, counselors, speech pathologists, and social workers.

ACKNOWLEDGMENTS

I would like to acknowledge the contribution of Chapters 5 and 6 by Dr. Laura Menikoff of the New York City Board of Education and Queens College of the City University of New York. I would like to thank Virginia Lanigan and staff at Allyn & Bacon for their assistance and support. I would also like to thank the reviewers of this book: Robbie Ludy, Buena Vista University; Craig Rice, Providence College; and Judy A. Smith, California State University, Fullerton.

David S. Goh

CHAPTER ONE

AN INTRODUCTION TO CONTEMPORARY SCHOOL TESTING AND ASSESSMENT

The use of tests is a long-standing practice in education. The modern history of testing can be traced back to the beginning of the twentieth century when Alfred Binet designed the first test of intelligence to identify children with mental retardation for special education. At about the same time, E. L. Thorndike also began to develop standardized achievement tests to measure student academic performance. Over the past one hundred years, the practice of testing in schools has expanded considerably in its focus, scope, and applications. Numerous tests are now available to measure a great variety of attributes and behaviors of students. Tests today are used widely not only with the general mainstream population but also with a diversity of nontraditional populations including students with disabilities and English language learners whose native language is not English. Standardized tests and teacher-made classroom tests are administered to millions of students each year. Tests play an important role in the education of all students. It is not uncommon for a student to be administered various achievement, aptitude, vocational, or psychological tests during the course of his or her school career. Indeed, testing has become an important part of the education process.

This book deals with a significant aspect of testing—the use of accommodations and other alternative procedures in assessing students in the educational setting. It covers when, how, and to whom these procedures should be given in educational testing and assessment. The book addresses two specific populations: students with disabilities and English language learning students, or English language learners (ELLs; see Chapter 2 for a definition of ELLs). We will provide a systematic discussion on the professional use of testing accommodations and other alternative procedures in assessing

1

these students as well as the many issues related to this practice. In this chapter of introduction, we provide the readers with some basic knowledge about the use of tests and assessments in contemporary education. The topics covered here include testing and assessment, uses of tests in education, contemporary developments affecting assessment in education, including diverse learners in large-scale assessment, and recent trends in school assessment.

TESTING AND ASSESSMENT

The terms *testing* and *assessment* are frequently seen in modern education literature and are sometimes used interchangeably. Many people often think that *assessment* is simply a more fashionable term for *testing* and mistakenly assume that assessing a student's performance means giving the student a test. However, these terms are not synonymous. Although both refer to gathering data for evaluation purposes, testing and assessment represent two different notions.

Testing implies the administration of a test in order to obtain a score to describe a person's attribute or behavior. A test is a set of uniform stimuli (e.g., items, tasks, questions) that aims to measure a specified construct (e.g., aptitude, achievement). Most tests used in the schools for measuring academic performance are paper-and-pencil instruments. Test scores on these tests are used to draw inferences about a student's achievement in nontesting, real-life situations. For example, if a fifth-grade student scores high on a reading test, we would infer that he or she has good reading ability for his or her grade placement.

Assessment, on the other hand, is a broader term that covers a variety of techniques used to gather information. It is viewed as a process of collecting a multitude of data to make decisions about a student. The data collection procedures can be formal or informal, and the information gathered can be quantitative or nonquantitative in nature. Under this broad definition, testing, as a formal data collection procedure, is a part of the assessment process. Other commonly used assessment procedures include review of school records, observations, interviews, and evaluation of work samples or task performance. The variety of procedures is necessary in assessing student performance, because many worthwhile learning outcomes are not best measured by traditional paper-and-pencil tests (Popham, 1999).

Testing and assessment also differ in the way that their results are used. Test scores alone are seldom sufficient for arriving at important decisions about students. On the other hand, assessment includes the process of integrating results from various procedures to provide a basis for making important instructional, curriculum, or placement decisions about students. The *Standards for Educational and Psychological Testing* (AERA, APA, & NCME, 1999) refer to assessment as a process that integrates test information and information from other sources in making decisions about a person. Depending on the purpose of evaluation or the type of decisions to be made about a student, different formal or informal procedures may be used to gather the necessary assessment data.

USES OF TESTS IN EDUCATION

Tests are used for a variety of purposes in educational settings. In the classroom situation, teacher-made tests are primarily tools for student evaluation. In other situations, standardized tests monitor student progress, diagnose student academic or behavioral problems, evaluate instructional effectiveness, and so forth. In all situations, it is best to use test scores in conjunction with other assessment data in making important educational decisions, such as the six major types of decisions that follow.

Evaluation Decisions

Tests are widely used to evaluate student performance in areas of educational and psychological functioning. Some tests are designed to measure academic knowledge and skills, whereas others measure aptitude, intelligence, or personality attributes. Teachers use tests to determine whether students have acquired the expected learning outcomes or are making satisfactory progress. Teachers also use tests regularly to assign grades to students. Other school professionals (e.g., counselors, psychologists) use standardized tests to determine students' functioning levels as well as strengths and weaknesses in various cognitive and noncognitive (e.g., interests, self-concept, adaptive behaviors, etc.) domains. Such test results are usually maintained in school files to monitor students' progress throughout the span of their educational careers.

Classification or Placement Decisions

For effective instruction, students sometimes are grouped into different instructional levels or programs in which they are most likely to succeed. These decisions are usually made with the aid of test results. For example, achievement test scores can be used to place individual students in particular programs (e.g., remedial reading) or course sequences (e.g., beginning, intermediate, advanced) that best suit their needs. Classification or placement decisions are made by school administrators, psychologists, counselors, or committees, rather than by individual teachers (Worthen, White, Fan, & Sudweeks, 1999).

Instructional or Interventional Decisions

Teachers and other school professionals often utilize tests to collect information to plan for instruction or intervention. For example, teachers use results from classroom tests to determine the effectiveness of their students' learning. They also use test results to decide when to begin the next instructional steps or whether instructional changes are warranted, and if so what changes should be made to enhance student learning. Similarly, psychologists employ tests to identify students who are exhibiting specific learning or behavior difficulties. Once the problems are identified, test results and other assessment data can help them design and implement interventions specific to individual students.

Diagnostic Decisions

Programs in most schools address a wide range of functioning levels of students. For diagnostic purpose, tests and other assessment data are used together to determine whether a student has a special talent, disability, or other special need, in light of established diagnostic criteria. Furthermore, test results can assist in determining the nature and extent of a student's special ability or disability, as well as how the particular condition might affect the student's functioning. Subsequently, this information is utilized to determine whether the student is eligible for special services. When a student is diagnosed to have a specific disability, the assessment data are also used to develop the Individual Educational Program (IEP) for the student as part of the special services he or she receives. A child study team or committee makes the diagnostic decisions.

Program Evaluation Decisions

In addition to evaluating individual students, tests can be used to monitor the outcome of school programs and make decisions regarding how well a school program is succeeding. Test results may also be utilized to indicate how students in a given class, school, or school district perform in relation to other students who take the same test at the local, state, or national level. Such program evaluation data help in determining the merit of particular programs or schools and enable policy makers to make sound decisions on curriculum matters, funding allocations, and so on. (Gardner, 1991).

Selection and Certification Decisions

Selection and certification are uses of tests to classify students into different categories (e.g., accept or nonaccept, certified or noncertified). Standardized test results constitute a major source of data for making both types of decisions. Selection involves obtaining entry into a program or institute. For example, SAT scores are one type of data that is considered by college admissions officials in accepting students into colleges. In an employment setting, psychological tests are sometimes used to help select applicants for job positions. Certification implies classifying persons on a pass or fail basis, in terms of meeting or failing to meet acceptable minimum competence required for credentialing decisions (e.g., grade promotion, graduation, the practice of a profession). For example, standardized achievement tests are used to certify a student's acquisition of knowledge or competence for high school graduation. Teacher certification examinations are used to certify qualified persons to teach. Both selection and certification uses of tests imply that test results help in predicting future success in some programs or activities.

CONTEMPORARY DEVELOPMENTS AFFECTING ASSESSMENT IN EDUCATION

An ongoing movement of educational reform since the 1980s has as its primary goal the improvement of the public education system to enhance student academic performance. This movement aims to impact the education of all students including students with disabilities and English language learners (ELLs). In this section, we will discuss two developments that have affected the use of tests and assessments in education: standards-based education reform and inclusive education reform.

Standards-Based Education Reform

Standards-based education reform refers to efforts to improve overall educational quality by setting high academic achievement standards and then holding educators and students accountable for meeting those standards (Schulte, Villwock, Wichard, and Stallings, 2001). By the early 1980s, studies indicated that students in the United States were lagging behind their counterparts in other countries with respect to academic achievement and that

U.S. students lacked sufficient skills to enter the workforce (Geisinger, 1992; Keith, Reimers, Fehrmann, Pottebaum, & Aubey, 1986; Steinberg, 1987; Stevenson, Lee, & Stigler, 1986; Stigler, Lee, Lucker, & Stevenson, 1982). The publication of *A Nation at Risk: The Imperative for Educational Reform* in the early 1980s (National Commission on Excellence in Education, 1983) issued a warning about the weakening of the U.S. education system at that time and addressed the need to restructure the nation's schools (Tirozzi & Uro, 1997). *A Nation at Risk* challenged public schools by recommending increased learning time, strengthened graduation requirements, and higher standards. Since then a number of reform efforts have been adopted in public education. These include raising academic standards and expectations, emphasis on educational accountability, increased use of testing and outcomes assessment, incentives for improved performance, and innovations in teacher training. (Kubiszyn & Borick, 2003).

In 1989, six national education goals were developed, which focused on implementing high academic standards among all students in the United States. In 1994, Congress passed the Goals 2000: Educate America Act, providing a framework for educational reform consistent with the national education goals. Inherent in this Act were the establishment of high academic standards and the active involvement of parents, educators, and communities in accomplishing the national goals. Also, the 1994 Improving America's Schools Act requires states to develop standards in core academic subject areas. Conseqently, all fifty states have developed challenging standards, commonly known as content standards and performance standards. Content standards specify what the students should know and be able to do in specific subject areas. Performance standards describe the performance students must achieve at various levels of proficiency. These academic standards set expectations of students and are used to inform instruction and assessment.

Educational Accountability

An important component of standards-based education reform is educational accountability. With the raising of standards and expectations comes increased concern about the accountability of student achievement toward these expectations. Accountability has always been valued and considered as necessary in public education. However, the focus of educational accountability in the past had been on the process of achieving educational goals and objectives. In the recent educational reform movement, this focus has shifted to the outcomes of school instruction. Federal legislations require each state to implement a system of accountability for schools and districts to ensure all students are meeting challenging state academic standards. Schools must demonstrate that they are meeting the high standards and document their progress through student performance on state assessments. In addition, consequences are often attached to student performance expectations at both policy and practice levels in the accountability system (Erikson, Ysseldyke, Thurlow, & Elliott, 1998). It is believed that people accomplish more when goals are clarified and the consequences of their performance are understood (Lashway, 1999).

An effective educational accountability system should contain certain essential elements. For example, five such elements are identified in a model accountability system (Southern Regional Education Board, 1998). (1) Rigorous content standards must be established so teachers and students know where to focus their attention. (2) Student performance must be measured to provide concrete evidence of student progress. (3) Professional development needs to be aligned with the standards to help schools develop the capacity to meet the expectations. (4) Results should be publicly reported to put pressure on individual schools to meet the standards. (5) Results should be linked to rewards, sanctions, and targeted assistance. Most states have developed accountability systems that contain some, if not all, of these elements. A number of states have included rewards and sanctions as a part of their accountability systems that are directed toward individual students, schools, and school districts (Erickson et al., 1998; Olsen, 1999). The goal is to build schools that can effectively produce high educational outcomes.

High-stakes Testing

In standards-based reform, testing and assessment are used to collect data on student progress and document educational accountability. To meet the demands of accountability, states have instituted mandatory large-scale testing programs to measure student achievement. These are called standards-based assessments and are developed using content standards (which specify what the students should know and be able to do) created by the states as a basis. They usually measure student knowledge and skills in various core subject areas. A common test is administered at specified intervals, such as fourth, eighth, and eleventh grades (Rivera, Vincent, Hafner, & LaCelle-Peterson, 1997; Shaul, 1999). Most states use group-administered standardized measures in their testing programs. Several states use portfolios, performance tasks, and other forms of educational assessment.

Several reasons exist for using mandatory large-scale testing programs. One reason is the belief that such testing is necessary to improve student performance and ensure that students are making progress toward meeting the standards. Another reason is that large-scale testing will provide data for states and school districts to monitor the advancement of schools and determine a school's position compared to other schools (Tirozzi & Uro, 1997). In addition, these testing data can be used to evaluate school programs designed to facilitate instructional improvement for various student groups (Chase, 1999).

Certain uses of large-scale achievement test scores are called "high stakes" if they carry important educational, financial, or social consequences for students or schools (AERA, 2000). Results from high-stakes tests are used to make crucial educational decisions for students, such as grade promotion, retention, high school graduation, or selection for special programs or services. Results from high-stakes tests can also lead to major consequences for schools. For example, high school–wide scores may bring financial rewards or other incentives to a school or school staff, or low scores may result in a school being taken over by state educational agencies (Erickson et al., 1998).

Policy makers first produced high-stakes tests as a means of targeting children at risk of school failure and identifying students with special needs. Eventually, high-stakes assessments were used to create annual profiles of school accountability and to increase the overall educational attainment of all students (Tapper, 1997). Currently, high-stakes testing is viewed as an efficient way of ensuring the effectiveness of school systems. Legislative and political support is strong for accountability and high-stakes testing and will remain so for the foreseeable future (Braden, 2002).

Implications for Diverse Learners

The movement of standards-based reform has direct implications for diverse learners, including students with disabilities and ELLs. Goals 2000 demonstrates a commitment to equity and excellence by setting high academic standards for all students (Salvia & Ysseldyke, 1995). Students with disabilities and ELLs are to be held accountable to the high standards and expectations. In the meantime, the performances of these students are to be measured along with that of their mainstream peers (Hanley, 1995).

For diverse learners to benefit from standards-based reform, they should be included in the development of the standards and provided with high-quality instruction to achieve challenging expectations. In addition, performances of these students should be assessed by reliable, valid, and fair procedures. However, some concerns exist about how standards-based reform is implemented for students with disabilities and ELLs. One concern is that often diverse learners are not considered in developing state and district standards. Therefore, some standards may not apply to students with disabilities or ELLs. States and districts need to modify or expand these standards to make them more appropriate for these diverse students. Another concern is that standards are intended to be the lynchpin in reform efforts, aligning curriculum, instruction, and assessment. That is, standards should be used to guide curriculum and instruction and serve as a foundation on which assessment is based. Unfortunately, these elements often remain disconnected from one another, which negatively impacts the education of all students (Braden, 2002; Lagurada, Breckenridge, Hightower, & Adelman, 1994; Menken, 2000). This is particularly a problem for students with disabilities and ELLs. For example, given the discontinuity frequently observed between special education and general education (Reschly & Ysseldyke, 1995), it is questionable whether students with disabilities have adequate access to general curriculum to meet general education standards and expectations. Similarly, although common high standards are set for all students, it cannot be assumed that curricular changes that contribute to the success of mainstream students will also work for ELLs (Rivera & LaCelle-Paterson, 1993). Special considerations must be given to the particular needs and strengths of these students in developing curriculum materials and instructional practices that will help them achieve high academic standards.

A related concern involves the issues of quality of education and opportunity to learn that are available to diverse learners. If high-quality instruction is not used for students with disabilities or ELLs, or if these students are not given the opportunity to learn the curricular material, then it would be inappropriate to hold them accountable for meeting the high standards. Often educators and parents are concerned that ELLs are being held accountable for high standards, but the accountability demand has not been supported by adequate resources in the schools they attend. For example, many urban schools that enroll large numbers of ELLs often have less qualified teachers and limited materials, equipment, laboratories, and other physical resources. Also, students in these schools are less likely to be included in rigorous courses that are geared to high standards. Under such situations, it would be difficult to hold these students accountable for the same high standards set forth for mainstream students (National Urban League, 1999; O'Malley & Valdez-Pierce, 1994). Thus, challenging academic standards must be supported by high-quality instruction and opportunity to learn for students with disabilities and ELLs. If high standards are implemented without adequate support, the results could be punitive and nonachievable for diverse learners.

Finally, there is a concern about using standardized large-scale tests to make high-stakes decisions. Many believe that a single objective test provides only a limited sample of knowledge and skills that is not comprehensive enough to base important educational decisions on (Darling-Hammond, 2002; National Council of Teachers of Mathematics, 2001; Smith & Frey, 2000). Also, overreliance on such test scores for making high-stakes decisions may lead to an obsession on test preparation and, thereby, a narrowing of curriculum taught to the students. More class time is spent on test preparation and less time is devoted to other curriculum materials and improving learning (Jorgenson & Vanosdall, 2002; Orfield & Ward, 2000). In the meantime, more traditional forms of teaching are used, focusing on drill and practice and rote memorization (Passman, 2001). This presents a particular problem for students with disabilities and ELLs who need more valuable learning time. Furthermore, in many cases large-scale tests administered in the standard fashion do not provide an equitable assessment of the knowledge and skills of students with disabilities and ELLs. Often these students are unable to demonstrate what they know and can do, due to the disabilities or language barriers that they have. When used inappropriately, high-stakes tests could produce unreliable and invalid results and yield negative consequences for these students (AERA, 2000; Darling-Hammond, 1994b; Schrag, 2000; Tapper, 1997; Wilson & Dickson, 1991). Thurlow and Johnson (2002) contend that as a result of high-stakes testing, the number of students with disabilities may increase due to more referrals to special education. Similarly, more ELLs may be placed in low-track classes because of their low scores on high-stakes tests. To avoid these negative consequences, innovative assessments are needed to provide students with disabilities and ELLs a fair opportunity to demonstrate their knowledge and skills. These may include the use of testing accommodations and, if necessary, other alternative assessment procedures. Federal and state laws now mandate that testing accomodations and alternate assessment be used whenever necessary in testing students with disabilities and ELLs to facilitate equitable and valid assessment.

Inclusive Education Reform

Inclusive education, a movement that calls for reform in special education delivery, has gained considerable momentum since the early 1990s. The concept of inclusive education can be traced back to the Education for All Handicapped Children Act of 1975, which mandated that all students must be served in the least restrictive environment. Hence, special education service delivery within the general education classroom has become more prevalent. The Individuals with Disabilities Education Act (IDEA) of 1990 and the Amendments to IDEA of 1997 further emphasize the need to serve students with disabilities in the general education setting whenever possible. The idea of placing students with disabilities in general education environments with their peers without disabilities has become known as inclusion. According to the Association of Learning Disabilities (1993), inclusion is defined as the instruction of all students, with and without disabilities, in the general education classroom, unless substantial evidence is provided to show that such a placement would not be in a student's best interests. Thurlow, Ysseldyke, and Silverstein (1993) state that under inclusion, students with disabilities are served whenever possible in general education classrooms in inclusive neighborhood schools and community settings. In an inclusive school, a unified system allows all students to receive the necessary educational services that they require without being labeled and without being removed from the general education classroom (Malarz, 1996).

The inclusive education movement has led to increased participation of students with disabilities in general education settings and in the general education curriculum. According to data from the U.S. Department of Education, in 1996 more than 45 percent of students with disabilities ages 6 to 21 in public schools were educated in general education classrooms. This was a 20 percent increase from 25 percent of special education students educated in general education in 1986. Conversely, the percentage of students with disabilities served in resource rooms and other special education settings decreased during the same period (U.S. Department of Education, 1999b). These trends have been continuing. In many states, a majority of students with disabilities spend some or all of their time in general education settings. These students vary in age and disability groupings. Schools must now address the special needs of these students in the general education classroom.

Inclusion of students with disabilities in general education settings has many advantages. It allows the alignment of special education programs and general education curriculum, raises the expectations of student performance, provides opportunities for students with disabilities to learn and be assessed alongside their typical peers without disabilities, and increases school-level accountability for educational results (U.S. Department of Education, 1999b). However, including students with disabilities in general education settings also presents significant challenges to students with disabilities as well as teachers who teach them in the general education classroom. For students with disabilities, achieving success in the general education classroom is a challenge itself, which becomes even more arduous when they are held responsible for the same high standards set for their peers without disabilities. Considering their disabilities, it is imperative that instructional and curriculum modifications be made to assist these students to achieve effectively. Similarly, accommodations should be provided whenever necessary for students with disabilities in both classroom testing and large-scale assessment to evaluate and monitor their progress.

It is obvious that inclusive education cannot be appropriately implemented without proper supports and services. Efforts must be made to assemble and reorganize the appropriate staff and resources within the schools to deliver more inclusive, coordinated services for all students (Will, 1986). A key issue is the training that general education teachers have and the support that they receive in teaching students with disabilities within their class-rooms. Many general education teachers believe they do not possess the training to teach these students within their classes (Werts, Wolery, Snyder, Caldwell, & Salisbury, 1996). General education teachers also cannot be expected to teach students with disabilities effectively without the necessary supports from special educators and other personnel. Proper training and supports should be provided to general education teachers as well as others (e.g., special education teachers, paraprofessionals) who work with students with disabilities in the general education classroom. For example, general education teachers need to be trained and encouraged to modify lessons, teaching strategies, and tests to meet the special needs of students with dis-abilities. Likewise, other school professionals (e.g., special educators, school psychologists, speech therapists) should be trained with competence in using accommodations and other alternative procedures in assessing achievement and progress of students with disabilities.

INCLUDING DIVERSE LEARNERS IN LARGE-SCALE ASSESSMENT

An issue surrounding mandated state or district-wide large-scale testing is the educational representation of students with disabilities and ELLs. In the past, many students with disabilities and ELLs have been exempted from large-scale testing programs. Due to the low scores often received by diverse learners on standardized tests, school districts feared that including scores of students with disabilities and ELLs would lower the average scores of the schools. Also, educators and parents were not aware of the various testing accommodations, modifications, and adaptations that can and should be used with these students. As a result, until recent years there had been a lack of large-scale assessment data on these students for accountability purposes (Erickson et al., 1998; Lam, 1993).

Federal and state laws now mandate the inclusion of all students in state or district-wide assessments, via either standardized testing or alterna-tive methods of evaluation. The Amendments to the Individuals with Dis-abilities Education Act (IDEA) of 1997 require that students with disabilities must be included in state assessment and that accommodations or alternative assessment be used when necessary (Heubert & Hauser, 1999). They also require that the achievement of students with disabilities be reported in the same way and with the same regularity as students without disabilities. Similarly, the No Child Left Behind Act of 2001 requires that students whose native language is not English be assessed in a manner that produces the most valid results. The Act also calls for states to include ELLs along with other students in state testing programs and to report results separately. The rationale for these legislative mandates is that a biased picture of local, state, or national performance may be presented if students with disabilities or ELLs are not included in state or district-wide assessment. Including all students in testing will present a more accurate picture of the performance of the entire student population (Erickson et al., 1998; Kleinert, Kennedy, & Kearns, 1999). In addition, such data will benefit students with disabilities and ELLs by providing the schools with a means of determining what types of services these students may need.

Subsequently, states and school districts have attempted to develop and apply assessments that will accommodate all students, as well as to seek out ways to provide an account of the results of these assessments. Accurate measurement of the knowledge and skills of students with disabilities or ELLs is essential if the resultant data are to be meaningfully included in the accountability systems. Unfortunately, there is presently a lack of national uniform guidelines in including diverse learners in large-scale assessments and in reporting their assessment results. (See Chapter 3 for further discussion of this topic.)

RECENT TRENDS IN SCHOOL ASSESSMENT

As mentioned earlier, tests are a major source of information for making various important educational decisions. In the recent standards-based assessment, tests are also widely used as a tool in measuring student achievement. Most tests used in national, state, and district-wide mandatory assessment programs are standardized tests. However, standardized tests are not without shortcomings and they are useful only within limits (Gredler, 1999). Over the years, a number of trends have evolved in school assessment to counteract the limitations of standardized tests and to improve the data gathering process, in order to produce more reliable, valid, and useful results. These trends apply to not only large-scale assessment but also classroom testing and individual assessment of students for more specialized purposes (e.g., diagnosis, intervention). Five major trends are described next: (1) using multiple approaches and measures, (2) reducing bias in tests and assessments, (3) using accommodations in testing diverse learners, (4) emphasizing assessment of performance, and (5) linking assessment to intervention.

Using Multiple Approaches and Measures

There is a general consensus that educational decisions about students should be made based on concrete data from high-quality assessments with good reliability and validity. Further, educators also agree that such decisions should not be made by relying on only a single measure or test score. Despite the wide use of standardized tests in education, test scores should not be used exclusively as the only data source to draw inferences about students. For example, scores from state or district-wide achievement tests alone should not be used to make decisions involving crucial outcomes. Rather, different up-to-date approaches and measures should be adopted in collecting assessment data. Examples include norm-referenced tests, criterion-referenced tests, multiple-choice tests, writing samples, interviews, naturalistic observations, and behavioral rating scales. The use of this multiple-method approach is supported by current federal legislations (e.g., Amendments to Individuals with Disabilities Education Act of 1997) and professional standards (e.g., *Standards for Educational and Psychological Testing* [AERA, APA, & NCME, 1999]). When tests are used in ways that meet relevant psychometric and professional standards, the information they yield can be combined with other assessment data for making important decisions that are beneficial to students or school programs. Using multiple approaches and measures in school assessment requires professional training and qualification on the part of the school personnel for astute analysis, interpretation, and integration of the assessment data.

Reducing Bias in Tests and Assessments

Standardized tests have long been criticized for their potential bias against ethnic and language minority students (Darling-Hammond, 1994a; Lam, 1993; Supovitz & Brennan, 1997; Worthen, 1993). Differences sometimes exist among ethnic and cultural groups that may affect the kinds of knowledge acquired by students. This is not recognized in standardized tests, which are based primarily on the mainstream culture. As a result, standardized tests provide narrow and often inaccurate portraits of the abilities and achievement of ELLs (Falk, 1994). The use of standardized tests can produce adverse effects on these students. For example, research has shown that ethnic and language minority students are disproportionately represented in special education, remedial, and lower-track classes because of their low scores on standardized tests. This impacts on the learning opportunities that these students receive. For example, students in the lower tracks have limited access to high-quality knowledge, teachers, and resources (Garcia, 1994). There is a clear need to reduce and eliminate bias in tests and other types of assessments. One way to do this is to take into consideration the characteristics of students from diverse backgrounds (e.g., abilities, disabilities, attitudes, strengths, socioeconomic factors) in the construction and norming of tests. Another way is to train qualified test users who can make sound, professional judgments in interpreting test results from ethnic and language minority students.

Using Accommodations in Testing Diverse Learners

Historically, testing accommodations have been used in individual testing to make it possible for individuals with disabilities to take standardized tests. As part of the standards-based assessment, there has been a "renewed" interest in the use of testing accommodations not only for students with disabilities but also for ELLs. This is necessary because many of these students cannot take tests under standard administration due to the effects of their disabilities and language barriers. The purpose of using accommodations is to increase the validity of test results, so that the results may accurately reflect the construct (e.g., aptitude or achievement) measured by the test, rather than the disabilities or language barriers of the students. Nevertheless, using testing accommodations is a far more complex issue than it appears. Currently, the knowledge that is needed to guide best practices in the use of testing accommodation is yet to be fully established. Effective use of accommodations requires a clear understanding of the specific accommodations that are needed by a student with disability or an ELL whose native language is not English, as well as adequate knowledge about the effects of the selected accommodations on test scores. The practice of testing accommodations for diverse learners will continue to improve as more advances are made on the professional, psychometric, and technological aspects of their use. These issues are discussed throughout the latter chapters of the book.

Emphasizing Assessment of Performance

Emphasis on the assessment of performance gained popularity in the 1990s. It is viewed as an alternative to traditional standardized testing. Proponents of this approach believe that it is important to require students to perform actual tasks or carry out activities in the real world as a way of demonstrating what they know and can do (Chase, 1999). Standardized tests, which rely heavily on the multiple-choice format, measure solely facts and simple cognitive skills and do not allow students to demonstrate their knowledge about and competence in actual tasks. Many important aspects of learning that take place in the classroom—such as how students think, what they understand, or the strategies they use in problem solving—are not assessed by standardized tests. Convinced that these limitations are inherent in standardized tests, some educators have emphasized direct assessment of performance as a way of measuring student achievement. Major types of this alternative approach include the so-called performance assessment and portfolio assessment. A variety of techniques (e.g., demonstrations, performance tasks, interviews, observations, ratings, checklists) can be used to assess actual performance or learning outcomes of students. By doing so, these tools have the benefit of evaluating thinking, reasoning, and other higher-order cognitive capabilities, which students need to develop for future success. However, some unresolved technical issues (e.g., reliability, validity) still remain in direct assessment of performance. We will discuss this topic thoroughly in Chapter 8.

Linking Assessment to Intervention

One of the primary purposes of assessment is to obtain information that can be used in designing effective interventions. Although standardized tests can be used to serve many purposes (see earlier section Uses of Tests in Education), they have been considered weak in producing useful information to guide the development of intervention (Engel, 1994; Shavelson, Baxter, & Gao, 1993). Traditionally, standardized tests are known to be valuable for classification, diagnostic, and placement purposes. That is, they show high utility in classifying students into different groups and in determining student eligibility for special programs or services. However, standardized tests until recently have not placed great emphasis on generating test results that can be readily used in developing instructional, remedial, or other interventional programs. To compensate for this limitation, there is presently an emphasis on linking assessment to intervention in school assessment. Major standardized cognitive and achievement tests are seeking ways to link test results to intervention. Assessment approaches that view assessment and intervention as a continuum (e.g., performance assessment, behavioral assessment) are also gaining recognition and popularity. By linking assessment to intervention, teachers may use assessment information to help them in planning and improving students' instructional programs. Similarly, psychologists may use assessment data to assist them in designing interventions that can effectively treat students' learning and behavioral difficulties.

SUMMARY

Educational and psychological testing has become an important part of the education process. Although the terms are sometimes used interchangeably, *testing* and *assessment* are not synonymous. Testing refers to the use of a test to obtain a score to describe a person's attribute or behavior. Assessment is a broader term that covers a variety of procedures used to gather information for decision making.

Tests are used in making different types of decisions about students and schools. These include evaluation decisions, classification or placement decisions, instructional or interventional decisions, diagnostic decisions, program evaluation decisions, and selection and certification decisions.

The standards-based educational reform and the inclusive education reform have impacted on the testing practice in education. Goals 2000 set high standards for all students, including students with disabilities and English language learners (ELLS). The current emphasis on educational accountability focuses on outcomes of school instruction. States are using high-stakes testing as a measure to improve education. The reform in special education service delivery has called for the inclusion of students with special needs in general education classrooms.

The reform movements in general education and special education have direct implications for students with disabilities and ELLs. One concern is the lack of close alignment of standards to curriculum, instruction, and assessment for these diverse learners. Another concern involves the issue of quality of instruction and opportunity to learn that are available to these diverse learners to meet high standards. Still another concern calls into question equity assessment of diverse learners through high-stakes testing.

Finally, five major trends in current school assessment have developed. They are using multiple approaches and measures, reducing bias in tests and assessments, using accommodations in testing diverse learners, emphasizing assessment of performance, and linking assessment to intervention.

CHAPTER TWO

DIVERSE LEARNERS, STANDARDIZED TESTS, AND TESTING ACCOMMODATIONS

As is commonly known, diverse learners are often challenged by their disabilities or different linguistic and cultural backgrounds in taking standardized tests. This chapter covers the basic concepts about diverse learners, standardized tests, and testing accommodations. The purpose is to provide the readers with essential information to form a foundation on which further knowledge can be built about actual uses of testing accommodations, applications, and related issues. The specific topics covered in this chapter are diverse learners defined, general requirements of assessment, characteristics of standardized tests, types of standardized tests, using testing accommodations for diverse learners, and legal bases for testing accommodations.

DIVERSE LEARNERS DEFINED

This book is entitled *Assessment Accommodations for Diverse Learners. Diverse learners* is used as a broad term to include a diversity of students who are eligible to receive accommodations in taking large-scale assessments, individual standardized tests, or teacher-made classroom tests. Specifically, the term is intended to represent two primary student populations: students with disabilities and English language learning students, or English language learners (ELLs). Diverse learners, obviously, also include students with disabilities who are English language learners and ELLs who have disabilities. These subsets of students are included in *students with disabilities* and *ELLs* throughout the discussion in the book. The definitions of these two primary types of diverse learners follow.

Students with Disabilities

As many as one in seven Americans has a physical or mental disability that interferes with activities of daily living (O'Keefe, 1994). Under both Section 504 of the Rehabilitation Act and the Americans with Disabilities Act (ADA) of 1990, a person is considered to be disabled if he or she (1) has a physical or mental impairment that substantially limits one or more life activities (e.g., learning, test taking), (2) has a record of such an impairment, or (3) is regarded as having such an impairment. In further explaining this definition of disability, ADA specifies impairment as any physiological disorder or condition, cosmetic disfigurement, anatomical loss affecting one or more of the body systems, or any mental or psychological disorder. Included in mental impairment are conditions such as mental retardation, organic brain syndrome, emotional or mental illness, specific learning disability, or attention-deficit/hyperactivity disorder (Foote, 2000).

The Individuals with Disabilities Education Act (IDEA) does not give a generic definition of disability. That is, there is no single definition of disability given in the IDEA. Instead it lists thirteen separate categories of disabilities under which students may be eligible for special education and related services because of mental, physical, or emotional reasons. In each disability, the student's condition has adversely affected his or her educational performance. The IDEA categories are generally adopted by all states and incorporated into state laws and practice. Each category represents a special type of physical or mental disability. A student's disability status is determined by a multidisciplinary committee, based on a multidimensional comprehensive assessment. The thirteen categories follow:

- *Autism:* a developmental disability significantly affecting verbal and nonverbal communication and social interaction, generally evident before age 3.
- *Deafness:* a hearing impairment that is so severe that the student is impaired in processing linguistic information through hearing, with or without amplification.
- *Deaf-blindness:* simultaneous hearing and visual impairments.
- *Emotional disturbance:* a disability whereby a student of typical intelligence has difficulty, over time and to a marked degree, building satisfactory interpersonal relationships; responds inappropriately behaviorally or emotionally under normal circumstances; demonstrates a pervasive mood of unhappiness; or has a tendency to develop physical symptoms or fears.
- *Hearing impairment:* an impairment in hearing, whether permanent or fluctuating, that is not included under deafness.

- *Mental retardation:* significant subaverage general intellectual functioning existing concurrently with deficits in adaptive behavior and manifested during the developmental period.
- *Multiple disabilities:* the manifestation of two or more disabilities (e.g., mental retardation-blindness), the combination of which requires special accommodation for maximal learning.
- *Orthopedic impairment:* physical disabilities, including congenital impairments (e.g., club foot), impairments caused by disease (e.g., poliomyelitis), and impairments from other causes (e.g., cerebral palsy).
- *Other health impairment:* having limited strength, vitality, or alertness due to chronic or acute health problems (e.g., asthma, heart condition, attention-deficit/hyperactivity disorder).
- *Specific learning disability:* a disorder in one or more of the basic psychological processes involved in understanding or in using language, spoken or written, which may manifest itself in an imperfect ability to listen, think, speak, read, write, spell, or do mathematical calculations.
- *Speech or language impairment:* a communication disorder such as stuttering, impaired articulation, a language impairment, or a voice impairment.
- *Traumatic brain injury:* an acquired injury to the brain caused by an external physical force or by a certain medical condition (e.g., brain tumor) resulting in total or partial functional disability or psychosocial impairment, or both.
- *Visual impairment:* a visual difficulty (including both partial sight and blindness) that, even with correction, adversely affects a student's educational performance.

English Language Learners

Many terms have been used in describing students whose native language is not English. Some commonly seen terms include *English Language Learner (ELL), Limited English Proficient (LEP) student, English Speaker of Other Languages, Second-language Learner, student of diverse linguistic backgrounds,* among others. Although the federal legal definition refers to students as LEP, the term *ELL* has been used recently because it focuses on potentials and achievement rather then limitation (C. Loop, personal communication, November 20, 2002).

The Improving America's Schools Act of 1994 defined students with limited English proficiency in three alternative ways. The student was not born in the United States or whose native language is a language other than English and comes from an environment in which a language other than English is dominant; or the student is a Native American or Alaskan Native who is a native resident of the outlying areas and comes from an environment in which a language other than English has had a significant impact on the individual's level of English language proficiency; or the student is migratory and whose native language is other than English and comes from an environment in which a language other than English is dominant. In addition, the student has sufficient difficulty speaking, reading, writing, or understanding the English language, and these difficulties may deny such individual the opportunity to learn successfully in classrooms in which the language of instruction is English or to participate fully in our society. Briefly, the definition contains two essential elements: (1) the student's native language is other than English, and (2) the student is having difficulty in an English-only classroom due to his or her limited ability to speak and understand English. If a student meets both criteria, he or she can be considered limited English proficient. The No Child Left Behind Act of 2001 continues to use the term *limited English proficient.* In this legislation, Title III is for Language Instruction for Limited English Proficient and Immigrant Students, and Title VII is for Native Americans including Alaskan and Hawaiian students.

There is no federal mandate as to which term should be used in addressing this student population. However, many school districts and researchers have adopted ELL because it stresses a learning status rather than a limitation. The number of ELLs in the U.S. public school system has grown steadily in the recent past. In the 2000–2001 school year an estimated 4,584,946 ELLs were enrolled in the public schools, representing approximately 9.6 percent of the total school enrollment of prekindergarten through grade 12 (Kindler, 2002).

The term *English language learners* is used in this book in discussing testing accommodations and alternative assessments. ELLs conveys a concept that these students are in the process of learning English and, to varying degrees, may be challenged by language barriers in taking standardized tests. ELLs may range from students who are just beginning to learn English to those who have already developed considerable proficiency (LaCelle-Peterson & Rivera, 1994).

Two particular points should be noted in referring to ELLs as a population. First, unlike in the area of disabilities, no federal mandates have been established to regulate the identification and assessment of students whose native language is not English. As a result, states vary considerably in the terminologies and definitions they use in addressing this student population (Goh, Zupnik, & Mendez, 2001). This indicates that *ELL* as a term does not have a nationally uniform definition. Second, besides sharing a common characteristic that they need to increase their proficiency in English, ELLs are an immensely heterogeneous group. ELLs differ widely in such aspects of their language, ethnicity, cultural background, educational orientation, socio-economic status, family history, values, attitudes, and adjustment style (LaCelle-Peterson & Rivera, 1994). These considerable within-group differences must be recognized and considered in working with ELLs in the schools.

GENERAL REQUIREMENTS OF ASSESSMENT

Determination of a student's status of disability or ELL must be done in an objective and accurate manner by a committee of school professionals involving teachers, administrators, psychologists, speech therapists, social workers, and counselors, depending on the need of the student under consideration (Cohen & Spenciner, 1998). The assessment results from the committee are discussed with the student's parents and consent from the parents is obtained before a final decision is made about the student. The *Federal Registrar* (1992) indicates the following general requirements for assessment of students with disabilities. The principles underlying many of these requirements also apply to ELL students. In general, assessment procedures used for determining disability or ELL status must be reliable, valid, fair, and equitable.

- The test be administered in the student's native language or preferred mode of communication.
- The test be validated for the purpose that is being used.
- The tests be administered by trained personnel in conformance with instructions from the test publisher.
- The assessment yield not merely an intelligence quotient but additional information about the student's educational needs.
- The assessment of students with impaired sensory, manual, or speaking skills be completed with tests that are selected and administered to reflect the student's aptitude and achievement level (or other factor) accurately. The tests should not reflect the student's impaired sensory, manual, or speaking skills.
- No single test be used to determine a student's eligibility for special education services.
- The students be assessed in all areas related to the suspected disability, including, where appropriate, health, vision, hearing, social and emotional status, general intelligence, academic performance, communicative status, and motor abilities.
- The assessment be made by a multidisciplinary team, including at least one member with knowledge in the suspected areas of disability. (*Federal Registrar*, 1992, Sec. 300.532; Cohen & Spenciner, 1998)

CHARACTERISTICS OF STANDARDIZED TESTS

Standardized tests and teacher-made classroom tests are the most widely used tools in school assessment. Cronbach (1984) defines a test as a systematic procedure for observing a person's behavior and describing it with the use of a numerical scale or category system. The *Standards for Educational and Psychological Tests* (AERA, APA, NCME, 1999) define a test as an evaluation device or procedure in which a sample of the examinee's behavior in a specified domain is obtained and subsequently evaluated and scored using a standard process. These definitions indicate several characteristics that are essential to a test. First, a test provides a sample of behavior from which inferences are drawn about a test taker's attributes or performance. Thus, the behavior sampled on a test should be representative of the attributes or performance that the test is designed to measure. On a reading test, for example, we would want to collect a sample of reading behavior that is representative of the test taker's reading ability and performance. Second, a test uses an objective scoring procedure to evaluate and quantify examinee responses. This may be done quantitatively or nonquantitatively. For instance, some test results are scored in numbers (e.g., number of correct items, percentile scores, standard scores), while others are presented in categories (e.g., pass or fail).

Third, a test uses a standard set of procedures for test administration, scoring, and interpretation. That is, the test is administered to all examinees using the same procedure under the same condition. Also, test responses are scored and interpreted using the same criteria. The standard procedures of test administration and scoring enable test users or teachers to compare the test performance of different test takers. Another characteristic of a test is the standard to which a test taker's score is compared. On teacher-made classroom tests, a student's performance is usually compared to the performance of the whole class. On standardized tests, a test taker's performance is compared to that of a standardization sample.

Standardized tests are designed for use with a large population. These tests differ greatly from teacher-made tests and other nonstandardized tests in the ways they are developed and used. A strict and extensive standardization process is followed in standardizing these tests. During the test construction stage, the test developer formulates specific test directions as part of the standardization process. Test directions include particular details and instructions with regard to the materials to be used; instructions and demonstrations that should be presented by the examiner; time limits of test administration; methods in which the examiner should handle examinee questions; scoring criteria and procedures; and any other information necessary for the administration and scoring of the test (Schmidt, 1999). The test is then administered to a large, representative sample within a given population following the specific test directions. This sample is known as the standardization sample. Based on the test results of the standardization sample, norms are established. When an individual examinee takes the test, his or her performance is compared with the norms. The result is interpreted to indicate the examinee's relative standing with reference to the standardization or normative sample.

Reliability and validity are two additional qualities that a test must possess. Reliability refers to the consistency or stability of test scores received by the same student. If a test does not measure consistently, we would not have confidence on the accuracy of its measurement. Then the test results cannot be given much credibility. Validity, on the other hand, is defined as the degree to which a test measures what it purports to measure. Validity of test scores reflects the degree of truthfulness of the inferences that can be drawn from the scores. Without validity, a test score would be meaningless and have no value. Reliability is considered a prerequisite of validity; that is, test scores must be reliable before they can be valid. Test scores that are not reliable can never be valid. Evidence of both reliability and validity should be established before a standardized test is released for general use (AERA, APA, & NCME, 1999). We will return to the discussion of standardization, reliability, and validity in greater detail in Chapter 4.

TYPES OF STANDARDIZED TESTS

Numerous tests are used in the schools, which can be classified into different types or categories. One way to classify tests is by the construct the test purports to measure. Using this method, tests can be organized into achievement tests, aptitude or intelligence tests, personality inventories, projective techniques, interest inventories, attitude measures, and so forth. Each of these types of tests may be further divided into subcategories. For example, individual tests are designed for administration in a one-on-one situation. Group tests are designed for group administration.

Individual tests are typically used for clinical purposes, such as making a diagnosis of a disability or disorder or determining strengths and weaknesses in a specific area of functioning (e.g., intelligence, achievement). These tests are administered to one student at a time. The test user should have considerable training in test administration, scoring, and interpretation. Group tests, on the other hand, are designed primarily as instruments for mass testing (Anastasi & Urbina, 1997). They are largely pencil-and-paper measures suitable for administration to large or small groups of students at the same time. The majority of tests used in schools are group tests. The recent large-scale tests used by states are also group tests. Group tests are fairly easy to administer and score, and their use does not require much special training on the part of the examiners. Some group tests may also be computer administered and scored.

Tests may also be grouped into speed tests and power tests. A speed test is designed to measure the speed or rate of performance, rather than the acquisition or mastery of knowledge. Typically, speed tests include very easy items so every test taker knows the answers. This way, only speed of response is measured by the test. On the other hand, a power test is designed to measure the knowledge of the test taker, regardless of his or her speed of performance. Power tests contain items with varying degrees of difficulty and allow enough time for test takers to attempt all items. Performance is based on how well a student can answer the items, instead of how fast he or she can perform. However, most tests used in the schools measure both knowledge and speed as factors on test performance. Specifically, these tests are designed to measure students' knowledge in a domain of content and a time limit is set for the students to complete the test. In other words, a student's score is influenced by both accuracy and speed of his or her answers. On such tests, although a student may have the necessary knowledge required to answer the test items correctly, the student may not receive a high score if he or she works in a slow speed and is unable to complete many items within the time limit.

Another way to classify tests is by the measurement theory that underlies a test. Based on this consideration, tests may be categorized into norm-referenced tests (NRT) and criterion-referenced tests (CRT). The major difference between NRT and CRT lies in the standard used in interpreting test performance. In NRT, a student's performance is compared to that of other students in a group. Specifically, interpretation of scores is made by comparing the student's performance to the average of performance of other similar students on the test or to the norm of a standardization sample. It indicates the student's status in a group or how well the student has performed with respect to the rest of the group. NRT is by far the most common approach to test interpretation. However, it should be noted that because NRT compares a student's performance to the normative group, language, culture, and socioeconomic status differences between the student and the normative group could affect the student's score (Kubiszyn & Borich, 2003). CRT, also known as domain-referenced tests, employs a different frame of reference in test interpretation than does NRT. In this approach, a performance standard called criterion is established prior to testing to indicate mastery of the specific content domain covered by the test. A student's performance is compared to the preestablished criterion, rather than to the performance of other students. Interpretation of CRT results yield specific information regarding the student's proficiency in or mastery of the measured skills. In recent years, states have begun to develop minimum competence tests to assess students' performance, which are designed and used based on the theory of criterion-referenced measurement.

USING TESTING ACCOMMODATIONS FOR DIVERSE LEARNERS

This section begins to introduce the readers to the use of testing accommodations for students with disabilities and ELLs. We cover these two topics: why use testing accommodations and testing accommodations explained.

Why Use Testing Accommodations?

It would be ideal if a test could assure accurate measurement for all students, regardless of gender, ethnicity, linguistic or cultural background, or disability. Unfortunately, this has not been the case. Because tests are standardized primarily on the mainstream population, they provide a more adequate measure for mainstream students than for students who are not part of the mainstream population, such as students with disabilities or ELLs (also see Chapter 1). In addition, although standardized tests are designed to assess each student in the same manner with the intent to provide a fair comparison among test takers, this is not always the case for students with disabilities or ELLs. In fact, for some students with disabilities or ELLs, standardized test administration does not provide an equal opportunity for them to demonstrate their abilities and skills as for their mainstream peers. This directly affects the validity of the test results and often produces an underestimation of the abilities measured for these students. There are several reasons for these results.

Taking standardized tests requires certain functional skills (e.g., physical, sensory, linguistic, etc.) to understand and respond to the test stimuli. Some students with disabilities or ELLs have a lack of such skills, which prevents them from performing optimally on the tests. For example, a blind student would be unable to take a test that requires vision. A hearing impaired student would be unable to understand auditorily presented test questions. A student with severe speech impairment would not do well on test items that require orally responses. Likewise, an ELL with little English skills would be unable to understand and respond to test items that require a high level of

English proficiency. When standardized tests are used in each of these examples, the test results would reflect more of the effects of the test taker's disability or language barrier than of his or her true abilities.

The issue of lack of requisite functional skills is sometimes further complicated by some attendant characteristics that students with disabilities or ELLs have. Scruggs, Bennion, and Lifson (1985) report that many learning disabled students may not have the attentional, memory, organizational, reading, and/or writing skills to perform at their optimal levels on standardized tests. Culbertson and Jalongo (1999) also indicate that students with disabilities are likely to use poor test-taking skills and ineffective learning strategies on formal tests (e.g., they are less likely to attend carefully to specific format demands). Other similar issues exist with English language learners. For example, Lam (1993) reports that ELL test takers often do not have the "test sophistication" and motivation necessary to perform well on standardized tests. Also, many ELLs tend to work in a slower rate and do not pace themselves well during testing. Consequently, they are unable to complete all test items within the time limits allowed and would receive lower scores than that they might deserve (Scruggs, Bennion, & Lifson, 1985). Sometimes, it is difficult to determine whether the low score is due to the student's lack of knowledge required on the test or lack of effective test-taking skills.

An additional problem comes from the norms used to score standardized test results. Appropriate norms are essential when using standardized tests to assess any students. Unfortunately, few standardized tests are standardized on students with disabilities or ELLs. The validity of test scores obtained by students with disabilities or ELLs using mainstream norms is questionable.

From this discussion, it can be seen that standardized tests may be invalid and unfair measures in assessing students with disabilities and ELLs. The true abilities of these students may be shrouded under the difficulties they experience in taking the tests. To remedy these difficulties and to "level the playing field," appropriate testing accommodations should be used in standardized testing to offer an equal opportunity for these students to demonstrate their optimal performance as do mainstream students.

Testing Accommodations Explained

Traditionally, testing accommodations have been used as a way of helping students with disabilities to perform on standardized tests. Thurlow, Scott, and Ysseldyke (1995) report that there has been great variability in the terminology used to describe changes made in the administration of standardized tests to students with disabilities. "Among the terms used to convey the concept of accommodations are: nonstandard administration, mediation, modification, alteration, and adaptation" (p. 3). Other terms have been used as well, such as *accommodated tests, modified tests, nonstandard test administration*, and *alternating testing techniques.* A review of the literature indicates the most commonly used terms are *accommodation, modification*, and *adaptation*, which are sometimes used interchangeably and at other times convey different meanings. For example, testing accommodations sometimes refers to changes made in the testing environment or facility, such as allowing a student to take a test in an alternative location or providing special lighting or special acoustics during testing. Testing modifications and adaptations, on the other hand, are associated with changes that are made to the actual test format or content (Thurlow et al., 1993). For example, a standardized test is changed into Braille or large print for administration to blind and visually impaired students. Or, an interpreter is used to help administering tests to an ELL in his or her native language. In addition to its use in special education, *test adaptation* is a common term used in cross-cultural assessment. It indicates that a test is translated from a source language into a target language and that necessary modifications are made to the test to make it better fit the target culture.

However, in most of the literature the terms *accommodation, modification*, and *adaptation* are used interchangeably. Collectively, they refer to any changes made to testing procedures or formats that provide students with disabilities equal opportunity to participate in testing situations (New York Education Department, 1995). The purpose is to make the test environment, content, or format more suitable and accessible to students with special needs. This broad concept of accommodation is also reflected in the 1990 Americans with Disabilities Act's definition of "reasonable accommodation," which includes (1) making existing facilities readily accessible to and usable by individuals with disabilities; and (2) appropriate adjustment or modifications of examinations, training materials or policies, the provision of qualified readers or interpreters, and other similar accommodations for individuals with disabilities. The *Standards for Educational and Psychological Testing* (AERA, APA, & NCME, 1999) describe testing accommodation as "any action taken in response to a determination that an individual's disability requires a departure from established testing protocol" (p. 101). We adopt this broad definition and expand it to include ELLs, in addition to students with disabilities. Furthermore, because there is no formal consensus on the use of the different terms, we choose to use *testing accommodations* as a generic term throughout this book, but use it interchangeably, occasionally as appropriate, with terms such as *modified tests* and *nonstandard test administration* in different contexts.

LEGAL BASES FOR TESTING ACCOMMODATIONS

Both constitutional and statutory laws have shaped policy regarding testing students with disabilities (Thurlow, Ysseldyke, & Silverstein, 1995) and ELLs. The equal protection and due process clauses of the Fourteenth Amendment to the U.S. Constitution are of particular importance and play a crucial role in policy for diverse learners. These clauses consist of two constitutional rights: that individuals will have (1) equal protection of the law, which in educational terms means that all individuals will have an equal educational opportunity, and (2) due process when a government or state action "adversely affects an individual" or attempts "to deprive a person of a property [e.g., a high school diploma] or liberty interest" (Phillips, 1992 cited in Thurlow, Ysseldyke, & Silverstein, 1995).

Legislations Pertaining to Students with Disabilities

Legal protection for students with disabilities to receive equal opportunities to participate in assessments as mainstream students has increased over the years. Statutory laws that are of relevance to testing students with disabilities include Section 504 of the Rehabilitation Act of 1973 (P.L. 93-112), the Education for All Handicapped Children Act of 1975 (P.L. 94-142), the Individuals with Disabilities Education Act of 1990 (P.L. 101-476) and its reauthorization of 1997 (P.L. 105-17), and the Americans with Disabilities Act of 1990 (P.L. 101-336).

Section 504 of the Rehabilitation Act of 1973 guarantees the right to free and appropriate public education to all people with disabilities. The Act established a mandate to end discrimination and bring individuals with disabilities into the mainstream of American society (Gordon, Stump, & Glaser, 1996). A person with a disability cannot be denied the opportunity to participate in a program or activity that receives federal assistance. In 1977, the U.S. Department of Health, Education, and Welfare issued regulations to implement Section 504. These regulations mandate that admissions tests for students with disabilities be valid and reflect what the test was intended to measure rather than the student's disability (Mehrens, 1997). Section 504 further requires that an institution may not use a test that has a disproportionate adverse effect on handicapped persons unless it has been validated for that population. The importance of Section 504 in testing is generally recognized as marking the beginning of the development of testing accommodations (Willingham, 1988).

The passage of the Education for All Handicapped Children Act of 1975, also known as P.L. 94-142, led to mandates requiring all children with disabilities to receive a free, appropriate public education. The Act requires that all tests and evaluation procedures be nondiscriminatory. Tests that are selected for students with disabilities from diverse backgrounds cannot be racially, culturally, or linguistically biased and, if necessary, must be administered in the native language or main source of communication that the student uses. In 1990, the Individuals with Disabilities Education Act (IDEA) was passed as a successor to P.L. 94-142. The IDEA further addresses the rights for students with disabilities, especially when evaluations are used to determine eligibility for special education services. However, both P.L. 94-142 and IDEA do not specifically address the topic of testing modifications (Thurlow, Ysseldyke, and Silverstein, 1995). The 1997 Amendments to the IDEA require states to include students with disabilities in state and district-wide testing and to provide these students with appropriate testing accommodations, where necessary. Furthermore, they mandate the use of alternative assessments for those students who cannot participate in state and district-wide assessment programs.

The Americans with Disabilities Act (ADA) of 1990 also has made a major impact on the testing of individuals with disabilities. This law maintains that taking tests for qualification and advancement is essential to many occupations. Individuals with disabilities have the right to apply and participate in licensing, certification, and/or credentialing examinations, despite their impairment. The ADA requires that accommodations and adaptations be made by businesses and agencies receiving federal funds so as not to bar individuals with disabilities from attempting to pass credentialing exams. Any test or course to be used for credentialing, licensing, or certification must be offered in a manner accessible to those with disabilities. It also requires that the agency responsible for administering such tests must provide the test taker with the disability with aids and/or modifications and cannot charge this individual for the accommodations made. The Act stresses the importance that the test result must accurately reflect the ability of the test taker and not be a reflection of the specific disability at hand (Ranseen, 1998; Sauter & McPeek, 1993; Thurlow, Ysseldyke, & Silverstein, 1995).

Legislations Pertaining to ELLs

Compared to legislation on testing students with disabilities, fewer statutory laws pertain to testing ELLs. The major federal education legislation that addresses ELLs include the Civil Rights Act of 1964, the Bilingual Education Act of 1968, the Improving America's Schools Act of 1994 (P.L. 103-382), and the No Child Left Behind Act of 2001 (P.L. 107-110).

Title VI of the Civil Rights Act prohibits discrimination in assigning students to schools, classes, or courses of study in programs or activities that receive federal financial assistance. School districts are responsible for providing equal educational opportunity to national origin minority children with limited English proficiency. Under Title VI, students cannot be excluded from effective participation in school because of inability to speak and understand English.

The Bilingual Education Act of 1968 is an amendment to the Elementary and Secondary Education Act (ESEA) of 1965. The Bilingual Education Act mandates that school districts that receive federal funding for bilingual programs must follow nondiscriminatory evaluation and placement procedures in assigning students to such programs. ELLs should not be denied the opportunity to learn successfully in classrooms in which the language of instruction is English or to participate fully in society.

The Improving America's Schools Act of 1994, a reauthorization of the ESEA, requires schools to set high standards for student achievement, including ELLs, and use appropriate assessments to measure student progress toward those standards. The Act also requires that ELLs be assessed in a manner that produces the most accurate results. In addition, school districts are required to provide information on the ELLs' progress in math, English proficiency, and reading to the U.S. Department of Education (Gomez, 1997).

The No Child Left Behind Act (NCLB) is the 2001 reauthorization of the ESEA. Two of the ten Titles of NCLB are devoted to the education of ELLs. Title III of the NCLB is entitled "Language Instruction for Limited English Proficient and Immigrant Students" and Title VII is entitled "Indian, Native Hawaiian and Alaska Native Education." The Act emphasizes the need for full opportunity for every student, including ELLs, to achieve high standards. It also requires that ELLs be included along with other students in state testing programs and results reported separately. Furthermore, NCLB requires assessments using tests written in English for students who have attended schools in the United States for three or more consecutive years. States also must annually assess English proficiency for all ELLs beginning with the 2002–2003 school year.

Legislations Pertaining to All Students

In 1994, the Congress passed the Goals 2000: Educate America Act (P.L. 103-227) that calls for the implementation of high academic standards among all the nation's students (also see Chapter 1). It contains a number of activities that were conducted to advance the development of content, performance, assessment, and opportunity to learn standards in support of the six national education goals. The Goals 2000 legislation encourages nondiscriminatory approaches to assessment and calls for adequate assessment and data collection systems be used to measure the progress of students with disabilities and ELLs at the local, state, and national levels (Hanley, 1995).

The No Child Left Behind Act of 2001 is a landmark education reform law. Its intent is to improve the performance of all elementary and secondary schools while at the same time ensuring that no child is trapped in a failing school. One of the four basic principles underlying the Act is stronger accountability for results. Title 1 of the NCLB requires states to implement statewide accountability systems that are based on challenging standards. It emphasizes that state and district-wide assessments should include all students, and that schools should be required to meet adequate yearly progress by increasing student test scores (National Association of School Psychologists, 2002). The goal is for every student, including students with disabilities and ELLs, to achieve high standards and demonstrate achievement through these assessments. Furthermore, NCLB calls for all students to be included in annual assessments in reading and mathematics in grades 3 through 8 beginning in the 2005–2006 school year. State assessment results must be broken out by poverty, race, ethnicity, disability, and limited English proficiency. This mandate of accountability will allow the state to track progress of students with disabilities and ELLs relative to other students. In addition, students must have the opportunity to learn materials covered in the testing programs, and accommodations must be provided to those students needing them for standardized test participation (Klotz & Canter, 2002).

Summary of Legal Bases for Testing Accommodations

From the legislations reviewed in this section, it can be seen that the idea of testing accommodations grew out of laws instituted since the 1970s to reduce discrimination against individuals with disabilities. The focus of the existing legislations is on the right of all students to an equal opportunity to education and assessment. Schools must provide students with disabilities and ELLs with the same opportunities to be assessed in a nondiscriminatory manner as their mainstream counterparts. In summary, the various federal statutes require that (1) students with disabilities and ELLs be provided the opportunity to participate in reliable and valid assessments; (2) these students be supplied with reasonable testing accommodations during testing or with alternative assessment, where necessary; and (3) all test results should accurately reflect the aptitude and achievement of the student, rather than his or her disabilities or limited English language skills.

SUMMARY

A person with disability is someone who has a physical or mental impairment that significantly interferes with his or her life activities. The IDEA specifies thirteen separate categories of disabilities under which students may be eligible for special education and other related services. An English language learner is a student whose native language is not English and who is in the process of learning English. The student may be experiencing difficulty in an English-only classroom due to his or her limited English language skills. Despite some common characteristics shared by students within each of the two populations, it is important to recognize that wide individual differences exist among students with disabilities as well as among ELLs.

Assessment procedures used for determining disability or ELL status of a student must be reliable, valid, fair, and equitable. This process involves teachers, administrators, and other school professionals (e.g., school psychologists, social workers), as well as parents.

All standardized tests and teacher-made classroom tests aim to systematically sample test takers' behaviors. A standard set of procedures is used for test administration, scoring, and interpretation. Standardized tests differ from teacher-made classroom tests in that they are subjected to a strict and extensive process of standardization in test development and norming. Evidence of reliability and validity should be available before a standardized test is released for general use.

Tests may be classified in many ways: by the construct it purports to measure, by the administration procedure involved, by the time limit allowed for test takers to respond, and by the measurement theory that underlies the test, among others.

Taking standardized or teacher-made tests under standard conditions requires certain requisite functional skills. Sometimes there are difficulties for students with disabilities or ELLs to demonstrate their true abilities on such tests. For example, these students may not have the necessary physical, sensory, or language skills to understand or respond to the test stimuli. The norms may not be suitable for use with these students. Because of these reasons, testing accommodations should be provided to students with disabilities or ELLs, in order to produce accurate measures of the students' knowledge and competence.

Testing accommodations are changes made to test format, content, or administration procedures to enable students with disabilities or ELLs to perform on standardized tests. The term *accommodations* is sometimes used interchangeably with *modifications,* or *adaptations.*

Legislations over the past thirty years have provided a legal basis for the use of testing accommodations for students with disabilities or ELLs. Among the federal laws, Section 504 of the Rehabilitation Act is recognized as marking the beginning of the development of testing accommodations. All of the laws require that test results should accurately reflect the measured attribute of the student, rather than his or her disability or language barrier.

CHAPTER THREE

PROFESSIONAL USES OF TESTING ACCOMMODATIONS

Although the importance of accurately assessing diverse learners on standardized tests is widely recognized, some questions remain about how to use testing accommodations in school assessments. Accommodations should not be used freely simply because a student has a disability or limited English language skills. Rather, it is important to employ them in an appropriate and fair manner to achieve the most valid measurement of a student's abilities and achievement. This chapter provides a systematic discussion on the professional use of testing accommodations in various school assessment situations. The following topics are included: purpose of using accommodations in testing, basic considerations in using testing accommodations, types of testing accommodations, selecting testing accommodations, requesting and granting accommodations, interpreting results from accommodated testing, reporting assessment data from diverse learners, and research on the use of testing accommodations in various school assessments.

PURPOSE OF USING ACCOMMODATIONS IN TESTING

Two important questions to consider in testing students with disabilities or ELLs are "Can the test be administered to the student under the standard test condition?" and "If not, what can and should be done in administering the test to the student?" To answer these questions, the student's special abilities, disabilities, characteristics, and background should be considered (Geisinger, 1994a). If the student does not have the requisite skills (e.g., physical, sensory, linguistic, etc.) to meet the demand of a test, or if certain characteristics of the student significantly interfere with his or her performance on the test under the standard administration, then the student cannot be appropriately and meaningfully assessed. It would be necessary to take steps to accommodate the special needs of the student during testing. When this occurs, an important question to consider is "What accommodation(s) is (are) acceptable in testing a diverse learner, without affecting the reliability and validity of the test results?"

The purpose of using accommodations is to reduce the effects of the disability or language barrier that a diverse learner has in taking an individual test, a teacher-made classroom test, or a large-scale test. It is hoped that when provided with appropriate accommodations, the student's special qualities would not unfairly restrict his or her test performance. The ultimate goal is to ensure a valid assessment of the construct (e.g., ability, achievement) that the test purports to measure in the student. That is, the test results should accurately reflect the student's measured ability or achievement, not his or her disability or limited English language skills.

Not all students with disabilities or ELLs need accommodations in taking various tests. These diverse learners may be grouped into three categories with regard to their participation in individual, classroom, or large-scale assessments: (1) those who can take tests under standard test administration, (2) those who can take tests but require special accommodations, and (3) those who cannot take tests under standard administration and must be assessed by alternative procedures (Lam, 1993; Ysseldyke, Thurlow, McGrew, & Vanderwood, 1994; AERA, APA, & NCME, 1999). Many students with very mild disabilities or ELLs with satisfactory English proficiency fall in the first category. Tests may be administered to these students in the standard fashion, because their special characteristics do not interfere with their performance on the tests. The second category includes students who exhibit disabilities or limited English proficiency that make it difficult for them to take tests under standard conditions. For example, standardized tests, which are designed for use with the general population, pose unusual demands on these students due to the nature of the students' special sensory, motor, language, or psychological qualities. These special qualities often adversely affect the students' performance and prevent them from producing maximum performance on the tests. Therefore, testing accommodations become necessary to provide these students an equal opportunity to demonstrate their true abilities as their general education peers. Included in the third category are students with severe disabilities or minimum English language proficiency who are unable to take tests under standard administration, even with accommodations. Due to the significant extent of their disabilities or English language barriers, or the lack of appropriate accommodation technology, tests cannot be administered to these students. Instead, alternative assessments should be used to evaluate these students. Chapter 8 is devoted to the discussion of some major alternative assessment procedures.

BASIC CONSIDERATIONS IN USING TESTING ACCOMMODATIONS

Several important considerations need to be taken into account in using accommodations in testing or assessment. The accommodations (1) must be appropriate and meet the individual need of the student test taker, (2) should be used in a fair manner to all students, and (3) should not be provided in certain assessment situations. These considerations are discussed next.

Accommodations Should Be Appropriate and Individualized

Testing accommodations provided to students with disabilities or ELLs should be appropriate and meet the individual needs of these students. Depending on the disabilities or English language skills of a student, it may be suitable to make accommodations or modifications to the testing environment, administration procedures, format, and/or content of a test. For example, a Braille or large print version of a test may be used for students who are blind or have severe visual impairment. Modifications can be made to the test format to help make the test protocol less confusing to students with learning disabilities and enable them to concentrate better on the test questions. Similarly, a bilingual interpreter may be used in administering tests to ELLs. All of these, when used appropriately, allow the true ability and competency of the diverse learners to be assessed.

Testing accommodations should also be individualized in order to be effective. Each student who is labeled to have a disability or to be an ELL is unique from other students with disabilities or ELLs. Special testing accommodations need to be tailored to meet each student's unique needs. It is obvious that testing accommodations for one type of disability cannot be assumed to apply to other types of disabilities. Furthermore, accommodations suitable for one particular student with a disability cannot be assumed to apply to other students within the same disability category. For example, not all blind students would benefit from testing in Braille; not all ELLs would need an interpreter in taking a test. It is unrealistic to expect that all ELLs would require the same accommodations (Liu, Anderson, Swierzbin, & Thurlow, 1999).

Accommodations Should Be Used in a Fair Manner to All Students

A vital consideration in using testing accommodations is fairness. As indicated in Chapter 2, the purpose of using accommodations is to ensure an even playing field by providing students with disabilities or ELLs an equal opportunity to perform on tests as their general population peers. However, it is important that testing accommodations not be used in an excessive manner to provide these students an unfair advantage over other students who do not receive accommodations. Fairness requires that no specific groups of students are getting special treatment that presents an unfair disadvantage over other students (Bernstein, 1989; Heubert & Hauser, 1999; Hishinuma, 1995). Accordingly, testing accommodations must be provided only to those students with disabilities or ELLs who genuinely need them and in a manner not to exceed what they need.

When Not to Provide Accommodations in Assessment

Despite the need for using accommodations to offset the disadvantages students with disabilities or ELLs have in taking tests under standard administration, accommodations should not be used in certain situations. One such case is when tests are used to assess a specific ability or diagnose a disability or disorder. If a test is designed to measure a construct that requires the student to be functional in a particular area of ability, and if the test is used to assess whether the student is impaired in the ability or to assess the level of impairment, then testing accommodations should not be provided. For example, no accommodation should be made for a student with visual impairment if the test is designed to assess his or her ability to read regular print. Nor should accommodations be allowed for a student with hearing impairment if the test is intended to measure his or her ability to understand spoken language. In addition, when the purpose of a test is to diagnose a disability or disorder, it would be inappropriate to make modifications to that test if such modifications make it impossible to measure certain characteristics or skills that are required in the diagnostic criteria. The diagnosis of a sensory, learning, or psychological disorder is made on the basis that a student manifests deficiencies in particular skills or characteristics. Therefore, it is essential to assess these characteristics or skills during testing. Allowing testing accommodations may preclude the opportunity for the examiner to assess the presence or absence of the skills to be addressed and make it impossible to render an accurate diagnosis. For example, allowing extra time on timed tests would make it difficult to determine whether a processing difficulty indeed exists in a student with learning disability (AERA, APA, & NCME, 1999).

TYPES OF TESTING ACCOMMODATIONS

As indicated in Chapter 2, recent years have witnessed an increased awareness and use of testing accommodations in large-scale testing as well as in classroom testing. An impetus for this increase is the legislative mandate for students with disabilities and ELLs to participate in state and district-wide assessment programs. Another reason is the inclusive education movement that calls for students with disabilities to be educated and assessed in the general education classroom. While most of the testing accommodations have been developed for students with disabilities, some have been developed for ELLs. The rationales for the use of testing accommodations for these two student populations are similar. A review of the literature (e.g., AERA, APA, & NCME, 1999; Siskind, 1993; Thurlow, Liu, Erickson, Spicuzza, & El Sawaf, 1996; Thurlow, Ysseldyke, and Silverstein, 1995) indicates testing accommodations can be organized generally into several categories: (1) modification of setting, (2) modification of presentation format, (3) modification of response format, (4) modification of timing and scheduling, (5) using portions of a test or substitute tests, (6) testing of limits. This organizational scheme can be used to categorize testing accommodations applicable to students with disabilities as well as ELLs. In this section, the accommodations for the two student populations are discussed together under each category. Although some accommodations can be used for both student populations, others are suitable only to students with a particular type of disability or to ELLs with a certain level of English proficiency. Explanations of the six types of accommodations follow. Further discussions of their use with different specific types of diverse learners are provided in Chapters 5, 6, and 7.

Modification of Setting

Modification of setting, also known as setting accommodations, is associated with modifications in the location, environment, or condition of testing. Examples of this type of accommodations include testing in an alternative location, individual testing, small group testing, preferential seating, and using a bilingual test administrator. If a standard testing site is not readily accessible to special test takers (e.g., students with wheelchairs), modification of the architectural structure of the testing site should be made to improve accessibility. Special students may also be allowed to take the test in an alternative location or facility (e.g., home with supervision). Sometimes it is appropriate to change group test administration to individual administration for students who cannot take the test in a group setting, or for students whose participation in group testing would pose an interference to other test takers. For example, a student with a diagnosed attention-deficit/hyperactivity disorder (ADHD) may be allowed to take a test alone in a private room or test carrel. In addition, setting accommodation includes modifications of the testing environment to make it more conducive to optimal performance of diverse learners, such as using special lighting, special acoustics, amplification devices, adaptive furniture, or other equipment.

Modification of Presentation Format

Modifying the presentation format of tests is a much-reported type of testing accommodation. It involves changing the medium of test administration including test instructions, test items, or both. For example, for students who are blind or visually impaired, the test directions and items may be presented orally, in Braille, or in large print. For students who are deaf or hard of hearing, tests may be administered in sign language, in writing, or with manual demonstrations. Other modifications of presentation format include oral reading of directions, explaining directions, signing directions, reducing the number of items per page, increasing spacing between items, rearranging format of test questions, reordering of test items, and placing markers to maintain space. Some of these accommodations may be used for students with disabilities as well as ELLs. Other accommodations specific to ELLs include oral reading of test directions in the student's native language, written translation of the directions into the student's native language, use of a bilingual interpreter to render the questions into the student's native language, and use of a bilingual dictionary or spell checker.

Modification of Response Format

Modifying response format is used for students who are unable to respond to the test items in the standardized format. The response format is changed to allow the student to answer in his or her preferred modality of communication. For example, students with expressive language deficits may be allowed to write their answers or simply point to the preferred response. Students with motoric impairments who cannot mark responses or write answers may give their answers orally and have another person record them. Other often-used response accommodations for students with disabilities include marking responses on booklet, using computer or word processor for responding, using template for responding, and giving response in sign language. Some commonly used response accommodations for ELLs include using a bilingual dictionary, giving responses orally in the student's native language, writing answers in native language, and using an interpreter to write responses in English.

Modification of Timing and Scheduling

Modification of timing involves changing the time and scheduling requirements of testing, such as allowing additional time to complete the test, changing the time of day for test administration, offering breaks during test, administering test in multiple sessions, and modifying order of tests administered. These testing accommodations can be used for both students with disabilities and ELLs. A major timing accommodation is extended time. Some diverse learners, due to their disabilities or limited English language skills, have a slower speed in processing test information than their general education peers. These students need additional time than normally allowed on standardized tests to demonstrate what they know and can do. Students with sensory disabilities sometimes also need extended time to compensate for their disabilities. For example, reading Braille and using an audiocassette recorder in taking a test may take longer time than reading regular print. Another time accommodation is adjusting scheduling of testing. For some students, it may not be possible to administer a test in one session as called for by the standard administration procedure. Frequent breaks during testing may be necessary for students unable to sustain concentration for a significant amount of time or for those whose sustained effort is reduced by fatigue factor. In these situations, test administration may be conducted in multiple sessions or extended over several days.

Extended time is a most frequently requested accommodation. However, some unresolved issues exist in the use of this accommodation, especially in large-scale assessment. One issue involves determining the appropriate amount of extra time needed by a particular test taker. It would be desirable to offer just the right amount of time needed by the student, rather than simply allowing him or her a multiple of the standard time, as is done in most current practices. Another issue involves determining whether timing accommodation is truly needed by some students, especially those with certain psychological disorders such as ADHD and anxiety disorder (Ranseen, 1998). Further research is needed to establish a sound empirical basis for making these decisions.

Using Portions of a Test or Substitute Tests

Often a test or a test battery is comprised of multiple parts, each requiring a particular physical, sensory, or linguistic capability to perform. When a student's disability or English language level adversely interferes with his or her performance on a particular part of the test, that portion should be eliminated. The student should be administered only those portion(s) of the test that are not impacted by his or her disability or language barrier. For example, in testing a deaf student, the verbal scale of an intelligence test should be omitted, because the result is more likely to reflect the student's hearing impairment than his or her verbal cognitive ability. The performance scale, however, can be administered to measure nonverbal abilities, because the student has functional ability in processing visually presented information. Alternatively, it may be desirable to use a substitute test in place of the original test under consideration. For example, certain tests of cognitive abilities do not emphasize verbal responses. It is appropriate to use such a test or a test specifically designed to measure cognitive abilities of the deaf in this case. Likewise, a substitute test that does not require English language skills (e.g., a nonverbal intelligence test) can be used in assessing the cognitive abilities of students who have very limited English proficiency. However, one disadvantage of this approach is that it is often difficult to find substitute tests with adequate technical quality that are specifically designed for students with disabilities or ELLs (AERA, APA, & NCME, 1999).

Testing of Limits

Testing of limits may be used as an accommodation for diverse learners. In testing of limits, the test is first administered to the student using the standard test administration procedure. After the completion of the standard administration, the test is given again to the student with a series of help steps (e.g., providing additional cues or structure, eliminating time limits, asking probing questions) to determine whether the student can improve his or her performance with additional help (Sattler, 2001). Comparison of results between standard test administration and testing-of-limits administration often yields valuable insight regarding the student's true ability and what the student can or cannot do under different conditions. It should be noted, however, that testing-of-limits results need to be considered carefully because the second testing may reflect "learning" that occurred from the student's having had the opportunity to try the test during standard administration.

SELECTING TESTING ACCOMMODATIONS

Selection of testing accommodations for diverse learners should be made by a team of knowledgeable school professionals. These professionals review all available information about the student's unique needs to make decisions regarding testing modifications. A number of considerations come into play in this decision. These include the purpose of testing, the specific disability condition or language barrier that the student has, the testing accommodations available and their possible effects on test scores, and the student's past experience with and preference for particular accommodations. As mentioned earlier, accommodations should be made on an individual basis. Depending on the specific needs of a test taker, one or more testing accommodations may be chosen for use during testing.

The school professionals should first review the nature of the student's disability or the level of an ELL's English language skills and how it may adversely affect the student's performance under standard testing conditions. Students with disabilities or ELLs vary greatly in the nature and extent of their disabilities or English language skills. Knowing the specific nature of a student's disability or an ELL's level of English proficiency is essential in choosing the most appropriate testing accommodations for him or her. The school professionals should also consider whether a standardized test under consideration has a special version (e.g., Braille, audiocassette, translated versions) or special administration procedures designed for students with certain types of disabilities or language difficulties. Should such a special version be available, it is then important to determine whether that version is suitable for use with a particular student, and whether norms and interpretive guides are available for evaluating the test results (Geisinger, 1994a).

When special versions or special administration procedures are not available, the school professionals need to make their own selection of appropriate testing accommodations for specific students. This complex task requires knowledge about the accommodation needs by a student with disability or an ELL, the accommodations that are allowed by school policy, and the their effects on test scores. Knowledge on the proper use of various testing accommodations and how a specific one might affect the meaning of test outcomes is particularly crucial. Often providing accommodations may impact on more than one aspect of testing. For example, reading Braille or large print takes students with visual impairment longer to read than the same material presented in regular print to students without visual impairment. Such accommodations affect the time limits of a test and can have a significant effect on the meaning of test scores. Another example is that in translation of test directions into a signed language or a test taker's native language, an exact word-for-word translation is frequently not possible. Any changes made in the translation from the standardized directions may have a significant effect on the test results. School professionals responsible for selecting testing accommodations for students with disabilities or ELLs should appreciate the complexity of the issue and be fully knowledgeable about the effects of various accommodations on the meaning of test scores. Ideally, the goal is to select accommodations that do not significantly alter the validity of the test scores or to choose accommodations whose effects are known. Uncertainty has given rise to questions regarding the amount of knowledge school professionals usually possess about the influence of disabilities or limited English proficiency on test performance and about the effects of various test accommodations. These are difficulties often faced by school decision team members. To compensate for these difficulties, it is recommended that professionals responsible for making accommodation decisions should have such knowledge available to them through consultation with the empirical literature or through experts who are familiar with such literature (AERA, APA, & NCME, 1999).

Another factor that must be taken into consideration is the student's preference for and past experience with specific accommodations. Students with the same disability may have different experiences with certain types of accommodations. For instance, not all students with learning disabilities would find oral reading of test items to be a useful accommodation. The appropriateness of an accommodation to be used during testing may be determined by the type of adaptation that has been used in the past. For example, if an accommodation that has been used for a student with disability or an ELL for classroom instruction in the past, has been found effective and is preferred by the student, then the same accommodation should be considered for test taking. Relatedly, school professionals may also seek input from students themselves (or parents of students) on what accommodations they feel would be most beneficial to them taking tests, as well as their level of comfort with the accommodations (Liu, Thurlow, Erickson, Spicuzza, & Heinze, 1997). Overall, there should be some consistency between accommodations used during testing and those used in the classroom setting and other school activities.

REQUESTING AND GRANTING ACCOMMODATIONS

The practice of requesting and granting testing accommodations for students with disabilities is governed by federal (e.g., IDEA, Section 504) and state laws. Although the specific procedures vary somewhat from state to state, a fair degree of consistency exists about general policies and procedures. However, there is not such a parallel federal legislation for ELLs (Thurlow, Liu, Erickson, Spicuzza, & El Sawaf, 1996). As a result, considerable variation exists among the states and school districts in determining accommodations for ELLs.

Generally, a student with disability or an ELL may request accommodations in taking a test. School districts need to establish guidelines and administrative procedures for determining testing accommodations and include the guidelines in the district's assessment program. These guidelines should be used in granting accommodations to students with disabilities or ELLs. In the former case, with students with disabilities, a child study team initiates an individual evaluation to determine whether a student has a disability and the extent of the disability. Based on the findings of this evaluation, the child study team will determine the specific accommodations the student needs. In the case of ELLs, a team of school professionals should evaluate the student's proficiency in English as well as his or her native language and determine whether specific accommodations are needed for the student in taking a test. Once an accommodation decision is made, it should apply to all testing situations including individual testing, classroom testing, and large-scale testing. The decision then needs to be documented in the student's file, such as the Individual Educational Program (IEP) of a student with disability, and reviewed periodically.

In participating in state or district-wide assessment, there are four circumstances in which students with disabilities may be eligible to receive testing accommodations (New York State Education Department, 1995).

1. Students with disabilities whose IEP includes testing accommodations as determined by the child study team are eligible.
2. Students who are declassified by the child study team, yet the effects of the disability prevent the student from demonstrating certain knowledge or skills, may continue to receive testing accommodations for the balance of the student's public education.
3. Students who are determined to have a disability pursuant to Section 504 who do not require special education or related services may be entitled to testing accommodations, in order to benefit from all the programs and activities available to general education students.
4. Schools may modify testing procedures for general education students who experience temporary or long-term disabilities shortly before the administration of a large-scale assessment.

Requests for testing accommodations in taking large-scale assessments must be accompanied by written documentation of the student's disability and his or her eligibility for that particular accommodation. In most cases, a student requesting testing accommodations must have an IEP developed by the child study team under a state law or a Section 504 Accommodation Plan (504 Plan) developed by a Section 504 multidisciplinary team indicating his or her eligibility and need for particular testing accommodations. The IEP or 504 Plan specifies the accommodations that the student needs to demonstrate his or her competencies in important activities including classroom, district-wide, and state assessments. If a testing accommodation is specified within the IEP or 504 Plan, there should also be documentation of the extent and conditions under which this accommodation will be applied (Burns, 1998).

When a student requests accommodation from testing agencies outside of the school, the testing agencies usually ask that a letter be enclosed from the school the student is attending, which indicates that the student consistently receives a specific testing accommodation(s) during classroom tests and/or standardized tests provided by the school. The document should indicate under which testing conditions, or types of tests, the specific accommodation(s) is (are) necessary. If an individual is not currently attending school, and/or does not have an IEP or 504 Plan, other documentation must be provided from a qualified professional in the area of the disability to support the request. A qualified professional is someone who is licensed or certified to diagnose and treat the disability (e.g., physician, psychologist, learning specialist). The professional should provide proof of his or her training, credentials, and employment experience with the particular population of disability. Another instance when additional documentation may be needed is in the event that a student experiences disability shortly prior to taking a test or may have an undocumented disability. In these instances the testing agencies will require special documents from qualified professionals to support such requests. On receipt of the request and supporting documents, the testing agencies usually have professional experts review the student's request and determine whether to grant special testing accommodations (Burns, 1998).

Requested versus Reasonable Accommodations

One issue that requires special attention in determining testing accommodations for students with disabilities or ELLs is requested versus reasonable accommodations. This issue often occurs when a student participates in a state, district-wide, or commercial standardized testing program (e.g., SAT or ACT Assessment) and sometimes results in a conflict between the student and the organizations (e.g., schools, testing agencies) responsible for making accommodation decisions. Eligible students have the right to request a particular testing accommodation in taking a standardized test. The responsible organizations, on the other hand, have the responsibility to determine whether the requested accommodation is justified and appropriate. Only those requests that are deemed justified are accepted. If the request for a particular testing accommodation is not considered justified, then the requested accommodation is denied.

Ranseen (1998) identified two sources in which a conflict between requested and reasonable accommodations may arise: (1) the diagnosis of a mental disability that requires testing accommodations and (2) the rationale for and the reasonableness of the accommodations requested. Regarding the first source, the question is often raised about how a person was diagnosed as having a mental disability. A disorder that has drawn particular concern is learning disability. Because there is much disagreement about what exactly constitutes a learning disability and a lack of a standard procedure in diagnosing this disability, some students may be incorrectly diagnosed as having one. Therefore, it would be inappropriate to grant accommodation requests to all individuals who claim to have a "diagnosed" learning disability. The second source of conflict concerns the appropriateness of an accommodation request. The ADA requires that assessment of individuals with disabilities be conducted with reasonable accommodations. However, the word *reasonable* is ambiguous and often becomes a source of disagreement between testing organizations and persons requesting testing accommodations. For example, a student with ADHD may request to take a test in a distraction-free environment and with extended time. Although testing organizations generally would agree to allow the student to take a test in a quiet separate room, they may disagree with the request for extended time or with the amount of extended time that the student requests. When such a disagreement occurs, the test organization contacts the student requesting accommodations to reach an agreement. Also, a neutral third party who has training and experience in testing accommodations may be contacted to evaluate the case and render an appropriate decision. Deciding on the "reasonableness" of a testing accommodation sometimes can be controversial. Much knowledge about the effects of specific accommodations on the test outcomes (e.g., whether the accommodations change the validity of test scores) is required to act on such decisions. This issue is discussed in great detail in Chapter 4.

INTERPRETING RESULTS FROM ACCOMMODATED TESTING

When diverse learners are able to take tests under standard administration, test scores may be interpreted by employing the normal judgment process, with the school professional taking special care to follow recommendations offered in the test manual that apply to these students (Geisinger, 1994a). However, when accommodations are offered during testing to a student with disability or an ELL, the test administration becomes nonstandard. Interpretation of results from nonstandard test administration becomes a far more complex matter. Questions often arise over whether the accommodations are appropriate and if they significantly alter the meaning of test results. Interpretation of test scores on accommodated tests relies heavily on the professional judgment of the school professional involved. Two considerations are particularly feasible in interpreting such test scores.

First, interpretation of scores from accommodated testing should be guided by empirical findings. When tests are administered in nonstandard conditions, the test scores may not have the same meaning as scores on the same test administered under standard conditions, unless it can be demonstrated that the technical characteristics of the test are not affected by the accommodations employed. The *Standards for Educational and Psychological Testing* (AERA, APA, & NCME, 1999) recommend that interpretation of test results should be guided by empirical research on the reliability and validity of test scores on accommodated tests. When such empirical evidence is not available, interpretation should be done with caution. Standard 10.4 states,

> If modifications are made or recommended by test developers for test takers with disabilities, . . . evidence of validity should be provided whenever available. Unless evidence of validity for a given inference has been established for individuals with the specific disabilities, test developer should issue cautionary statement in manuals or supplementary materials regarding confidence in interpretations based on such test scores. (p. 106)

In the same vein, if accommodations are selected and made by individual test users, the test users should be aware that the scoring, norms, and interpretation are compromised (Geisinger, 1994a). The test users should seek empirical knowledge about the effects of the particular accommodations used to aid in the interpretation of scores. Does the nonstandard version of the test continue to assess the same construct measured by the original test? Are scores on the nonstandard and standard versions of the test comparable and do they have the same meaning? Again, great care should be taken in drawing inferences from the test results. In all cases, it is important to treat the interpretations as hypothetical rather than definitive. If necessary, the school professional should consult other qualified test experts who have training and experience on the questions under consideration.

The second consideration involves the use of appropriate norms in interpreting test scores. Norms represent the test performance of individuals in the standardization sample. Normative data are used to compare an examinee's performance to those in the general population. For a norm to be useful in interpreting test scores of students with disabilities or ELLs, a representative sample of such students should be included in the normative and validation samples of a standardized test. Furthermore, at each stage of test development and standardization, these subpopulations of students should be recognized and considered along with the general population. It is always desirable for the school professional to review the normative sample in the test manuals to see whether students with a particular type of disability or linguistic background were included. If not, it may be doubtful whether valid inferences may be drawn from test scores obtained by students with that particular type of disability or linguistic background.

Depending on the purpose of testing, scores of diverse learners on a test may be interpreted using general population norms, as well as specific subgroup norms. Subgroup norms are established to represent the performance of subpopulations of students such as those with certain types of disabilities or linguistic backgrounds. This type of specific norm is useful in interpreting a diverse learner's performance relative to students with similar disabilities or linguistic backgrounds. One problem of developing subgroup norms is that it is frequently difficult to obtain a sufficient number of participants to form a highly specific normative sample. Finally, it is important to remember norms are in no sense absolute or universal (Martino, 1999). Different norms merely offer different frames of reference for score comparison and interpretation. When both general norms and subgroup norms are available, it is beneficial to use both in interpreting the test scores and compare the results.

REPORTING ASSESSMENT DATA
FROM DIVERSE LEARNERS

Large-scale assessments are administered to numerous students each year in national, state, and district-wide assessment programs. Test scores of these assessments are used to make high-stakes decisions about students and schools (see Chapter 1). However, states and school districts differ in their practices of reporting scores of diverse learners in these assessment programs (Erickson, Ysseldyke, Thurlow, & Elliot, 1998; Johnston, 1998; Olsen, 1998). Sometimes a school may be concerned about the low score obtained by students with severe disabilities or students with very limited English skills and exclude them from score reporting, in order to raise the school's average scores. Disparities in score reporting practices inevitably call into question the validity of group comparisons among schools. For example, if one school includes students with disabilities in reporting its test scores and another school does not, the same inferences cannot be made about both schools. Reschly (1993) rightfully called for the development and implementation of universally accepted guidelines for reporting large-scale assessment results. If all states and districts follow the same guidelines, then comparison of test results between schools would not be compromised.

Legislation now has required that all students be included in state and district-wide assessment programs. In order to provide complete and accurate data for accountability purposes, assessment data of all students should be reported, including those with disabilities and ELLs. Generally, scores obtained in large-scale assessments are reported in both aggregated and disaggregated forms. In the aggregated form, test scores of students with disabilities or ELLs are combined with the scores of all other students, and the results are reported. This does not allow separate analyses for subpopulations of students, but provides a more broad-based, inclusive measure of school performance. On the other hand, disaggregation allows for the reporting of student assessment data by different classifications, such as students with and without disabilities. It permits the assessment data to be used to analyze and improve services for students with specific types of disabilities or linguistic backgrounds. However, research has reported that assessment data on students with various types of disabilities and ELLs are not always reported clearly. For example, Liu, Albus, and Thurlow (2000) found that although states frequently separate test scores by categories such as race and ethnicity, they do not always include a separate category for ELLs. Therefore, ELLs are often included with English proficient students and this makes it difficult to track ELLs' performance. Other researchers (e.g., August, Hakuta, Olgum, & Pomps, 1995; Lachat, 1999) also suggest separating ELLs even further by such variables as socioeconomic status, primary language, and amount of time the student has been in the United States and has been receiving English instruction. A disadvantage to disaggregating assessment scores, when used alone, is that students with disabilities or ELLs may continue to be segregated from the general student population. Another potential disadvantage is that if a group of students with a particular disability is very small in a school, disaggregation may reveal the identifications of specific students, which may constitute an invasion of privacy (Olson & Goldstein, 1997).

RESEARCH ON THE USE OF TESTING ACCOMMODATIONS IN VARIOUS SCHOOL ASSESSMENTS

After discussing the ways in which assessment accommodations should be used, we now turn to the topic of recent practices on the use of accommodations in various school evaluative activities, such as large-scale testing for different purposes and day-to-day classroom testing. Relevant research is reviewed on (1) state and school district policies and practices on the use of testing accommodations for diverse learners, (2) state and school district practices on reporting assessment results of diverse learners, and (3) the use of accommodations in classroom testing.

Policies and Practices on the Use of Testing Accommodations

The use of accommodations in statewide assessment continues to grow and change, and guidelines are updated every few years. Thurlow, Scott, and Ysseldyke (1995) reviewed state guidelines for accommodations in assessments for students with disabilities. They found that accommodation guidelines were provided by thirty-eight states. Within these states, the size and function of guidelines varied from state to state (e.g., one page in one state and seventeen in another state). In some states, accommodations depend on the purpose of assessment and/or the specific type of assessment being used, whereas in other states, the same guidelines are used regardless of the purpose or type of assessment. Furthermore, the specific testing accommodations allowed also varied from state to state. What might be acceptable in one state could be prohibited in another.

Testing policies are also available on a local level. Jayanthi, Epstein, Polloway, and Bursuck (1996) surveyed 214 school districts nationwide to study local testing policies for students with disabilities. Results indicated that about 60 percent of the school districts had a formal written policy on standardized testing, and 22 percent had a formal policy on nonstandardized testing. In addition, 61 percent of districts with standardized testing policies and 56 percent of districts with nonstandardized testing policies required that accommodations be made for students with disabilities. Some of the most commonly mentioned modifications included the use of a special administer, extended time, large print, aids, and a special administration site.

There are also inconsistencies among states in accommodation procedures used with ELLs. Thurlow, Liu, Erickson, Spicuzza, & El Sawaf (1996) examined state guidelines for accommodations allowed for ELLs taking state graduation exams. They found nine out of eighteen states with graduation exams did not list accommodations in their written documents, two states allowed alternative procedures, and three states allowed ELLs to be exempted from standardized tests. Furthermore, of the states that provided accommodations, they differed in the specific ones allowed and in the ways that eligibility for the accommodations was determined. This study found that the state guidelines were vague and the format of the guidelines varies enormously across states. Additionally, half of the states did not offer accommodations for ELLs at all. The authors stated that ELLs "do not have the same legislative support for accommodations as do students with disabilities.

Therefore, states are left to themselves in determine what types of accommodations they will allow" (Thurlow, Liu, Erickson, Spicuzza, & El Sawaf, 1996, p. 1). Liu, Thurlow, Erickson, Spicuzza, and Heinze (1997) reviewed a study done by the North Central Regional Educational Laboratory in 1996 that surveyed fifty states on their use of testing accommodations for ELLs on the National Assessment of Educational Progress (NAEP) exam. It was found that twenty-five states allowed accommodations for these students during testing. However, the states varied in the accommodations they use. Among the accommodations reported were administering the test in a separate setting, allowing a flexible testing schedule, the use of extra time, simplified directions, and small group administration. Another survey done by Rivera and Vincent (1997) found twenty-seven states allowed for testing accommodations for the ELL population on assessments. The most commonly used accommodation by the states was giving the students extra time. Four states had translated some standardized tests into various languages that were given to ELLs who were more competent in their native language as opposed to English. Several states also reported developing their own tests for use with ELLs.

Policies and Practices on Reporting Assessment Results

As mentioned earlier, students with disabilities and ELLs should be included in state and district-wide assessment programs and reasonable accommodations need to be made to enhance their participation in these assessments. However, varied data have been reported in this regard, and overall, these data indicate significant portions of the population of students with disabilities were excluded from large-scale assessments. Furthermore, when students with disabilities are included, their scores are often not reported (McGrew, Thurlow, Shriner, & Spiegal, 1992; Ysseldyke, Thurlow, McGrew, & Vanderwood, 1994). The reporting of ELLs' scores also varies from state to state. Johnston (1998) reported that although school districts are required to report all students' scores on standardized tests, some school districts resisted having scores of ELLs reported.

This problem also exists on the local level. In the Jayanthi, Epstein, Polloway, and Bursuck (1996) study mentioned earlier, the authors found about one-half of the school districts with testing policies did not include scores of students with disabilities in the district data set. Also, many students with disabilities were excluded from standardized testing altogether. The types of students exempted ranged from those with severe disabilities, to learning disabilities, to mild mental retardation, and to a number of other disabilities (e.g., multiple disabilities, emotional/behavior disorder, visual impairment, etc.). It is unclear why these school policies allowed for the exclusion of students with mild disabilities who should be able to participate in testing with appropriate accommodations. Furthermore, Thurlow, Ysseldyke, and Silverstein (1993) in their review of state guidelines found that states vary considerably in their guidelines for (1) making decisions about the inclusion/exclusion of students with disabilities in state and national testing programs and (2) determining the kinds of accommodations and modifications that are to be used during assessments.

From the research reviewed here, it is encouraging that a majority of states and school districts have policies regarding the use of accommodations for students with disabilities and including these students in the assessment programs. Comparatively, fewer states have established guidelines for the use of accommodations with ELLs. Unfortunately, considerable inconsistencies exist in policies and practices across states and school districts. The field would benefit greatly by formulating consistent guidelines for students with disabilities to receive accommodations and participate in assessment programs (Thurlow, Scott, & Ysseldyke, 1995). Likewise, the same type of universally accepted guidelines is also needed for the ELL population (Thurlow, Liu, Erickson, Spicuzza, & El Sawaf 1996). The recent legislations of the Amendments to the IDEA of 1997 and the No Child Left Behind Act of 2001 should provide an important impetus in facilitating the development of such guidelines.

Using Accommodations in Classroom Testing

Testing accommodations are intended to help diverse learners to effectively meet the demands of large-scale assessments as well as teacher-made classroom tests. One topic that has gained increased attention is the use of accommodations for students with disabilities in inclusive general education classrooms. The inclusion movement has resulted in more students with disabilities being integrated into general education classes, thereby increasing the responsibility of teachers to effectively meet the needs of these students in both instructional and evaluative activities. For classroom assessments, to have students with disabilities take the same tests as their peers without disabilities can place these students at a great disadvantage. Therefore, teacher-made classroom tests often are adapted to meet the needs of students with disabilities. The available literature has discussed various methods of making modifications in day-to-day classroom testing and encouraged teachers to become knowledgeable in this area. Nevertheless, successful implementation of the testing accommodations in the classroom is left to the teachers' discretion and is influenced by teachers' knowledge about and acceptability of these accommodations. A number of studies have examined teachers' perceptions and implementation of accommodations in classroom testing.

Teachers' Perceptions and Use of Testing Accommodations

Gajria, Salend, and Hemrick (1994) examined teachers' acceptability of test accommodations for mainstreamed students. They surveyed sixty-four general education teachers of grades 7 through 12. The participants were asked to respond to a questionnaire consisting of items relating to teacher knowledge of testing accommodations, common types of accommodations used in the general education classrooms, teachers' perceptions of integrity for specific testing accommodations, and the ease of use and effectiveness of testing accommodations. The results indicated that most of the teachers were familiar with modifications in test format and administration. They were less knowledgeable about the use of alternative scoring procedures. However, even though teachers were familiar with a variety of accommodations, they were reluctant to implement those they considered ineffective, difficult to implement, and a possible threat to the academic integrity of their examinations (e.g., give a sample test in advance, use alternative scoring procedures). Furthermore, teachers were more likely to use modifications in test design (e.g., typewritten rather than handwritten tests, well-spaced test items) that could be used uniformly with all students in the class. Comparatively, teachers were less likely to use accommodations specific to the needs of individual students (e.g., allowing students to dictate their responses, using technological equipment for presentation of test items and student responses).

In a similar study, Siskind (1993) compared the level of knowledge of testing accommodations between special and general education teachers. Sixty elementary, middle school, and high school teachers responded to questions about the permissibility of fifty-one possible testing accommodations. In contrast to the results of the study conducted by Gajria, Salend, and Hemrick (1994), Siskind found that both special and general educators lacked knowledge regarding some testing accommodations. Although a majority of the respondents were familiar with modifications in test setting and scheduling, they were less familiar with other modifications such as revised test directions, revised test format, revised answer mode, and mechanical and nonmechanical aid. Furthermore, with few exceptions, special educators were no more informed than general education teachers. The concern raised by these findings is that those teachers not aware of testing accommodations will be less likely to employ accommodations to entitled students. Siskind (1993) suggests frequent in-service training be provided to teachers as a possible remedy of this concern.

Jayanthi, Epstein, Polloway, and Bursuck (1996) conducted a national survey of general education teachers' perceptions of testing accommodations related to students with disabilities. Four hundred and one general education teachers participated in the study. The survey included questions relating to test administration, responsibility of providing accommodations, communication with parents regarding test accommodation, the fairness of making accommodations for students with disabilities, and the helpfulness and ease of making specific accommodations. The findings revealed that 47.1 percent of general education teachers were responsible for making testing accommodations in their classrooms, while 35.9 percent were joined by special education teachers in deciding which accommodations to make in general education classes. In addition, close to 60 percent of teachers indicated that students with disabilities were taking their general education tests in either the special education classroom or both the general and special education classrooms.

The teachers as a group rated the following testing accommodations as most helpful for students with disabilities: (1) providing one-on-one help with directions during test administration, (2) reading test questions to students, and (3) simplifying wording of test questions. However, many of the adaptations rated as being most helpful for students were not necessarily easy to make. Testing accommodations that were viewed as easy to make included (1) using black-and-white copies instead of dittos, (2) providing extra space on tests to answer questions, (3) using practice questions as a study guide, (4) giving open-book or open-notes tests, and (5) providing one-on-one help with directions during test administration. In addition, 66.6 percent of general education teachers indicated that it was not fair to make testing accommodations only for students with disabilities. A majority of these teachers believed that testing accommodations should be made available to other students who may need them (e.g., students with English as a second language, students at risk, students with an unidentified disability, slow learners) (Jayanthi, et al., 1996).

The implementation of testing accommodations, along with other testing practices, were investigated in a study conducted by Putnam (1992). Putnam utilized an open-ended survey to investigate the testing practices of 60 seventh-grade and 60 tenth-grade general education teachers with mainstreamed special education students in their classes. A section on the survey inquired about modifications to testing procedures such as giving smaller, more frequent tests and extended time. The results found that special education students who were mainstreamed in general education classrooms took an average of 11 classroom tests each marking period. The tests were rarely modified to meet the needs of the mainstreamed special education students. Only 52 percent of the teachers reported making occasional testing accommodations; the most commonly used accommodation being dividing a test into sections for easier overview and comprehension. Forty-three percent of the teachers reported reading a test orally to a student with mild disabilities, but this accommodation was used only once or twice a school year. In addition, 87 percent of the teachers provided assistance to students during a test, primarily reading directions to them. Just over 50 percent of the teachers allowed students to use some form of written assistance (e.g., students' class notes, textbook) during a test—again only once or twice a year. These results indicate that effective testing accommodations are not being frequently and consistently implemented to meet the needs of mainstreamed students in general education classrooms.

In summary, despite the availability of teacher-made testing accommodations for students with disabilities, some confusion still exists concerning which accommodations are reasonable, effective, and acceptable to teachers. Overall, general education teachers are not knowledgeable about many of the testing accommodations that can be used with students with disabilities in their classrooms. Some teachers perceive accommodations as nonpractical, unfair, and even compromising the integrity of their tests. The testing accommodations that are used tend to be those that are easy to implement and may be used with students without disabilities as well. General education teachers would rarely use individualized accommodations to meet the specific needs of students with disabilities. Given these findings, special efforts need to be made to enhance more frequent and consistent use of accommodations by teachers in day-to-day classroom testing.

Students' Perceptions of Testing Accommodations

Relative to studies on teachers' perceptions of testing accommodations, considerably less research has focused on student perceptions. Vaughn, Schumm, and Kouzekanani (1993) investigated the perceptions of mainstreamed students with learning disabilities regarding accommodations made by general education teachers for tests, homework, and instruction. The subjects consisted of 179 elementary, middle school, and high school students. The students were identified as learning disabled (LD), low achieving (LA), and average/high achieving (A/HA). The results of this study indicated that overall, students across the achievement groups (LD, LA, and A/HA) preferred the general education teacher who made accommodations when they have difficulty learning, although the students differed slightly on the types of accommodations preferred. The students with LD were found to be more likely to differ from their LA and A/HA peers on accommodation types in tests, homework, textbooks, and grouping. For example, elementary school students with LD indicated a stronger preference than LA and A/HA students for the opportunity to work in groups with different students. At the middle school and high school levels, LA and A/HA students, but not students with LD, preferred the teacher who made no accommodations in homework and textbooks. Also, students with LD viewed being treated the "same" for tests, homework, and textbooks as more important at the middle school and high school levels than at the elementary level. Compared to the teacher perceptions discussed in the previous section, the findings of Vaughn and colleagues (1993) show a generally favorable perception and acceptance of testing and instructional accommodations by mainstreamed students with learning disabilities. This student perception is worth noting and indicates the importance of accommodations in assisting students with disabilities in learning and testing situations.

SUMMARY

The purpose of using accommodations is to reduce the effects of the disabilities or language barriers of diverse learners in taking individual, classroom, or large-scale assessments to ensure reliable and valid results. However, not all students with disabilities or ELLs need accommodations in taking tests. Testing accommodations are designed primarily for use with those students who are capable of taking tests but whose special qualities adversely affect their performance under standard test administration.

Several basic considerations should be taken into account in using accommodations in assessment. Testing accommodations (1) must be individualized to meet the specific needs of students with disabilities or ELLs, (2) need to be used in a manner that is fair to all students, and (3) should not be used when the purpose of assessment is diagnostic. When used appropriately, these accommodations will help to ensure a valid assessment of a diverse learner's true abilities or achievement.

Testing accommodations can be organized into six categories: modification of setting, modification of presentation format, modification of response format, modification of timing and scheduling, using portions of a test or substitute tests, and testing of limits. Selection of testing accommodations for diverse learners should be made by knowledgeable school professionals. The decision must take into account factors such as purpose of testing, special characteristics of the student, effects of particular testing accommodations on test scores, and the student's previous experience with the accommodations under consideration.

Generally, certain students with disabilities or ELLs are entitled to accommodations in participating in various school assessments. Schools should develop guidelines in determining testing accommodations for qualified students. In almost all cases, testing accommodations are provided to students with disabilities based on their IEPs or Section 504 Accommodation Plans. However, testing accommodations may also be provided to qualified students under other conditions. "Requested versus reasonable accommodations" sometimes causes a conflict between students who request accommodations and the schools or testing agencies that are responsible for granting accommodations.

Interpretation of test scores obtained from accommodated tests should be done by qualified professionals with great caution. Empirical knowledge concerning the effects of the specific accommodations employed and the use of appropriate norms are important in drawing valid inferences from test results.

Recent legislations mandate that students with disabilities and ELLs should be included in large-scale assessment programs and results of their performance reported to provide complete and accurate data for accountability purposes. Data from these students may be reported in aggregated and disaggregated forms. However, states vary in their practices in reporting scores from students with disabilities as well as from ELLs.

Finally, a review of the literature on state and district accommodations policies and practices in large-scale testing reveals a lack of common guidelines on the use of accommodations in testing students with disabilities as well as ELLs. Furthermore, a review of the literature on the use of accommodations in day-to-day classroom testing indicates that there is some confusion among general education teachers concerning which accommodations are reasonable, effective, and acceptable. Teachers tend to use accommodations that are easy to implement and may be used with all students. They seldom tailor testing accommodations to meet the individual needs of the students with disabilities. On the other hand, students with disabilities seem to show a favorable perception and general acceptance of accommodations.

CHAPTER FOUR

PSYCHOMETRIC ISSUES IN THE USE OF TESTING ACCOMMODATIONS

The discussion in Chapter 3 about the professional use of testing accommodations in school assessments frequently reminded the readers that it is vital that the use of accommodations does not compromise the validity of test scores from nonstandard administration. This chapter presents a detailed discussion on various psychometric issues surrounding the use of testing accommodations. The objective is to provide the readers with the necessary information on examining how the use of accommodations may affect the technical aspects of testing and test scores. Whereas Chapter 3 emphasized the practical use of testing accommodations, this chapter focuses on the psychometric aspect of testing accommodations. The chapter covers the following topics: testing accommodations and psychometric soundness, standardization, reliabilities, validity, types of validity evidence, effects of accommodations on reliability and validity, effects of accommodations on test performance, and flagging of scores on accommodated tests.

TESTING ACCOMMODATIONS AND PSYCHOMETRIC SOUNDNESS

Federal and state laws have required that nonbiased procedures be used in assessing diverse learners. For example, IDEA requires that reasonable testing accommodations be made to eliminate discrimination and provide students with disabilities with the same opportunities as their counterparts in general education. Also, both the IDEA and the No Child Left Behind Act mandate that states establish procedures that assure tests and other evaluation materials are provided and administered in the child's native language; that no single procedure shall be the sole criterion for determining an appropriate educational program. Similarly, Section 504 of the Rehabilitation Act states that an institution may not use a test that has a disproportionate adverse effect on persons with disabilities unless it has been validated for that population. Consistent with these laws, the use of testing accommodations has been required in recent years in assessing students with disabilities and ELLs, in order to obtain a true estimate of the ability and achievement of these students.

However, concerns have been raised in the meantime that the use of testing accommodations on standardized tests can sometimes make technical aspects of the tests questionable. Specifically, changing standard test administration procedures and materials may decrease or even eliminate the reliability and validity of the test and render the results meaningless. Therefore, this creates a potential conflict between the use of testing accommodations and the psychometric soundness of assessment. Best practices call for a balance between the two, in that testing accommodations should be used in a manner that does not sacrifice the reliability and validity of the test results. To develop a full appreciation of this issue, let us examine the notions of standardization, reliability, and validity in a more thorough manner.

STANDARDIZATION

As mentioned in Chapter 2, a major characteristic of educational and psychological tests is standardization. According to Anastasi and Urbina (1997), standardization implies uniformity of procedures in administering a test and scoring the results. That is, the same testing conditions (e.g., test content and procedures) are applied to all examinees taking the test. The conditions do not vary from one examiner and setting to another. The conditions also do not vary for different examinees. Placing all examinees under the same conditions in testing is similar to conducting a controlled laboratory experiment. Only under such a uniform situation can test scores from different examinees be compared in a meaningful manner. That is, differences in test scores may be interpreted to reflect differences between examinees in the construct or attribute measured by the test, rather than fluctuations in testing conditions.

However, standardization may pose a problem for diverse learners who exhibit different physical, sensory, linguistic, cultural, or psychological qualities from the general population. This is because some of the students with disabilities or ELLs may not have the requisite skills (e.g., sensory, motor, linguistic) in taking the tests. As a result, special accommodations need to be made in testing these students.

Theoretically, all testing accommodations represent a departure from the standard test administration. In some situations, testing accommodations neither drastically change the testing procedures nor significantly affect the validity of the test results. For example, allowing a student to take a group achievement test in an individual setting would not likely change the meaning of the test scores. In other situations, however, testing accommodations may constitute major changes in the standard administration procedure that is essential to the reliability and validity of test results. These modifications may alter or damage the technical aspects of the assessment and produce questionable test results. Therefore, when test accommodations are used with students with disabilities or ELLs, their effects on the validity of test scores should be carefully examined.

RELIABILITY

Reliability refers to the consistency and stability of test scores. It indicates how consistently a test measures a construct or attribute of interest. When a test has high reliability, it produces the same or very consistent results when used with the same examinee. Contrarily, a test with low reliability would produce inconsistent or different results on the same student. There are several ways to examine the reliability of a test, including comparing the scores obtained by the same examinees on different administrations of the same test, with different sets of items, or with different examiners or scorers.

It would not be difficult to see that when a test produces inconsistent results on the same student, all the different scores cannot be accurate. This indicates there are errors involved in the measurement. Therefore, reliability can also be defined as the degree to which test scores are free from measurement errors. Sources of measurement errors include test administration (e.g., quality of the testing environment and examiner's adherence to test instructions), examinee characteristics (e.g., anxiety, motivation, attention, and fatigue level), test scoring (e.g., subjective judgment in scoring and computational errors), and attributes of the test (e.g., unrepresentative item sampling) (Gregory, 1996; Sax, 1989).

Geisinger (1994a) states that modifications to standard test administration may increase measurement errors and decrease test score reliability. For example, in using bilingual interpreters in testing ELLs, different interpreters may make different interpretations. Similarly, in testing students with visual impairments, different scribes may record responses differently. These examiner-related differences are likely to introduce errors into the testing process. When a modified version of a standardized test involves more measurement errors than the original test, the scores from the modified or accommodated test are less accurate in reflecting the construct or attribute being measured. This means that the scores from the accommodated and original versions are not comparable. Comparability of test scores is ensured only when the standardized and accommodated tests yield equivalent reliability and measurement errors.

VALIDITY

An even more important consideration in judging the value of a test is validity, which is defined as the degree to which a test measures what it purports to measure. For example, if a test were designed to measure reading ability, the test users would want to make sure it measures reading ability and not some other attribute or characteristic. With regard to test scores, validity reflects the degree of truthfulness of the inferences that can be drawn from test scores. For example, a valid reading test would enable its users to draw valid inferences from the test scores about students' reading abilities.

Messick (1980) posits that the validity of test scores may be affected by construct-irrelevant components and construct underrepresentation in measurement. Construct-irrelevant components are factors that are irrelevant to the construct being measured by a test. Construct underrepresentation occurs when a test fails to fully measure the construct it is intended to measure. Both construct-irrelevant components and construct underrepresentation may influence or even distort the validity of test scores of diverse learners on standardized tests. For example, when an ELL with minimum English proficiency is administered a standardized achievement test in English, the test may become a measure of literacy or language, instead of a skills assessment measure. The test is then considered to be invalid because it measures language, rather than the content it was originally intended to assess. The test results will most likely underestimate the student's achievement in the content area measured. In this situation, valid inferences about the student's academic skills cannot be drawn from the test scores (French, 1992; Lacelle-Peterson & Rivera, 1994; Zehler, Hopstock, Fleischman, & Grenick, 1994). Similarly, the special physical and psychological qualities that students with disabilities have often introduce construct-irrelevant variance in their scores on standardized tests.

The purpose of using accommodations in testing diverse learners is to neutralize the effects of their disabilities or lack of English language skills. The intent is also to ensure that the test results accurately reflect what is supposed to be measured, rather than the disability or language limitation of the student. With that said, however, it is also essential to maintain the validity of test scores on accommodated tests for diverse learners. Even if the standard test administration procedures have been modified, the test user should be able to make valid interpretations from the test scores about the construct or attribute measured by the test. This may not be achieved easily sometimes in testing diverse learners.

In other situations, depending on the intended use of the test, testing accommodations may decrease or even nullify the validity of test results. For example, if speed of performance is a vital component of the skills being assessed, then allowing for extended time may invalidate test results. Similarly, when a reading test is read to students suffering from learning disabilities and/or visual impairments, it ceases to be a measure of reading ability. Rather, the test has been changed into an auditory measure, thus invalidating the results. In other instances, modifying the content of a test (e.g., eliminating a portion of the test) would significantly alter what is measured and cause a problem of construct underrepresentation in test results.

The ADA requires reasonable accommodations for individuals with disabilities, but it also indicates that such accommodations should not fundamentally alter the construct or attribute being measured by the test. It is important to be able to make valid interpretations from the test scores of diverse learners who receive testing accommodations, just as it is crucial to be able to make the same interpretations with general education students who did not receive any accommodations. Proper use of testing accommodations will eliminate the effects of disabilities, language barriers, or other special qualities and give diverse learners an equal chance to display their true abilities. However, if employed arbitrarily or used inappropriately, testing accommodations can invalidate test scores.

TYPES OF VALIDITY EVIDENCE

All tests should establish evidence of validity for different uses and purposes of the test. The *Standards for Educational and Psychological Testing* (AREA, APA, & NCME, 1999) adopt construct validity as a unitary concept. That is, all tests are viewed as measures of some construct. A construct is defined as an attribute or characteristic that a test is designed to measure. It is essential that all tests measure what they intend to measure and achieve construct validity. Under this notion, there are not different separate types of validity, as traditionally thought. Rather, there are distinct types of evidence that one may use to assess the extent to which a test measures the construct it purports to measure. When testing accommodations are used with diverse learners, it is important to show that tests administered with and without accommodations are comparable in the constructs they measure. Here follows descriptions of the five types of validity evidence indicated in the 1999 *Standards*. Depending on the particular use of a test, one or more kinds of evidence may need to be established and documented.

Evidence Based on Test Content

Test content refers to "the themes, wording, and format of the test items, tasks, or questions on a test, as well as the guidelines for procedures regarding administration and scoring" (AREA, APA, & NCME, 1999, p. 11). It is important that the content of a test adequately samples the content of a particular subject matter or knowledge domain, so that a student's scores may be used to infer the knowledge he or she has on the subject matter measured by the test. Evidence based on test content may be arrived at by logical or empirical analysis about the relevance of the test content to the content of a particular domain of interest. For example, content experts may be used to judge the representativeness with which an item or task content covers a particular domain. When testing accommodations are made for students with disabilities or ELLs, evidence should be provided to show that the same content is being measured on both the standard and accommodated versions of the test.

In achievement testing, the notions of the so-called curricular validity and instructional validity (Mehrens and Lehman, 1988) also should be considered in gathering validity evidence based on test content. Curricular validity refers to the degree to which the test content is covered by the curriculum materials being adopted in a school. Instructional validity relates to the extent to which the test content is actually taught in a school. If a school wants to select a commercial standardized achievement test to be used with its students, it should ensure that the content of the test items adequately samples the curriculum material and instructions being provided to the students. The idea is to make sure the students have had an opportunity to learn the content being assessed on the test. It is especially critical that students with disabilities or ELLs have been exposed to the same educational opportunities to learn the content that the general education students have had.

Evidence Based on Response Processes

The concept of response processes is related to test content. Instead of measuring a direct content (e.g., knowledge, skills, or behaviors), a test may be designed to measure the processes that a student uses in arriving at a response. One example is a test of cognitive processes such as mathematical reasoning or problem solving. On such a test it is important that the test scores adequately reflect the reasoning or problem-solving abilities that a student has in mathematics, rather than some irrelevant construct components.

Evidence based on response processes generally comes from the careful analysis of the individual responses through observation, recording, and expert judgment (AREA, APA, & NCME, 1999). If a standardized test is designed to measure certain response processes, then these same processes also should be measured on the accommodated test for diverse learners. It is possible that in some situations testing accommodations used with diverse learners may change the response processes called for by a test. For example, the cognitive processes used by students without disabilities to interpret figures and graphs may be altered when the task is described verbally to students with visual impairments (Bennett, Rock, & Novatkoski, 1989; Geisinger, 1994a). Finally, as is true with test content, students with disabilities or ELLs should have been exposed to the response processes required in comprehending and processing the content material on the test.

Evidence Based on Internal Structure

Analysis of the internal structure of a test can indicate the degree to which the relationships among test items and test components conform to the construct measured by the test (AERA, APA, & NCME, 1999). These relationships should not change between a standardized test used with general population students and its accommodated version for diverse learners. Otherwise, valid interpretation of test results cannot be made for the diverse learners. Evidence based on internal structure is essential in determining whether items on the standard and accommodated versions of a test measure the same construct across students with and without disabilities, or with and without English language limitations.

One method to gather evidence based on internal structure is factor analysis. This is a statistical procedure that can be used for determining which items of a test cluster together, and thereby measuring the same underlying ability or characteristic. Findings from factor analysis can be used to determine whether the standard version of a test (used with the general population) and the accommodated versions of the test (used with specific groups of diverse learners) measure the same internal structure. If the results indicate equivalent factor structure between the two versions of the test, then this supports the idea that test scores on the accommodated version have the same meaning as scores on the standard version. Otherwise, the scores may have different meanings, and interpretation of test scores obtained from diverse learners under nonstandard test administration should be made with caution.

A second method is to examine item–test and component–test correlations. This indicates the relation between a particular item or subtest and the test as a whole. If the correlations for the standard and accommodated versions are about the same or highly similar, this gives evidence of test score validity for the diverse learners who receive testing accommodations. If the correlations are higher or lower for students with disabilities or ELLs than for general education students, the involved items or components may be more or less discriminating for the former groups.

A third method is differential item functioning (DIF). DIF analysis examines whether certain items on a test function differently (e.g., different average item scores, different rates of choosing various item options) for those students who received accommodations than for those students who did not. "Items identified as functioning differently are then evaluated by bias review panels to determine whether they are measuring irrelevant factors" (Pitoniak and Royer, 2001, p. 78). If DIF analysis reveals certain items have become more difficult or easier as a result of testing accommodations, then this would indicate that accommodations have an impact on the items and care should be exercised in drawing inferences from test scores on the accommodated test.

Evidence Based on Relations to Other Variables

Another source of validity is the relationship between test results and variables external to the test. External variables may be some relevant criteria that are hypothesized to measure the same constructs. Commonly used external criteria in school assessments include school grades, teacher ratings, disability diagnoses, and another established test. Generally, the test and the external criterion are administered at about the same time or at two different points in time. If high correlation is found between test scores and the criterion, the test is considered to be valid in measuring the construct it purports to measure.

Besides test–criteria relationships, validity evidence may be obtained from the relationship between a test and some external variables measuring different constructs. In this situation, one would expect the test and the external variable to have a low or no relationship. Whereas relationships between test scores and other measures of the same constructs provide convergent evidence, relationships between test scores and measures of different constructs provide discriminant evidence (AERA, APA, & NCME, 1999). When tests are used with students who require accommodations, correlations between accommodated test scores and the criterion measure should be the same as correlations between scores on the standard version and the criterion measure. For example, if scores on a standardized test have been found to be predictive of a future criterion (e.g., high school GPA), then the same predictive usefulness should be found for the accommodated tests.

Evidence Based on Consequences of Testing

The issue of consequences of testing has received considerable attention in recent years. It is possible that the use of tests may yield adverse consequences for identifiable groups of diverse learners. For example, it is historically known that disproportionately high numbers of African American and Latino students are placed in special education classes based on their test results. According to the 1999 *Standards* (AERA, APA, & NCME, 1999), such consequences do not in and of themselves indicate that a test is invalid. Further analysis is necessary to identify sources of the consequence. If differential consequence is due to different distributions of skills measured by a test, then the finding of group difference per se does not necessary imply that the test scores are invalid. For example, if a blind student scored low on a test of visual reasoning due to the lack of skills measured and consequently was placed in a special education class, this test consequence would not interfere with the valid interpretation of the test results.

On the other hand, if a student's low test score is not due to a lack of skills, as measured by the test, but can be traced to a source of invalidity such as construct underrepresentation or construct-irrelevant components, then validity would be called into question (AERA, APA, & NCME, 1999). Because test accommodations aim to reduce or remove sources of invalidity and increase validity of test scores of diverse learners, their use should serve to reduce adverse consequences on some groups of students (e.g., incorrectly placing ELLs in special education classes).

EFFECTS OF ACCOMMODATIONS ON RELIABILITY AND VALIDITY

A series of studies were conducted in the 1980s on exams administered by ETS and the College Board to validate tests modified for examinees with disabilities. These studies examined the comparability of the Scholastic Aptitude Test (SAT) and the Graduate Record Examination (GRE) administered to examinees without disabilities and the accommodated versions administered to four groups of examinees with disabilities: visual impairment, hearing impairment, physical impairment, and learning disability. Generally, the results of these studies found that the use of accommodations with examinees with disabilities on the SAT and GRE did not impair the comparability of reliability and validity to the examinees without disabilities.

One of these studies was reported by Bennett, Rock, Kaplan, and Jirele (1988), who looked at the reliability of the SAT and GRE administered to examinees with and without disabilities. Their results indicated that the standard errors of measurement of tests administered with various accommodations (e.g., Braille, extended time, cassette tape) for the four groups of examinees with disabilities were almost identical to that of the examinees without disabilities. Similar but somewhat less positive findings were revealed in studies examining the validity of the SAT and GRE administered with testing accommodations. Specifically, comparable factor structure (Bennett, Rock, Kaplan, 1987; Rock, Bennett, & Jirele, 1988), item functioning (Bennett, Rock, Kaplan, & Jirele, 1988; Bennett, Rock, & Novatkoski, 1989), and predictive usefulness (Braun, Ragosta, and Kaplan, 1988) were found between the standard and nonstandard versions of both the SAT and GRE.

It should be noted, however, that minor exceptions to the general findings were noted in these studies. For example, Bennett and colleagues (1988) found that, after accommodation, some items on the SAT became more difficult for students with disabilities while other items became easier. Braun, Ragosta, and Kaplan (1988) also found that in some cases nonstandard administrations of the SAT and GRE resulted in slight over- and underprediction of average grades in college and graduate school. Specifically, SAT scores underpredicted college GPAs for individuals with hearing impairment, while scores for individuals with physical impairment and individuals with learning disabilities were overpredicted.

Besides the SAT and GRE research, a few studies (Koretz, 1997; Koretz & Hamilton, 1999; as cited in Pitoniak & Royer, 2001) have examined the validity of statewide assessments administered to students with disabilities. The first finding of these studies was that differential item functioning was present on selected items on various parts of a statewide assessment between accommodated students with disabilities and students without disabilities who did not receive accommodations. While most of these items were differentially more difficult for students with disabilities, some of the items were found to be differentially easy. The second finding revealed that nonsimilar item–test and component–test correlations were found on some parts of the assessment between students with and without disabilities. The authors suggested that the use of testing accommodations for students with disabilities could interfere with the validity of the assessment.

Thus, the available research seems to suggest that the reliability and validity of the accommodated versions of the SAT and GRE for examinees with disabilities do not differ appreciably from those of the original forms. However, the findings may not be generalized to statewide or other types of assessments. More research is needed in this area to establish equivalent reliability and validity between standard and accommodated versions of various types of tests.

EFFECTS OF ACCOMMODATIONS ON TEST PERFORMANCE

A fair amount of empirical research is now available on the effects of accommodations on test scores of students with disabilities. A good portion of this research, especially the earlier studies, has been conducted on the SAT and GRE. The more recent research has included statewide and other types of assessments (e.g., performance assessment). The available research has examined the effects of a variety of testing accommodations used with diverse learners. This section reviews some major research on three types of assessments: SAT and GRE, statewide assessments, and other assessments. In addition, studies on the effects of extended time are reviewed in a separate section, because it is probably the most widely used and controversial testing accommodation.

Scholastic Aptitude Test and Graduation Record Examination

The series of SAT and GRE studies mentioned earlier also examined the effects of various accommodations (e.g., Braille, large print type, cassette tape, extended time) on the test performance of students with disabilities. The general findings indicate that the mean SAT scores for the examinees with visual impairments and the examinees with physical impairments tested with accommodations were comparable to those of the examinees without disabilities. However, the mean SAT scores for the examinees with hearing impairments was one standard deviation below the mean of the examinees without disabilities, and the mean for the examinees with learning disabilities was two-thirds of a standard deviation below the examinees without disabilities (Bennett et al., 1988).

Similar patterns were noted on the GRE as well. Braun, Ragosta, and Kaplan (1988) reported that the mean GRE-V scores for the examinees with physical impairments and examinees with visual impairments were similar to those of the examinees without disabilities, but the mean GRE-Q scores for these two groups of examinees with disabilities were slightly lower (one-quarter to three-quarters standard deviations) than the sample without disabilities.

The studies also showed examinees with disabilities (e.g., LD) who received special administrations of the SAT and GRE to have higher scores than did examinees with the same disabilities (e.g., LD) who received regular administrations. These results indicate that while some test accommodations do increase the scores of students with disabilities, they do not always rise the scores to the level of examinees without disabilities.

Statewide Assessments

Two similar studies by Grise, Beattie, and Algozzine (1982; and Beattie, Grise & Algozzine 1983) evaluated the effects of several testing accommodations on the Florida State Student Assessment Test (SSAT). The 1982 study included 344 fifth-grade students with learning disabilities and the 1983 study included 345 third-grade students with learning disabilities. The content of the test was not altered in both studies. The changes made to the tests included using arrows and stop signs to guide students through the test, ordering items in terms of level of difficulty, allowing complete sentences to be on one line, placing reading comprehension passages in shaded boxes, preparing examples for each set of items pertaining to a particular skill, increasing example/item ratio, and altering answer formats. In addition, the modified SSAT was printed in two different versions: one with standard print and the other with large print in 18-point type.

Both studies yielded similar results. Modifications made on the SSAT enhanced the test performance of students with learning disabilities. More students with learning disabilities who received the accommodated version of the test demonstrated mastery of the skills as compared to the students with learning disabilities taking the standard version. In some cases, 20 percent to 30 percent more students reached mastery levels with accommodation than when the test was taken under standard conditions. However, enlargement of type size did not have a significant effect on test performance. The overall mean scores of students tested using the regular print version were not significantly different from those of students tested with the large print tests.

Tindal, Heath, Hollenbeck, Almond, and Harniss (1998) studied the effects of a response accommodation and a presentation accommodation on a statewide math and reading assessment. The participants were 481 fourth-grade students; 84 percent of the sample was in general education and 16 percent from special education. A between-group experimental design was used to compare the performance of special education students who received accommodations and general education students who did not receive accommodations. The response accommodation allowed the students to directly mark the test booklet, and the presentation accommodation had the teacher orally read the test to the students.

The results indicated that scores on both the reading and math tests were not influenced by the response accommodation. Marking the test booklet directly (the accommodation condition) was generally not any more effective than bubbling in answers on a separate sheet (the standard condition). However, students in special education performed significantly higher when the math test was read to them by a trained teacher than when they read the test themselves. This improvement was found only for special education students, not for general education students.

At least one study, however, found that testing accommodations might actually decrease the performance of students with disabilities on large-scale assessments. Mick (1989) examined the effects of accommodations made on the minimum competency test on the overall performance of seventy-six high school sophomores. Thirty-six students with learning disabilities (LD) and forty students with educable mental retardation (EMR) were administered both an accommodated version and a standard version of the minimum competency test (MCT). In this case, the Instructional Objectives Exchange (IOX) Basic Skill Test: Reading was used as the MCT of choice. The accommodated version of the test included moderately increased print size, unjustified lines for reading phrases (e.g., sentences were kept complete on one line), and writing responses directly on the test booklet.

Results of this study revealed that both the students with LD and EMR performed significantly better on the standard version of the IOX than on the accommodated version. Mick (1989) suggests that this unexpected result might have been due to the fact that secondary students are already "test wise." In other words, high school students that are repeatedly exposed to the standardized test format may not be accustomed to more accommodated versions of the same tests. The researcher also noted that conclusions must be cautiously drawn from the results of this study due to difficulty in constructing two equivalent forms of the test, as well as the relatively small sample size.

Other Assessment Measures

Two recent studies investigated the effects of test accommodations on nontraditional tests. Fuchs, Fuchs, Eaton, Hamlett, and Karns (2000) used an experimental design to study the effects of testing accommodations on curriculum-based measurement (CBM) scores of students with and without learning disabilities. The participants were 373 fourth- and fifth-grade students, of whom 192 were identified to have a learning disability (LD) and

181 were without learning disability (non-LD). Three types of mathematics CBM were used: computations, concepts and applications, and problem solving. These CBMs were administered to each examinee under a standard condition and various accommodated test conditions as follows: computations (with extended time), concepts and applications (with extended time, with calculator, and with reading aloud to students), and problem solving (with extended time, with calculator, with reading aloud to students, and with encoding).

The researchers used the subsample of non-LD students to estimate the "typical boost" that would be expected for each accommodation. They then compared the accommodation boost of students with LD to the typical boost to determine whether a greater-than-expected boost existed for each student with a disability. Overall, non-LD students outperformed students with LD on all three types of CBM under the standard condition. With regard to the effects of testing accommodations, students with LD did not benefit differentially from the accommodations on either the computations or concepts and applications CBM. On the problem-solving CBM, however, students with LD benefited more than non-LD students from extended time, reading aloud, and encoding accommodations.

In a different experimental study, Elliott, Kratochwill, and McKevitt (2001) analyzed the effects of testing accommodations on test performance of students with and without disabilities. The participants included 100 fourth graders, of whom 41 were students with disabilities (24 students with LD and 17 students had various other disabilities) and 59 were students without disabilities. The study used a between-series design featuring alternating treatment design elements. All 41 students with disabilities received individualized accommodations specified in their Individualized Education Programs (IEP). The students without disabilities were randomly assigned to one of the three comparison conditions: 25 in a no accommodation condition, 20 in a standard accommodation package condition (e.g., extra time, assistance with directions, reading support, and verbal encouragement of effort), and 14 in a teacher-recommended accommodations condition (e.g., individualized accommodations as recommended by the teacher). The dependent measures were scores on math and science performance tasks.

Results indicated that more than 75 percent of the individualized test accommodations for students with disabilities had a moderate or large effect on test scores. However, the effect of individualized accommodations was not positive for a small percentage (less than 20 percent) of the students. Unexpectedly, the authors also found that testing accommodations had a lesser but significant effect on the scores of about 50 percent of the students without disabilities (Elliott, Kratochwill, & McKevitt, 2001).

Effects of Extended Time

More studies are available that test the effectiveness of extended time than any other modifications. Also, there is more research on extended time conducted on students with learning disabilities than on students with other disabilities. Comparatively, there is a lack of research examining the effects of extended time on ELLs. The time factor is believed to bias the results of diverse learners on standardized tests, due to either their slower speed in processing information or limited English language skills. When no extra time was given to these students, the slower speed of their performance may introduce construct-irrelevant variance and interfere with the validity of the test scores. As a result, the scores may not accurately reflect the true level of knowledge and skills of these students.

Mixed findings have been reported on the effect of extended time on the SAT and GRE. A few earlier studies investigated whether test timing might have an effect on the SAT and GRE scores of ethnic minority students. For example, Wild, Durso, and Rubin (1982) surmised that certain examinee subgroups might be given too little time to complete the GRE. They studied the effect of increasing the time allowed per item on scores of different demographic subgroups defined by race, sex, and number of years that have elapsed since the baccalaureate degree was obtained. The results showed that although a larger portion of the examinees completed the verbal and quantitative portions of the GRE when given additional time, this extra time did not significantly affect the scores of any of the groups. Evans (1980) found similar results on the SAT in that extended time did not differentially affect the scores of groups defined by ethnicity, sex, rural or urban residency, and years out of school.

However, studies on individuals with disabilities have yielded different findings. Centra (1986) conducted a study to determine the effects of extended time on SAT for students with learning disabilities (LD). Results showed that LD students' performance improved when given extra time and that the increase in their scores was greater than that for students without disabilities tested with extra time. These results suggest that the additional time is needed to reduce the effects of the examinee's disability. Many students with LD have slower reading rates than do students without disabilities. Thus, these students are able to respond to only a limited number of questions during a standard administration of the SAT. The increased time allows them to reach the final questions on the test, thus providing them with the same opportunity as students without disabilities.

Camara (1998) in a more recent study reported similar findings. The study compared the effects of extended time on the SAT for examinees with and without learning disabilities. It was found that examinees with LD scored higher with extended time than without extended time, and this gain of scores is greater than that for examinees without LD. The author also found a direct relationship between the score gains increased and the amount of extended time provided to the students with LD—as extended time increased, the score gains of students with LD also increased proportionately. Camara (1998) noted, however, that overuse of extended time may give students with LD an unfair advantage to increase their scores and may change the construct being measured by the test.

Besides the SAT and GRE studies, the effects of extended time on test performance have also been investigated in other settings. On the elementary school level, Munger and Lloyd (1991) administered the Iowa Test of Basic Skills to 212 fifth-grade students, of whom 6 had physical impairments, 94 had learning disabilities, and 112 had no disability. One form of the test was administered to the students under timed condition and a parallel form was administered under untimed condition.

The results revealed that the mean number of items completed by the two groups was approximately equal. The two groups could not be discriminated on the number of items attempted under timed condition. However, students without disabilities scored significantly higher than students with disabilities under both timed and untimed conditions. For either group, there was no significant score difference between timed and untimed conditions. There was neither evidence of a difference in test speededness for the two groups nor evidence indicating additional time would differentially affect the performance of students with and without disabilities. These findings are in partial agreement with some of the findings revealed in the study by Fuchs and colleagues (2000), in which extended time did not increase test performance on two of the three math CBMs. These researchers observed that because students in their sample with learning disabilities had limited mathematics competence, these students were unable to use the additional time allowed to answer more items correctly.

On the college level, Baldwin, Murfin, Ross, Seidel, Clements, & Morris (1989) examined the effects of extended time on the performance of 171 "marginal" college freshmen on the Nelson-Denny Reading Test (NDRT). The sample consisted of fifty-two honors students, fifty-four students enrolled in a developmental reading course, and sixty-five international students in the developmental reading course who scored lower than average on the Test of English as a Foreign Language (TOEFL). The NDRT is regularly used as a placement test for reading in colleges and universities. It is comprised of a vocabulary section with a 15-minute time limit and a comprehension section with a 20-minute time limit. Subjects were randomly assigned to one of the two treatment groups. The regular time treatment group took the NDRT under the standard time limits. The extended time group was given a 50 percent increase in the standard time with 22 minutes for the vocabulary section and 30 minutes for the comprehension section. The scores of the two groups were compared to determine whether there was an interaction between testing time and subject groups.

The results indicted that the extended time treatment group had higher mean scores and completed more items than did the regular time group. The timed format of the NDRT suppressed the scores of the international and developmental readers in contrast to those of the honors students. Furthermore, the vocabulary subtest was found to be a speed test for all groups.

Runyan (1991) provided additional support for extended time testing accommodation in college students. In this study, the Nelson-Denny Reading Test was administered to sixteen college students with learning disabilities and fifteen normally achieving college students under timed and extra-time conditions. Results indicated that the reading rate was significantly higher for the normally achieving students compared to that of the students with learning disabilities. Students with learning disabilities scored significantly lower than the normally achieving students under timed conditions. However, when given extra time, students with learning disabilities performed as well as their normally achieving peers. Furthermore, normally achieving students did not perform significantly better when given the extended time.

Finally, Alster (1997) compared the performance of forty-four community college students with disabilities and forty-four students without disabilities on an algebra test under timed and extended timed conditions. Two comparable versions of the test were used, one administered under timed conditions and the other administered under extended time conditions. Under timed conditions, students with learning disabilities (LD) scored significantly lower than did students without learning disabilities. The scores of students with LD increased significantly with extended time, and there was no significant difference between the extended time scores of students with and without LD as well as between the scores of the students with LD under the extended time conditions and the scores of students without LD under the timed conditions.

To sum up the findings of the research just reviewed, the majority of the studies indicate that students with disabilities score lower than students without disabilities on standardized tests. Generally, testing accommodations are found to be helpful in reducing the effect of disabilities and in enhancing the test performance of students with disabilities. However, the results are also somewhat varied. The assumption that testing modifications are beneficial is not always supported by empirical findings. It is difficult to draw conclusions across studies due to the different designs, sample sizes, dependent measures, and other technical qualities of the studies. The issue is further complicated because a wide spectrum of factors (e.g., intended use of tests, types of accommodations, nature and extent of disabilities, other student characteristics) may interact and affect the findings of the research. As Elliott, Kratochwill, and McKevitt (2001) correctly point out, more experimental research is needed to produce clearer and more definitive results on the effects of testing accommodations on test results. Such research should prove most useful in guiding the selection of appropriate testing accommodations for use with diverse learners, as well as in interpreting their test results.

FLAGGING OF SCORES ON ACCOMMODATED TESTS

Empirical research on the effects of testing accommodations provides a necessary basis in judging score comparability between standard and accommodated test administrations. Unfortunately, due to the still limited research available, it is often difficult to determine whether scores for diverse learners taking a test under accommodated testing conditions are equivalent or comparable in meaning to those obtained by general education students taking the test under standard conditions. This directly affects the way by which scores obtained under accommodated conditions should be reported.

The practice of reporting test scores varies in different contexts (AREA, APA, & NCME, 1999). In individual testing, the testing accommodations used in administering tests to students with disabilities or ELLs are typically described in the test report. Further, the possible effects of the accommodations on the validity of the scores are discussed. If the validity of the test scores obtained under accommodated test administration is called into question, then test results are reported with appropriate qualifications and sometimes qualitatively rather than quantitatively.

The practice of reporting test scores in large-scale testing is different, however. Traditionally, when scores from a nonstandard test administration are reported, the score report contains some types of designation (e.g., an asterisk next to the score) indicating testing accommodations were used. This procedure is known as the flagging of test scores. However, often the score report gives no explanation about the nature of the testing accommodations used and their possible effects on the validity of the test scores. This practice has generated some controversy and debate. Proponents believe flagging is necessary. Not doing so would violate professional principles and mislead the users of test scores (e.g., making the users believe that the test takers can do something that in fact they cannot do).

Opponents, on the other hand, argue that flagging of test scores reveals that an examinee has a disability, is a violation of privacy, and is contrary to the Americans with Disabilities Act. Flagging may also prompt invalid inferences about the test scores or prejudice. Laws protecting the rights of persons with disabilities in many instances would bar the use of any sort of score flagging that has the effect of identifying an examinee as a person with disability.

The 1999 *Standards for Educational and Psychological Testing* acknowledge the conflict between the need to identify test scores as obtained under nonstandard administration and the need to maintain privacy of the examinees as required by federal and state laws, and recommend that professional and ethical considerations should be weighted to arrive at a solution in each testing situation. The *Standards* posit that the flagging of test scores by using asterisks or other nonspecific symbols (which indicate only that a test's administration has been modified and do not provide additional information as to the nature of the modifications) invites confusion and may contribute to bias. Such practices should not be continued. Instead, depending on the knowledge available about the effects of testing accommodations used with particular students, scores from nonstandard administration may be reported in two different ways. First, when there is evidence to demonstrate that scores from nonstandard test administration are comparable to those from standard administration, there is no need to note or describe the accommodations. On the other hand, when such evidence is lacking, then the nature of the testing accommodations used (e.g., extended time, test-translated) should be explained when reporting test scores, if doing so is permitted by law, "to assist test users properly to interpret and act on test scores" (AERA, APA, & NCME, 1999, p. 108). Furthermore, test reports should avoid any references to the nature of the examinee's disability and, whenever possible, also offer interpretations in light of research on the accommodations.

SUMMARY

Although testing accommodations are intended to provide diverse learners an opportunity to demonstrate their best performance on various school assessments, there is a concern that any departure from standard test administration may decrease the reliability and validity of test scores.

Reliability refers to the stability and consistency of test scores. When testing accommodations are used, the nonstandard version of a test may contain more measurement errors than the original test. When this occurs, scores on the accommodated test are less accurate in reflecting the construct being measured. Methods of examining reliability of a test include comparing the scores obtained by the same test takers on different administrations of the same test, with different sets of items, or with different examiners or scores.

Validity refers to the degree of truthfulness of the inferences that can be drawn from test scores. If used appropriately, testing accommodations should increase the validity of test scores obtained by students with disabilities or ELLs. However, if employed arbitrarily and inappropriately, testing accommodations may reduce or even nullify the validity of test results. There are five types of validity evidence: evidence based on test content, evidence based on response processes, evidence based on internal structure, evidence based on relations to other variables, and evidence based on consequences of testing.

Only limited empirical research is available on the effect of testing accommodations on the reliability and validity of test scores obtained by diverse learners. Generally, the available research indicates that the use of testing accommodations with examinees with disabilities on the SAT and GRE did not significantly impair the comparability of reliability and validity to examinees without disabilities. However, these findings are not to be generalized to statewide or other types of assessments.

Research also has been conducted to examine the effects of various accommodations on the performance of students with disabilities on SAT and GRE, state tests, and other assessments. The findings are mixed. Whereas some accommodations have been found to increase test performance of students with disabilities, other accommodations have shown no significant effects. It is difficult to draw conclusions across studies due to the different designs, sample size, dependent measures, and other technical qualities of the studies. More experimental research is needed in this area.

Finally, flagging of test scores in large-scale testing has been a controversial issue. The 1999 *Standards for Educational and Psychological Testing* recommend that if comparability can be demonstrated between standard and nonstandard test administrations, there is no need to flag. However, if the test results are not comparable, then the testing accommodations used should be noted and explained, if doing so is permitted by law.

CHAPTER FIVE

USING ACCOMMODATIONS FOR STUDENTS WITH SENSORY AND/OR PHYSICAL DISABILITIES

LAURA MENIKOFF

This chapter provides the readers with information on current practices in accommodations when testing students who have visual impairments, hearing impairments, or physical disabilities. The number of students with these disabling conditions is few when compared to the more prevalent presence of students with learning disabilities, speech and language disorders, and emotional or behavioral disabilities. Although these disabilities are discussed separately, many students with multiple disabilities have two or more of these disorders. This chapter includes the following topics: blind and visual impairment, deaf and hard of hearing, physical disabilities, empirical research on the effects of testing accommodations, and some concluding remarks and recommendations. For each disability the chapter provides information on currently accepted definitions and classification systems, the diagnostic criteria that must be present as the rationale for the requested accommodations, and methods of accommodation. After addressing the three areas of disability separately, there will be a brief description of several empirical studies involving the effects of testing accommodations on student performance. It will become apparent that there has been a paucity of empirical investigations in this field.

BLIND AND VISUAL IMPAIRMENT

Visual impairment is a low incidence condition within the school population, making up less than 1 percent of the school-age group (American Printing

House for the Blind, 1996), and it is estimated to involve less than 0.5 percent of the population of students receiving special education services (U.S. Department of Education, 1999). About three-quarters of the students with visual impairments have some usable vision for learning and performing daily activities. Although some individuals are blind from birth, serious visual impairment more commonly develops during adulthood as a result of disease, physical trauma, and degenerative eye conditions. Over half of the students with visual disability have at least one other disabling condition.

A number of visually impaired students may be identified in the preschool years or on entering the elementary grades. Among the many tasks a student encounters in school that place new demands on the visual system are the following: a heavy load of close-up and distance reading, attention to the details of shapes, letter discrimination, sorting, classifying, and copying from the board. An observant teacher may be concerned about learning progress in general and may be attuned to various signs of visual difficulty. A referral for a vision exam may be required by the school due to such signs of visual problems as excessive rubbing of the eyes, squinting, blinking, or favoring one eye while reading. Additionally, a student may demonstrate difficulty copying print from the board, have trouble recognizing letters, tend to reverse written letters, and present a general avoidance of reading (Salvia & Ysseldyke, 2001; Sattler, 2001). In general, the multidisciplinary evaluation team will request an eye exam to assess sensory functioning prior to conducting other measures of academic functioning.

Definitions and Diagnostic Criteria

The legal definition of visual impairment and blindness, established by the federal government, is generally used to establish eligibility for governmental stipends and access to various support services. The legal definition of visual impairment characterizes vision in terms of acuity and visual field. The functional level of both of these domains is determined by an ophthalmologist. Visual acuity is usually determined by having a person read the lines of letters on a wall chart placed at a distance of 20 feet from where the individual is seated. A person with normal vision can read letters of a standard font at a distance of 20 feet. This is termed 20/20 vision. An individual is considered partially sighted if, even with correction in the better eye, he or she can see at 20 feet what a person with normal vision can see at 70 feet. Partially sighted vision ranges between an acuity of 20/70 and 20/200. A person is considered legally blind if, even with corrective lenses, the person has a measured acuity of 20/200 or less in the better eye. Visual field refers to the peripheral visual display, or the panoramic view, that can be scanned when looking straight ahead. A person with a normal visual field can scan a visual panorama extending 160 degrees. A person is considered legally blind if the visual field is limited to not more than 20 degrees.

The legal definition of visual impairment and blindness is limited in its practical application for educational decisions because it makes no reference as to the manner in which the individual functions on a daily basis with the measured degree of available vision. Within the educational context, the most commonly applied definition of visual impairment is that stated within the Individuals with Disabilities Education Act of 1990. This definition addresses the impact of vision on a child's educational performance. The visual impairment must be so severe, that even with correction, the student's educational performance is adversely affected. Visual impairment includes both partial sight and blindness.

In the spirit of the IDEA, educators define visual impairment in terms of the student's capacity to use print or tactual methods for learning. Distinctions are made among students who have low vision, those who are functionally blind, and those who are totally blind. Students characterized as having low vision are able to use print with magnification aids or may use a combination of Braille and print in order to learn. For low-vision students, a specialist may assist the student and teacher in determining how to use the residual vision efficiently by performing systematic observations of a student's response to the variables of print contrast, lighting conditions, type size, and so forth. Students who are functionally blind tend to use their functional or residual vision for daily operations such as making change, mobility, and housekeeping; however, they use Braille for receptive and expressive print communication. Finally, totally blind students learn through auditory and tactual modalities. The visual channel is not available as a means of learning about the academic or larger environmental context.

The Need for Testing Accommodations

It is generally accepted that most standardized cognitive and achievement tests have not been developed for, or standardized with, individuals who are blind or visually impaired, nor is the traditional paper-and-pencil test accessible to many students with visual impairments. Thus, many of these students require modifications to the test presentation and response format such that each student can demonstrate knowledge or skill via his or her dominant receptive or expressive learning modality. This may mean that the test is presented orally and the student responds verbally, that tactual materials are integral to the testing process, or that the test booklet and response mode incorporate enlarged print or Braille symbols.

The Educational Testing Service (ETS) study conducted by Ragosta and Wendler (1992), designed to develop guidelines for time extensions for students taking the Scholastic Aptitude Test (SAT), suggested that students with visual impairments using adapted test formats required the most time in order to complete the test, and more time than did other groups of students with disabilities. The authors of the study did not investigate whether the slower pace of test taking was primarily attributable to the characteristics of the disability or to the test format itself.

It is also evident that students who are blind from birth often have limited concept development and reduced descriptive terminology for concepts that relate to spatial relationships. Consequently, particular subtests or test items may be inappropriate to administer to a student with serious visual limitations (Sattler, 2001).

An educator specializing in the needs of students with visual impairment can assist in the gathering of other useful data related to testing including the student's response to glare and contrast, the student's response to levels of lighting, and the presence of monocular or binocular vision that may affect the placement of materials and impact further on the amount of time the student takes to read text (Bradley-Johnson, 1995).

Methods of Accommodation

In some cases, students with low vision may be able to take tests under standard test administration; however, many individuals with visual impairments take standardized tests with accommodations. The testing accommodation is offered in order to lessen the influence of the visual impairment on the demonstration of knowledge, skills, and competencies. The following types of accommodations include modifications to the setting, modifications of timing and scheduling, and modifications of the test presentation and response format.

The following material includes testing accommodation procedures for students with visual impairments that appear in professional literature and the publications of major testing centers (e.g., Bradley-Johnson, 1995; New York State Education Department, 1995; Sattler, 2001; Thurlow, Hurley, Spicuzza, & El Sawaf, 1996; Tindal & Fuchs, 1999).

Setting Modifications

Students may require testing in a separate location due to the fact that either extended time, special lighting, oral presentation of items, and/or special magnification equipment is necessary. The room should be as free from auditory distraction as possible, because visually impaired students rely on audition, any extraneous auditory stimuli will be confusing and possibly diminish performance. Some students with low vision need bright illumination, whereas others prefer dim or natural light.

Timing and Scheduling Modifications

Adequate time must be allowed to establish rapport between the assessment professional and the student. Due to the fact that students with visual impairments generally work at a slower pace than peers without disabilities, time extension is a frequently offered testing accommodation. The assessment professional should monitor the student for fatigue and pacing. Reading aloud to the student, and reading Braille takes considerably longer than does independent reading. It is better to have breaks between short testing sessions rather than one long session (Bradley-Johnson & Harris, 1990). The student's IEP or Section 504 Plan should indicate the degree of time extension (e.g., time and a half or double time) and other modifications in test scheduling. For very long tests, it is possible that an exam may be taken during two sessions over the course of consecutive days.

Presentation Modifications

Many students with mild to moderate vision loss may be able to take tests under standardized conditions with the aid of magnification devices. Yet, for other students who have difficulty reading print of standard size and/or tracking the printed lines, there are several available alterations to test format. These include the transcription of text into Braille or large type, increasing the spacing between items, and placing a reduced number of items on each page. In some cases it is not possible to transcribe an item from letters to Braille without losing the original intent of that item. In these cases, the items should be eliminated from the test administration.

When testing students with severely limited vision or total blindness, an assessment professional may select to administer only the verbal domain of a test. Although it is permissible to repeat or simplify directions under some circumstances, the presentation of test instructions should be modified as little as possible in order to maintain the validity of the test. Oral passages and test items must be read verbatim. All components of the test should be read in a neutral tone of voice.

Relatively recent advances in technology for blind and visually impaired students have increased access to the educational and workplace setting. Among the high-tech electronic devices are optical scanners, speech synthesizers capable of scanning text, closed circuit televisions that enlarge print, Braille embossers, and compact note takers. Low-tech assistive equipment includes the Perkins Brailler, the Braille slate and stylus, magnification aids, and specially designed illumination equipment (Turnbull, Turnbull, Shank, Smith, & Leal, 2002).

Response Modifications

Students who are totally blind may respond to items either verbally or in Braille. Braille response booklets may be used and credit should be given for an accurate response in any accepted modality. Students with partial vision may need to circle or underline responses directly in the answer booklet as compared to bubbling in responses on a computer scoring response sheet.

DEAF AND HARD OF HEARING

In 2000, the National Center for Health Statistics counted 22 million Americans with hearing impairments. Although hearing impairments are common in older adults, deafness and hearing impairment are considered low-incidence conditions among school-age children. It is estimated that during the 1996–1997 school year about 1.1 million students below the age of 21 received support services to address mild to severe hearing impairment (National Center for Education Statistics, 2000). This figure does not include those students for whom the hearing impairment is secondary to one or more primary disabilities (Schildroth & Hotto, 1994).

Many children are not identified as having a hearing loss until infancy or toddlerhood. Parents begin to observe a pattern of unresponsiveness to loud noises, to familiar voices, or to the calling of the child's name when the child is not directly facing the person. At that point, a pediatrician may provide a referral to a hearing specialist.

Yet other children draw the attention of preschool and primary grade teachers as they begin school and exhibit some of the classic signs of hearing problems. The initial referral problem may involve receptive and expressive language concerns, fluctuating hearing, inconsistent focusing behaviors, and peer interaction problems. More specifically, a child may be referred for a hearing evaluation due to difficulty in understanding and following spoken directions, not responding when called on, requiring frequent repetition of questions, and noninvolvement in group discussions. The student may have speech articulation problems and subsequent difficulty in grasping phonemic awareness concepts. The student often seems to be daydreaming or withdrawn, and/or does not make transitions well between activities (Salvia & Ysseldyke, 2001; Sattler, 2001). As is the case with vision, the multidisciplinary assessment team will initially require a report from a hearing specialist prior to gathering data on educational and psychological functioning.

Definitions and Diagnostic Criteria

As with visual impairment, there is a quantitatively based definition as well as an educationally based definition of hearing impairment. The medical definition categorizes a person's response to sound along a continuum from normal hearing to deafness. There are numerical indices relating the student's ability to hear sounds of certain intensities (loudness) at different frequencies (pitch). A person with a zero decibel loss is regarded as having normal hearing. A 16- to 25-decibel hearing loss is considered a mild hearing deficit. This means that a faint sound heard easily by a person with normal hearing must be amplified to a volume of 16 to 25 decibels to be perceived. A 41- to 55-decibel hearing loss is a moderate hearing deficit. A 70-decibel hearing loss is considered a severe hearing loss, whereas at a 90-decibel hearing loss a person is considered to be deaf, as he or she can no longer perceive meaningful input from auditory stimuli.

The definition favored by educators is that provided by the Individuals with Disabilities Education Act, which states that a student is considered to be deaf if he or she has a hearing loss so severe that the processing of linguistic information through hearing with or without the aid of amplification is seriously impaired, and the student's educational performance is severely affected. A student who is hearing impaired has an impairment of hearing, whether permanent or fluctuating, that severely impedes the child's educational performance, but is not included within the definition of deafness (IDEA, 1990).

The Need for Testing Accommodations

The assessment professional must be aware that few standardized educational and psychological tests have been developed specifically for, or standardized with, students who have moderate or profound hearing impairments. Because of the broad expressive and receptive linguistic deficits in lipreading, writing, reading, and spelling, students who are deaf tend to perform more poorly on standardized tests than do students from other disability groups (Freeman, 1989; Gordon, Stump, & Glaser, 1996).

Although these students have visual access to text, the average student has a constrained competency with Standard English that is in sharp opposition to the highly verbally loaded tests used by many school assessment professionals. These tests require a relatively sophisticated level of expressive and receptive vocabulary, as well as an ability to flexibly adapt to the structure of oral and written English (Gordon, Stump, & Glaser, 1996). Many students with moderate to profound hearing loss have learned English as a second language during school. For a segment of these students the dominant modality for social communication and learning may be one of a variety of manual sign language systems. These sign languages have their own grammatical structure, which is often reflected in student responses in testing situations. Additionally, due to poorly articulated speech and limited oral expressive skill, it is not uncommon for the assessment professional to have difficulty comprehending the responses of many students with severe hearing loss. Conversely, it is uncommon for students with hearing impairments to be reluctant to express their confusion in comprehending the assessment professional's articulations or test item content (Sattler, 2001).

In making testing accommodation decisions for students who have a significant hearing loss, it is important to get the input from medical professionals (i.e., audiologists) as well as the observations and recommendations of teachers, related service providers, and family members who are most familiar with the student during instruction, socializing, and daily living activities.

Methods of Accommodation

Most students with hearing impairments who have more than a mild hearing loss require some form of testing accommodation. The testing accommodation is offered in order to lessen the influence of the hearing impairment on the demonstration of the student's knowledge and skills. The following types of accommodations include modifications to the setting in which the testing takes place, modifications to timing and scheduling, and modifications to the test presentation and response format.

The following material includes testing modification procedures for students with hearing impairments that appear in professional literature and the publications of major testing centers (e.g., Freeman, 1989; Gordon, Stump, & Glaser, 1996; New York State Education Department, 1998; Thurlow, Hurley, Spicuzza, & El Sawaf, 1996; Tindal & Fuchs, 1999).

Setting Modifications

Students may require testing in a separate location due to the factors of extended time and the assistance of a proctor or an interpreter in order to have the material presented in the student's dominant learning modality. The setting should be free from clutter and distraction, particularly extraneous auditory stimuli, because the student must be able to use his or her residual hearing at an optimal level.

Timing and Scheduling Modifications

Students with moderate or severe hearing impairments generally require time extensions for the completion of a test. The students may require breaks during testing due to fatigue. It is possible in the circumstance of a lengthy examination that the test may be given over the course of two consecutive days.

Presentation Modifications

All directions should be written in text or signed words. Some students may require the use of an interpreter for test taking. This is particularly true of students who lost hearing prior to the acquisition of speech and may have a limited grasp of Standard English concepts. A total communication system that combines speech, manual signing, finger spelling, writing, and gestures has been shown to be effective for students who are deaf or hard of hearing (Sattler, 2001; Sullivan, 1982). Other researchers have suggested the use of a combination of signing and captioning for test presentation (Buills & Reiman, 1992).

A variety of high-tech devices have been developed to amplify the residual hearing of students with hearing impairments. The most commonly employed assistive equipment includes hearing aids, FM units, and closed captioning systems.

Response Modifications

Some students may prefer to respond to test items in a sign or total communication system, rather than by providing oral responses. For this purpose an interpreter may serve as a translator or as a scribe for the student. A correct response in any communication modality is to be given credit.

Using Portions of a Test

In some cases it is useful to eliminate those portions of the test that include a good deal of verbally mediated material and administer only the performance scale of these instruments. Even with this consideration, caution should be made in the quantitative interpretation of these performances.

PHYSICAL DISABILITIES

Despite the fact that children with physical disabilities represent a small proportion of the students being served by the nation's schools, a growing number of students with a variety of physical disabilities are enrolled as medical advances have improved the odds of surviving birth traumas, congenital anomalies, childhood disease, and debilitating accidents. It is estimated that about 0.54 percent of children between the ages of 6 and 21 have physical or health impairments (U.S. Department of Education, 1999). Although most students with a physical disability do not have cognitive impairment and function adequately under standard testing conditions, some students may have a physical disability in conjunction with a psychological or sensory condition.

Among the more frequently encountered physical disorders that significantly impact the academic and daily performance of school children are spina biffida, cerebral palsy, epilepsy, muscular dystrophy, juvenile rheumatoid arthritis, fetal alcohol syndrome, and acquired immune deficiency syndrome. As one may gather from this listing, a good deal of diversity exists among the symptoms and effects of these conditions. This section of the chapter will focus on the common features of motor impairment, skeletal weakness, decreased mobility, and impaired communication facility. Depending on the cause and nature of the disability, some of these students may require reevaluations more frequently than will students with other disabling conditions (Christensen, 1990).

Definitions and Criteria

Here as well, a distinction is made between the medical and educational perspectives of students with severe skeletal, musculature, and health challenges. Medical professionals usually refer to orthopedic impairments as physical disabilities, whereas educators refer to a broader umbrella incorporating medical and health concerns as well as multiple disabilities. The spectrum of physical disabilities falls within the auspices of three IDEA categories—Orthopedically Impaired, Other Health Impaired, and Multiple Disabilities.

The IDEA states that students with orthopedic impairments generally have restricted mobility and/or ambulation that is so severe that the student's educational performance is significantly affected. The term *orthopedic impairment* includes defects caused by congenital anomaly (e.g., clubfoot, missing limb), defects caused by disease (e.g., polio, tuberculosis), and impairments with other etiologies (e.g., cerebral palsy, amputations, fractures).

The IDEA identifies a student as having an Other Health Impairment (OHI) when the student exhibits inadequate strength, vitality, or alertness, including a heightened alertness to environmental stimuli, to such a degree that the student's educational performance is adversely affected. The health impairment can be the result of chronic or acute health problems such as asthma, attention-deficit disorders, epilepsy, a heart condition, hemophilia, lead poisoning, leukemia, hepatitis, rheumatic fever, and sickle cell anemia.

Finally, the IDEA states that a child whose disorder falls under the category of Multiple Disabilities has coexisting disabling conditions (such as mental retardation–blindness, mental retardation–orthopedic impairment), the combination of which causes such severe educational needs that they cannot be accommodated in special education programs solely for one of the impairments. The term does not include deaf-blindness (IDEA, 1990; Salvia & Ysseldyke, 2001).

Physical impairments may exist from birth or may develop at a later point. They differ in terms of etiology, prevalence, age of onset, body area and functions affected, rate of progression, and educational implications. A medical professional documents the presence of such a condition and makes a clinical judgment regarding the severity and chronicity of the disability. The feedback from family members and school professionals who are familiar with the student provides important information about the student's adaptive functioning, as well as offering recommendations for accommodations to daily living, instruction, and testing.

The Need for Testing Accommodations

In the test selection phase of the evaluation, the multidisciplinary assessment team should be conscious that most standardized tests place significant response demands on fine motor and visual motor speed and coordination, expressive oral and written communication facility, and sustained focus. Any of these requirements may tax the student with a physical disability. Students who have hard-to-understand speech or who have limited capacity for oral language pose a particular challenge to assessment professionals seeking a valid measure of student knowledge and competence. Sattler (2001) comments that many students with physical disabilities share a sense of anxiety and self-consciousness in formal testing situations. They may be intimidated by the awkwardness of their movements and by the formidable scale of many tests. It is especially important for the assessment professionals to offer patience and encouragement to these students.

The multidisciplinary child study team making a decision regarding testing accommodations must have evidence from a medical professional regarded as a specialist in the area of the particular physical disability (e.g., orthopedist, pulmonary) and from an educational professional experienced with students having specific disabilities (e.g., physical therapist, occupational therapist) that there is a need for a particular type(s) of accommodations for optimal performance of the student under testing conditions. Additionally, the school professionals should document that the student has operated with, and benefits from, similar types of accommodations within the instructional context.

Methods of Accommodation

As suggested by Munger and Lloyd (1991), students with relatively minor physical disabilities may be able to take tests under standard conditions.

However, due to the diversity of type, location, and severity of physical disabilities, it is clear that the decision regarding testing accommodations will be tailored for each child. Students who have mobility as the predominant concern will need adaptations in positioning and/or response modes, as well as scheduling and setting modifications. Students with expressive communication problems will have to be provided with accommodations that facilitate the response options.

The following material includes testing accommodation procedures for students with physical disabilities that appear in professional literature and the publications of major testing centers (e.g., Christensen, 1990; New York State Education Department, 1998; Sattler, 2001; Thurlow, Hurley, Spicuzza, & El Sawaf, 1996; Tindal & Fuchs, 1999).

Setting Modifications

Some students may require testing in a separate location due to the factors of extended time, frequent breaks, special breathing and positioning equipment, and the presence of a proctor and, in some cases, a health paraprofessional. For wheelchair-bound students, the test site must have tables with sufficient height for wheelchair clearance. There must be physical access to testing facilities, handicapped parking, an elevator, and appropriate toileting facilities.

Timing and Scheduling Modifications

Students with serious physical disabilities generally require extended or waived time limits on standardized exams. Students with motor impairments and respiratory ailments tire easily and may require frequent repositioning, thus necessitating extended time either in the single-day administration with shorter testing periods or testing over a couple of days. The student's IEP or Section 504 Plan should indicate the degree of time extension, (e.g., time and a half or double time), and other modifications in test scheduling.

Presentation Modifications

The use of speeded tests tends to penalize these students rather than assessing their abilities and knowledge. These students often respond with physical awkwardness or have a delay between the presentation of the stimulus and the beginning of a response. Subtests that include bonus points for quick performance may be either eliminated from administration or given as untimed subtests in order to gather qualitative data about student performance. Items that demand responses that are not within the student's repertoire or that may be damaging to the student because of pressure on weak body parts should be eliminated from the item pool.

Adaptive equipment is a frequent accommodation for students with physical disabilities. The assessment professional must be familiar with the adaptive devices that facilitate independent daily instructional functioning for these students. Physical and occupational therapists are of significant help in recommending those strategies or devices that may be most useful in an individual assessment of abilities. Students with physical disabilities are able to use computers that are voice activated, controlled by eye gaze or pointers, and others by a specially placed switch. Students with communication concerns may employ a range of devices from high-tech augmentative communication systems to basic communication boards.

Response Modifications

For students with expressive language complications, augmentative communication devices and strategies that have been applied in the home and classroom may be implemented in testing. The techniques range from pointing, nodding, or eye gaze responding, to the relatively simple use of a low-tech picture board. Sattler (2001) provides guidelines for a structured "eye blink" technique useful for the administration of a multiple-choice picture test with students who have serious motor impairments as well as severe expressive language limitations. There is an array of high-tech computers designed to synthesize speech, allow a student to express basic needs, and generally increase independent communication.

Assistive devices to aid written communication are useful for students who have muscle weakness, involuntary movements, or limited fine motor coordination. Low-tech aids include mushroom-handled writing implements, trays with raised edges, slanted writing tables, and nonslide surfaces. Computers with expanded keypads and those that respond to a student's commands via nonverbal communication also facilitate written expression.

EMPIRICAL RESEARCH ON THE EFFECTS OF TESTING ACCOMMODATIONS

Up to this point there have been few published studies offering methodologically sound empirical research on the effects of testing accommodations on the performance of students with sensory or physical impairments. Most of the research has been conducted with groups of students classified as having learning disabilities. That body of work will be presented in the following chapter. This section offers a brief description of several studies that have incorporated small groups of students with sensory and motor impairments.

The earliest studies were conducted by the Educational Testing Service (ETS) and the American College Testing (ACT) program. ETS provided research data on the score and task comparability of standard and nonstandard versions of the Scholastic Aptitude Test and Graduate Record Examination (Willingham, Ragosta, Bennett, Braun, Rock, & Powers, 1988). The authors studied task comparability among the following four groups: students with hearing impairments, students with visual impairments, students with motor disabilities, and students with learning disabilities. The format modifications applied in the nonstandard test administrations were Braille, cassette recorded booklets, and enlarged print editions. The most important finding was that the dimension of predictive validity offered the strongest evidence of inequality among groups. When used as the sole predictor, the scores from nonstandard test administrations were less valid predictors of subsequent academic performance than were the scores for students without disabilities on standard test versions. Among the subgroups of students with disabilities, test scores significantly underestimated the academic performance of hearing impaired students who went on to colleges that offered appropriate support services, whereas test scores overestimated the academic performance of students with physical and learning disabilities (Braun, Ragosta, & Kaplan, 1986). When the scores from nonstandard administrations were combined with grade point averages from high school or college, there was reasonable accuracy of prediction for students with disabilities.

Munger and Lloyd (1991) involved students with learning disabilities and students with physical disabilities (neurological and orthopedic impairments) in a sample of fifth-grade students taking sections of the Iowa Test of Basic Skills under timed and untimed conditions. In the untimed condition students were allowed to take as much time as needed for the completion of the test. Each student was administered two forms of either subtest (timed and untimed) in counterbalanced succession with a short break between versions. The results indicated that for both subtests both groups of students were comparable in terms of test completion (90 percent criteria) and the number of items attempted. Timing appeared to have little effect on the performance of either group. Overall, Munger and Lloyd advocate for the inclusion of students with physical disabilities and learning disabilities in standardized testing. Thurlow, Hurley, Spicuzza, & El Sawaf, (1996) cautioned that the conclusions of this study are limited due to the fact that the researchers included only those students with disabilities who were capable of independent testing under timed conditions.

SOME CONCLUDING REMARKS AND RECOMMENDATIONS

Here are some general recommendations for considering reasonable testing accommodations when assessing students with moderate to severe sensory and/or physical disabilities. As previously stated, many of these students have co-occurring learning disabilities that further complicate decisions regarding test selection, administration, scoring, and interpretation.

- The interpretation of results and high-stakes decisions should be based on multiple sources of data. When making decisions about testing accommodations for these students, it is important to get input from medical professionals as well as the time-tested recommendations of family members, related service providers, and classroom teachers who make formal and informal observations of the student during instruction, socializing, and daily living activities.
- It is the responsibility of each member of the multidisciplinary assessment team to be informed about, and sensitive to, the unique personal characteristics of the students, as well as characteristic features of the disabilities that impact on learning.
- It is important for the assessment professional to offer patience and encouragement to these students. Due to the fact that many of these students feel awkward, self-conscious, and anxious under testing situations, it is crucial to allow ample time to establish rapport.
- Although some students with mild disabilities may be able to take the test under standard conditions, many students with sensory and physical disabilities will need the accommodation of assistive technology. The assessment professionals should be knowledgeable about recent advances within their areas of specialization.
- Students with sensory and physical impairments should have had previous exposure to testing conditions similar to those in the current assessment situation. They should also have been given direct instruction in general test-taking strategies in order to maximize their performance.

SUMMARY

The total number of students with visual impairments, hearing impairments, and physical disabilities is few when compared to the population of students with learning disabilities, speech and language disorders, and emotional or behavioral disabilities. Although there is a medical definition for each disorder, this definition is limited in its practical application for educational decisions because it makes no reference to the impact of the disability on learning and school performance. Within the educational context, the most commonly applied definition is that stated within the Individuals with Disabilities Education Act.

There are few standardized educational and psychological tests that have been developed specifically for students who have sensory or physical disabilities. Although some students with mild sensory impairments may be able to take tests under standardized conditions, due to the diverse, and often combined, physical, cognitive, affective, and communication challenges experienced by these students, it is often necessary for standardized testing procedures to be modified in order to get a valid measure of knowledge, skills, and competencies.

The methods of accommodations offered include modifications to the test setting, modifications to timing and scheduling, and modifications to test presentation and response format. The most commonly accepted test accommodations are testing in a separate location, having the test in a one-on-one setting or with a small group of students having similar mandate, and the accommodation of extended time. The specific accommodations to test presentation or response demands vary with the capability of the student and the nature of the disability.

At this moment in time, there appears to be a general consensus on the part of testing organizations, state education departments, classroom professionals, and parents that these students should have fair access to all aspects of instruction and evaluation. Despite the broad acceptance of testing accommodations for students with sensory and physical disabilities, there has been little research to provide empirical evidence of the hypothesized benefits to test performance by these students.

USING ACCOMMODATIONS FOR STUDENTS WITH LEARNING, COGNITIVE, AND BEHAVIORAL DISABILITIES

LAURA MENIKOFF

This chapter addresses testing accommodations for students with learning disabilities, students with mental retardation, students with attention-deficit/hyperactivity disorder, and students classified as having behavioral and emotional disorders. The diagnosis and assessment of children with psychological disorders related to learning, attention, and behavior is more complex than that related to the sensory and physical disabilities addressed in the previous chapter. Whereas a consensus exists about the need for testing accommodations for a sector of students with sensory impairment, there is controversy surrounding the need for testing accommodations for students with learning, cognitive, and behavioral disabilities. This is due in part to the debate among mental health professionals and public policy makers regarding assessment methods, identification, appropriate educational placement, and funding allotment. No less significant are the perceptions and attitudes held by parents and teachers about labeling children, including or excluding them from mainstream practices, and special education options. Additionally, there are the factors of culture, developmental context, and co-occurring diagnoses that make the initial diagnosis somewhat less reliable than those based on sensory and physiological criteria.

The chapter includes the following topics: learning disabilities, mental retardation, attention-deficit/hyperactivity disorder, behavioral and emotional disturbance, empirical research on the effects of testing accommodations, and some concluding remarks and recommendations. Each section will begin with a brief overview followed by a description of the diagnostic features and classification systems associated with that disorder. A rationale will be provided as to why some students may need accommodations when taking standardized or classroom tests. Information will be provided about appropriate methods of accommodation and a brief survey of empirical research on testing accommodations.

LEARNING DISABILITIES

Learning disabilities have been termed *the invisible disability* and have been recognized as representing the largest and fastest growing classification category for students receiving special education services. Approximately 5 percent of the students in the public schools are classified as having a learning disability (American Psychiatric Association, 2000). Many students with mild learning disabilities receive support services within the general education classroom, whereas those students who have more severe learning disabilities may receive instruction within self-contained classrooms. A learning disability is conceptualized as a disorder of the central nervous system that impairs an individual's ability to process information presented linguistically and/or visually (American Psychiatric Association, 2000). Many of these students have a concurrent diagnosis of a sensory, behavioral, attentional, or mood disorder that further impacts adversely on learning.

A child who is subsequently diagnosed with a learning disability may initially be referred for an evaluation during the early to mid–elementary school years. The early signs of a learning disability may be reflected by uneven development within the domains of gross and fine motor skills, expressive and receptive language, cognitive skills, socialization, and self-help. The teacher might report concerns about the child's limited progress and frustration in several academic areas. Common early warning signs of a learning disability include an inability to remember the alphabet despite frequent review, an inability to make consistent letter–sound correspondences, and difficulty writing letters and numbers by the end of the first grade. The child often has trouble retaining a skill or concept and requires a good deal of adult supervision and feedback to attend to and complete class work (American Psychiatric Association, 2000; National Association of School Psychologists, 1995; National Center for Learning Disabilities, 1999).

Diagnostic Features and Classification Systems

A student classified as having a learning disability exhibits a deficit in one or more of the basic psychological processes involved in understanding or using language, that may be evidenced in an impaired ability to listen, think, speak, read, write, spell, or to do mathematical calculations. The term excludes learning problems that are primarily caused by a sensory or motor disturbance, mental retardation, an emotional disturbance, or environmental, cultural, or economic disadvantage (Amendments to the IDEA, 1997).

Within the *Diagnostic and Statistical Manual of Mental Disorders—IV* (American Psychiatric Association, 2000), learning disabilities are referred to as learning disorders. The subtypes include Reading Disorder, Mathematics Disorder, Disorder of Written Expression, and Learning Disorder Not Otherwise Specified. The essential diagnostic features of these specific learning disorders include the following: (1) an academic skill deficit measured by a standardized test that is substantially below that expected based on the child's age, measured IQ, and exposure to school; (2) the level of academic skills must adversely affect academic performance and other life activities that require these abilities; (3) if a sensory or neurological deficit also exists, the academic skill deficit is beyond that expected due to the accompanying sensory or neurological impairment; and (4) cultural and emotional factors must not be primary causes for the discrepancy between aptitude and achievement.

The Need for Testing Accommodations

Although these students comprise a diverse group with dissimilar learning profiles, a number of general characteristics may seriously interfere with an accurate rendering of academic achievement and skill under standard testing conditions. As stated earlier, many students demonstrate a limited ability to remain on task and complete work independently. There is a tendency to be easily distracted and to make impulsive choices, and few students implement strategies that indicate planning or time management. Inherent in the criteria for classification are expressive and receptive language processing deficits that impede attainment on many school-related tests. Some students have a good deal of difficulty comprehending and retaining directions, and many have problems with sequential auditory and/or visual memory (National Center for Learning Disabilities, 1999).

Having the classification of a learning disability on an IEP or Section 504 Plan is necessary, but not sufficient documentation of the need of a testing accommodation. The requesting source may establish that the learning disability significantly limits the student's school functioning. The rationale for the testing accommodation is supported by evidence that the child currently receives, and has benefited from, similar accommodations during instruction and classroom exams (Educational Testing Service, 1998b).

Methods of Accommodation

Within the school setting many students with learning disabilities have IEPs mandating testing accommodations, most commonly the accommodations of extended time and a separate location. It is common practice to have a test proctor administer a test to a small group of students with similar mandates. There has been a small body of research that examined the effects of this practice on test score outcomes for students with learning disabilities (Centra, 1986; Munger & Lloyd, 1991; Perlman, Borger, Collins, Elenbogen, & Wood, 1996). The overall evidence regarding the benefits of time extensions are inconclusive. It is noted however, that qualitative variables such as motivation, effort, and self-confidence have not been assessed by researchers.

There has been even greater controversy over other forms of accommodations, particularly the reading aloud of test items, the use of calculators to perform math computations, and having students respond orally to tests of written composition. The debate centers on the issues of test integrity and validity of test results (Phillips, 1994). Proponents of testing accommodations argue that a student can use a calculator if the test is intended to measure a student's math concept knowledge rather than knowledge of math "facts," or that a student may provide an oral essay in lieu of a written essay if the dependent measures are idea generation, creativity, and text organization. Opponents argue that any change in standard procedure diminishes the psychometric strength of the test and provides results that are of questionable interpretative value (see Chapter 4). Much more research is needed to offer consistent evidence that resolves these issues.

The following material describes commonly allowed test accommodations that are used in instructional, local, and large-scale assessment settings for students classified as having a learning disability (Educational Testing Service, 1998b; Kirk, Gallagher, & Anastasiow, 2003; New York State Education Department, 1995).

Setting Modifications

A student may require testing in a separate location either individually or with a small group of students working under the same testing conditions due to the fact that many students with learning disabilities are unusually sensitive to, and distracted by, environmental stimuli. The setting should be as free of visual and auditory clutter as possible.

Timing and Scheduling Modifications

A student may require extended time and/or breaks during testing in order to complete the examination. Some students will need breaks between limited work sessions in order to maintain focus and effort. Furthermore, the time extension may reflect the additional time necessary for the assessment professional or proctor to repeat instructions or orally present items as mandated in particular cases. The student's IEP or Section 504 Plan must specify the degree of time extension required.

Presentation Modifications

Some students with learning disabilities have difficulty interpreting and retaining item response requirements. Some modifications that may facilitate interpretation and follow-through include the rewording of directions in simple language, underlining key words in directions, and providing a set of directions at the top of each page of text and at the point at which each new skill assessment is introduced.

A student may have either the test directions read aloud or the entire test read aloud within the format of a proctor–reader or a tape-recorded exam booklet. Due to the learning characteristics of delayed information processing, poor sequential memory, and inattention to details, this assistance will permit the student to hear the presented information more than once to possibly enhance the understanding of task directions or response requirements.

Due to difficulty with information processing and visual tracking, the format of the test may be modified to offer larger print, fewer lines of information on a page, or wider spaces between the lines of text.

A proctor may be used to administer the test to an individual student or to a group of students taking the test under similar testing condition. The proctor may reread, break down, and/or simplify directions; offer non-contingent encouragement; and remind the students to pace themselves as appropriate.

Response Modifications

Students may be permitted to write their responses in test booklets rather than on a separate answer sheet. Many students with learning disabilities tend to have substantially stronger expressive verbal abilities than written expression faculty. It may be beneficial to have these students respond orally rather than in the usual written format. This may necessitate either a proctor serving as a scribe or the use of a tape recorder. The modification in response modality may support a preferred response mode for the student as well as increase motivation and reduce anxiety (Horton & Lovitt, 1994; MacArthur & Graham, 1987).

The use of equipment and technical aids has been suggested as supporting the response efficiency, interest, and motivation of students with learning disabilities (Horton & Lovitt, 1994; MacArthur & Graham, 1987). The use of word processors, electronic note takers, and spell checkers in particular may assist students who have difficulty with the mechanics of writing and short-term memory.

MENTAL RETARDATION

According to the American Psychiatric Association (2000), there is no typical pattern of physical, behavioral, or personality features that characterize students with mental retardation. Students subsequently identified as mentally retarded are often initially referred for special education services due to general delays in academic achievement, learning rate, social and emotional functioning, and often physical development. It is estimated that about one percent of the population is classified as mentally retarded (American Psychiatric Association, 2000). Students with mental retardation are three to four times more likely than the general population to have a co-occurring mentally or physically disabling condition. This is hypothesized to be attributable to the diversity of identified and unknown etiologies that may result in mental retardation.

Diagnostic Features and Classification Systems

The federal guidelines established by the Amendments to the IDEA (1997) state that in order to receive a classification of mentally retarded, a student must demonstrate significantly subaverage intellectual functioning existing concurrently with deficits in adaptive behavior and having manifested during the developmental period. This deficit profile must significantly affect a child's educational performance as well as other important life functions. Intellectual functioning is generally determined by a student's performance on an individually administered intelligence test, whereas adaptive functioning may be established by adaptive behavior scales administered to third-party members (e.g.. family members, teachers, service providers) who can attest to the student's performance of habitual behaviors. Educational achievement tests and other indices of school performance document the student's educational attainment.

Mental retardation is often categorized by levels representing the severity of intellectual impairment. Mild mental retardation, by far the largest category, reflects an intelligence quotient (IQ) of 55 to approximately 70 on an individual intelligence test with a mean of 100 and a standard deviation of 15. Moderate mental retardation corresponds to an IQ of 40 to about 55. Severe mental retardation corresponds to an IQ of 25 to 40. Profound mental retardation is equated with an IQ below 25. The diagnosis of students within the severe and profound ranges of mental retardation is generally based on behavioral criteria because traditional IQ scales are inadequate measures of cognitive functioning at the extremes of the intellectual continuum (American Psychiatric Association, 2000).

Students with mild mental retardation often resemble their typically developing peers during the early school years in their development and facility with social and communication skills. They may acquire academic skills peaking at the sixth-grade level. Students with moderate mental retardation acquire communication skills during the early school years, but their interpersonal and social interpretations are less adequate as they become teenagers and adults. They can maintain self-care needs with some support. They tend to profit from vocational education and may attain a second-grade academic level. Students with severe mental retardation often have significant lags in communication and may develop limited communicative speech. With a good deal of instruction and practice, these students may attain some basic self-help skills. They do not profit from traditional school experiences, but can acquire some functional academics. Most students who are classified as profoundly mentally retarded exhibit concurrent neurological impairments that contribute to sensory motor and communication deficits. They may learn some basic self-care skills within a highly structured setting offering a high degree of adult support (American Psychiatric Association, 2000; Kirk, Gallagher, & Anastasiow, 2003; Vaughn, Bos, & Schumm, 2000).

Whereas the American Psychiatric Association categorizes mental retardation by levels of intellectual impairment, the American Association on Mental Retardation (1992) applies "Patterns and Intensity of Support Needed," which offers a continuum that ranges from intermittent supports to "pervasive," or a very high level of support to sustain daily functioning.

The Need for Testing Accommodations

The use of standardized tests with accommodations is most applicable to the evaluation of students who are mildly retarded and relatively independent. Students with moderate to profound intellectual impairments are generally evaluated via functional and/or contextual assessments combined with third-party observation rating scales and checklists. Many students with moderate to profound intellectual impairments also present with concurrent physical, sensory, neurological, and communication impairments that require alternative assessment procedures to be conducted by trained professionals operating within a multidisciplinary framework.

Among the learner characteristics that might support the need for testing accommodations for students with mild mental retardation are limited interpersonal and linguistic skills, and a slower than typical response rate. Some students may also exhibit poorly developed short-term memory and information processing facility. The rationale for the testing accommodation is supported by evidence that the child receives and has benefited from similar accommodations during instruction and classroom exams.

Methods of Accommodation

There has been little empirical investigation of the impact of testing accommodations on the test performance of students who are classified as having mental retardation. This may be due in part to the fact that many students with moderate to profound mental retardation have been exempted from standardized tests by the child study team. Furthermore, it is often recommended that a more valid profile can be gathered by a combination of third-party ratings, observations, and functional and ecological assessments. The studies that have been reported here primarily consider the impact of various types of reinforcers and reinforcement schedules on student performance on selected subtests of the Wechsler Intelligence Scale for Children-Revised (Johnson, Bradley-Johnson, McCarthy, & Jamie, 1984; Saigh & Payne, 1979; Terrell, Terrell, & Taylor, 1981; Young, Bradley-Johnson, & Johnson, 1982).

The lack of empirical evidence regarding the effects of other specific testing accommodations on standardized test performance suggests that the assessment professional must turn to the suggestions offered by educators who have worked with students with mental retardation on a regular basis (New York State Education Department, 1995; Sattler, 2001; Vaughn, Bos, & Schumm, 2000).

Setting Modifications
Students may benefit from testing in a separate location due to such learner characteristics as limitations in social skills, language processing and communication facility, limited perseverance, and low frustration tolerance. The setting should allow sufficient space for assistive devices to meet any physical challenges that may be present. The assessment professional should allow sufficient time for the establishment of rapport. The setting should be quiet and uncluttered of visual and auditory stimuli.

Timing and Scheduling Modifications
Extended testing time will usually be required because many students process and retain information poorly, or they do not perform well on measures of

processing speed and fine motor coordination. The student's IEP or Section 504 Plan should indicate the specific time extension permitted for the test administration.

Presentation Modifications

Some students with mental retardation exhibit low frustration tolerance for challenging items and consequently resist complying with test demands. Sattler (2001) suggests that the proctor and/or assessment professional allow adequate time to establish rapport, begin with items that afford successful responses, and then alternate between easy and challenging items in order to maintain positive affect and cooperation on the part of the examinee.

Some research suggests that the use of contingent tangible and social reinforcers for responding during testing can improve the test performance and attainment of mildly mentally retarded students (Johnson, Bradley-Johnson, McCarthy, & Jamie, 1984; Saigh & Payne, 1979; Young, Bradley-Johnson, & Johnson, 1982).

ATTENTION-DEFICIT/HYPERACTIVITY DISORDER

It is currently estimated that about 5 percent of the school-age population is classified as having Attention-Deficit/Hyperactivity Disorder (ADHD) (Robison, Sclar, Skaer, & Galin, 1999). Although ADHD is one of the fastest growing diagnoses, within the Individuals with Disabilities Education Act, ADHD is not considered as a separate category of disability. It is subsumed within the category of Other Health Impaired (OHI). The OHI designation given by the child study team entitles the student to receive an appropriate educational placement and related services (Aronofsy, 1992).

In order to receive the diagnosis of ADHD, the child study team must conduct a comprehensive evaluation to determine whether the student exhibits the characteristic symptoms of excessive inattention, impulsivity, and hyperactivity (American Psychiatric Association, 2000). The initial referral is often made at the end of preschool or in the early years of elementary school because of teacher concerns about behaviors such as frequent fidgeting or inability to stay in the seat, excessive off-task talking, poor focus, disorganization, low frustration tolerance, and poor academic achievement. The diagnosis is made more complex because of the confounding issues of cultural and developmental norms, family and teacher tolerance for behavior, and the co-occurrence with other disruptive and externalizing behavioral conditions such as Oppositional Defiant Disorder (ODD) and Conduct Disorder (CD).

Diagnostic Features and Classification Systems

A student diagnosed with ADHD must exhibit levels of inattention and/or hyperactivity-impulsivity to such a degree that academic and nonacademic daily functioning is adversely affected. The behavioral symptoms must have first occurred prior to age 7, be displayed for longer than six months, and occur in more than one setting. Additionally, the symptoms of inattention and hyperactivity-impulsivity must be more severe and frequent than that observed in individuals at a comparable level of development. It is also important to note that a cluster of behaviors demonstrating inattention, impulsivity, and/or hyperactivity must be evidenced in order for a child to receive this classification (American Psychiatric Association, 2000).

The three identified subtypes of this disorder are (1) Attention-Deficit/ Hyperactivity Disorder, Predominantly Inattentive Type; (2) Attention-Deficit/ Hyperactivity Disorder, Predominantly Hyperactive-Impulsive Type; and (3) Attention-Deficit Disorder, Combined Type. The diagnosis of the type of ADHD is based on the predominant presenting behaviors at the time of the evaluation. Most of the children evaluated by the child study team exhibit behavior consistent with the Attention-Deficit Disorder, Combined Type.

Students who exhibit predominantly inattentive symptoms are easily distracted, are forgetful, and have difficulty sustaining attention to the completion of an assignment or activity. They are disorganized, make many careless errors, and do not always appear to be listening when spoken to directly. Students who exhibit predominantly hyperactive behaviors are described as excessively fidgety and often leave their seat at inappropriate times. They may run out of or around the classroom and talk excessively. They have difficulty remaining engaged in quiet activities. Impulsive behavior is characterized by children who cannot wait for a turn, often respond or begin a task before questions or directions have been completed, and often intrude on others (American Psychiatric Association, 2000).

The Need for Testing Accommodations

Although about one-quarter of students with ADHD perform adequately in the school setting, there are many who remain poor achievers, exhibit low frustration tolerance, and demonstrate low motivation on academic assignments. The test performance of many of these students on standardized tests is consistent with their performance on classroom assignments and homework. Although the observations of testing behavior often reflect the attention-deficit condition, the assessment results may represent an underestimation of a child's true ability, knowledge, or skill. Testing accommodations may be necessary in order to minimize the effects of the inattention, hyperactivity, and impulsivity. Among the particular behaviors that interfere with test attainment are the inability to remain seated and sustain focus, and the failure to implement self-monitoring and other executive strategies.

Having the classification of Attention-Deficit/Hyperactivity Disorder on an IEP or Section 504 Plan is necessary but not sufficient documentation of the need for a testing accommodation. The requesting source may establish that the ADHD condition significantly limits the student's school functioning. The rationale for the testing accommodation is supported by evidence that the child currently receives and has benefited from similar accommodations during instruction and classroom exams (Educational Testing Service, 1998a).

Methods of Accommodation

The dearth of data on the use of testing accommodations with students classified as having ADHD reflects the uncommon application of testing accommodations until fairly recently. Attention-Deficit/Hyperactivity Disorder is rapidly becoming a more prominent diagnosis, and the controversy regarding stimulant medications has raised popular interest in its treatment. The effect of the medication has permitted more students to successfully take tests under standard conditions, but many students with ADHD remain unable to withstand the sustained vigilance necessary for lengthy assessments.

The following suggestions for accommodations are based on the recommendations of school professionals who work with students with ADHD on a daily basis, as well as reasonable testing accommodations cited in the publication manuals of large-scale assessment centers (Educational Testing Service, 1998a; Kirk, Gallagher, & Anastasiow, 2003; New York State Education Department, 1995; Spinelli, 1997).

Setting Modifications

Students with ADHD may require testing in a separate location due to their tendency to be easily distracted by extraneous stimuli as well as the fact that they benefit from frequent short breaks during tasks that require sustained effort and attention to details. The test site should be free from physical clutter and away from sources of extraneous sights or auditory stimuli.

Timing and Scheduling Modifications

Due to their general deficits in executive planning combined with an inability to remain seated, stay focused, and follow through until task completion, it may be beneficial to give students with ADHD frequent short breaks between completed test units (i.e., between subtests). During the breaks students may be prompted to exercise, take a walk, or converse. This break cycle should be explained to students in advance of the formal testing so that they know what to expect and understand the expectations of the examiner. The inclusion of break time may necessitate time extension for these students. The student's IEP or Section 504 Plan should indicate the specific time extension permitted for the test administration.

Presentation Modifications

Some students with attention disorders have difficulty integrating and retaining item response requirements. Some accommodations that may facilitate the interpretation and follow-through include the rewording of directions in simple language, underlining key words in directions, and providing a set of directions at the top of each page of text and at the point at which a new skill area is assessed.

A test administrator may facilitate higher attainment for some students taking an exam by determining when a break is needed, offering verbal reminders to the student to check his or her work, encouraging the student to continue, rewarding for sustained effort, and assisting the student in efficient time management during a multistep activity.

Although there is limited empirical data on the use of reinforcement during testing, it is common practice for teachers to use social and tangible reinforcement to maintain on-task behavior and increase the motivation of students with attention disorders during classroom instruction (Vaugh, Bos, & Schumm, 2000). The classroom teacher may provide information on the way in which reinforcement has been used effectively with a particular student.

Response Modifications

Students my be permitted to write their response in test booklets rather than on a separate answer sheet. Students with attention deficits tend to have limited self-monitoring skills and make careless errors. The use of a separate answer sheet adds to response demands and may result in errors that reflect skipped or misaligned responses rather than a lack of knowledge on the part of the examinee. The proctor may intermittently prompt students to check that they have responded to every question in a section of the examination.

Many students with attention deficit disorders also have learning disabilities. As stated earlier in this chapter, some of these students tend to have substantially stronger expressive verbal abilities than written expression faculty. It may be beneficial to have these students respond orally rather than in the usual written format. They may necessitate either a proctor serving as a scribe or the use of a tape recorder. The modification in response modality may support a preferred response mode for the students as well as increase motivation and reduce anxiety (Horton & Lovitt, 1994; MacArthur & Graham, 1987).

BEHAVIORAL AND EMOTIONAL DISTURBANCE

Students within the category of behaviorally and/or emotionally disturbed represent a diverse group. Estimates of the prevalence of school-age children classified as having behavioral or emotional disorders vary widely from 0.5 percent to 20 percent (Kauffman, 2001). The U.S. Department of Education (1999) indicates that approximately 0.7 percent of the national school-age population receive special education support services to address behavioral and emotional disturbances.

Coleman (1996) states that these students are being underidentified and inadequately served in the school system because of nonuniform criteria and a lack of consensus among professionals from different perspectives as to who should be classified as behaviorally and emotionally disturbed. Additionally, there is the social stigma attached to the label of behavioral and emotional disturbance and the related ambivalence of funding and service availability.

Parental ambivalence regarding the labeling of a student must not be minimized. Many parents recognize and accept that their child has trouble socializing and is unusually aggressive, anxious, or unhappy, yet they often reject the stigmatizing label of emotional disturbance, sometimes at the cost of not receiving additional services within the school.

Diagnostic Features and Classification Systems

In accordance with the definition established by the federal government in the IDEA, a student characterized as having emotional disturbance exhibits one or more of the following chronic concerns to a degree that is excessive for his or her developmental status and to an extent that adversely affects academic achievement: exhibits an inability to build and maintain satisfactory interpersonal relationships with peers and teachers, demonstrates inappropriate behaviors and feelings under normal circumstances, presents with a pervasive mood of unhappiness or depression, and evidences somatic symptoms in response to personal problems. The learning difficulties cannot be primarily the result of intellectual, sensory, or health factors (Amendments to the IDEA, 1997).

Students who are unusually aggressive and disruptive may be subsequently diagnosed with either Oppositional Defiant Disorder (ODD) or Conduct Disorder (CD). The essential feature of ODD is a recurrent pattern of negativistic, defiant, and hostile behavior toward authority figures that has persisted for at least six months. The essential feature of CD, considered more serious and confrontational than ODD, is a cluster of behaviors that fit into the categories of (1) aggression to people and animals, (2) destruction of property, (3) deceitfulness or theft, and/or (4) serious violation of rules (American Psychiatric Association, 2000).

Although most referrals are initiated by teacher concerns related to overtly aggressive and disruptive classroom behaviors, many students with an emotional or behavioral disorder demonstrate internalizing disorders such as anxieties, phobias, and depression that adversely affect their learning and socialization, but have less obvious impact on the dynamics of the classroom. Males tend to exhibit more externalizing disorders, whereas females tend to evidence the internalizing disorders that hinder functioning across the domains of daily functioning.

Although adults are more commonly classified as being depressed, many school-age children exhibit depressed affect, anxiety, and withdrawn behavior. Students experiencing depression may evidence a lack of drive, social avoidance, boredom, and somatic complaints. More frequent angry episodes and an increased tendency to cry easily also may reflect childhood depression. Both depression and anxiety in children and adolescents may be demonstrated by separation problems or by avoiding potentially uncomfortable situations.

The Need for Testing Accommodations

Students with behavioral and emotional disabilities present with diverse symptoms. Both externalizing and internalizing clusters of behaviors may result in performance on standardized tests that is inconsistent and more representative of the student's emotional or behavioral status than of the student's knowledge or skill level. Factors that may interfere with school achievements and daily life activities are the same factors that may hinder test performance. Among areas of concern relevant to assessment are a failure to develop satisfying interpersonal relationships, inappropriate behaviors and feelings in everyday situations, extreme mood alterations, and physical symptoms and/or avoidant behaviors in response to fear and anxiety (American Psychiatric Association, 2000; Coleman, 1996).

Students who exhibit externalizing behaviors sometimes feel particularly sensitive and threatened by the test itself and by the perceived consequences of the testing. They may have a sense of impending doom as a consequence of the testing. They may be wary of self-disclosure and the intimacy of the testing situation. Rapport, albeit especially important, may be difficult to establish. The assessment professional should be patient, calm, and clearly explain the purpose and procedures of testing in order to create an environment that promotes trust (Sattler, 2001).

Having the classification of an emotional or behavioral disorder on an IEP or Section 504 Plan is necessary but not sufficient documentation of the need for a testing accommodation. The requesting source may establish that the emotional or behavioral condition significantly limits the student's school functioning. The rationale for the testing accommodation is supported by evidence that the child receives and has benefited from similar accommodations during instruction and classroom exams.

Methods of Accommodation

There has been limited empirical investigation of the application of testing accommodations for students classified as having emotional or behavioral disabilities. Although many of these students are of average intelligence, they often perform poorly under standard conditions, and in many cases have a chronic pattern of school failure. The following descriptions of possible testing accommodations for these students is culled from the literature on recommended practice for educators who instruct and assess these students on an ongoing basis (Coleman, 1996; Sattler, 2001; New York State Education Department, 1995; Vaughn, Bos, & Schumm, 2000).

Setting Modifications
Students may benefit from testing in a separate location due to such learner characteristics as impulsivity, limited perseverance, low frustration tolerance, noncompliance, and fearfulness. The setting should be quiet and uncluttered of visual and auditory stimuli.

Timing and Scheduling Modifications
It may be necessary for the test to be administered under extended time conditions due to such diverse learner characteristics as avoidance, frustration, noncompliance, and wariness. It is crucial that the assessment professional attempts to develop rapport prior to formal testing in order to establish trust. The student may need short breaks during the testing, or in cases of extreme noncompliance or nonparticipation, the test may need to be conducted over the course of two days. The degree of time extension must be specified on the student's IEP or Section 504 Plan.

Presentation Modifications
Due to concerns about trust, anticipated failure, and self-revelation, it may take longer than usual to develop rapport with the examinee. Input from a classroom teacher will assist the examiner in developing a constructive working relationship with the examinee.

Many students with behavioral and emotional disorders have poor social skills, limited self-monitoring ability, a depressed or unusually high activity level, and negative behaviors. Some students will benefit from having a proctor determine when a break my be needed, to offer verbal encouragement for effort, and to prompt the student to monitor work as appropriate.

The effect of various reinforcers on test performance has received little attention from researchers, yet is is effectively integrated in general and special education instructional settings (Vaughn, Bos, & Schumm, 2000). The examiner should be aware of developmental and cultural guidelines when selecting the reinforcer. It is helpful to consult with the classroom teacher as to what reinforcer has been effective for a particular student.

EMPIRICAL RESEARCH ON THE EFFECTS OF TESTING ACCOMMODATIONS

There have been two related research questions posed in the area of testing accommodations. One question of interest focuses on the effects of testing accommodations on the technical integrity of the assessment measures.

The other line of research addresses the effects of testing accommodations on the outcome performance of groups of students with and without disabilities. The data presented in this chapter emphasize the second area of research, particularly as testing accommodations impact on the outcome measures for students with learning, cognitive, and behavioral disabilities.

A comprehensive review of the empirical literature on testing accommodations for students with disabilities, published in 1996 by the National Center on Educational Outcomes (NCEO), indicates that very few empirical studies have been conducted. The authors note (Thurlow, Hurley, Spicuzza, & El Sawaf, 1996) the great majority of empirical research studies on testing accommodations have been done with participants classified as learning disabled. Extremely few studies use participants with other exceptionalities. The reported studies demonstrate a good deal of heterogeneity in terms of sample size, stated purpose, and the demographic characteristics of participants. Many of the earliest studies, conducted in the 1980s, have methodological flaws (Thurlow, Hurley, Spicuzza, & El Sawaf, 1996). Some lack control group conditions and others fail to include a general education comparison group. The latter point is particularly noteworthy due to an implicit assumption in the use of testing accommodations that students with disabilities should benefit to a greater degree than peers in the nonclassified group, thus demonstrating an interaction effect (Phillips, 1994).

Timing and Scheduling Modifications

Centra (1986) examined the effects of extended time on scores on the Scholastic Aptitude Test (SAT). When the investigator controlled for growth in student ability, practice effects, and measurement error, the mean group increase with extended time was between 30 and 38 points. It was noted that the scores for students with learning disabilities increased in direct proportion to the amount of extra time used to complete the exam.

Similar studies on the effects of timing modifications on student scores on the Iowa Test of Basic Skills (ITBS) were conducted by Munger and Lloyd (1991) and Perlman, Borger, Collins, Elenbogen, and Wood (1996). Both research projects resulted in positive yet inconclusive findings on the effects of timing extensions. The study by Munger and Lloyd employed fifth-grade students, some with learning disabilities and others with physical disabilities. The participants in the Perlman and colleagues study included fourth-grade and eighth-grade students with learning disabilities. In both studies the participants were given the ITBS under either standard time conditions or extended time conditions. In the Munger and Lloyd (1991) study, the researchers found no distinction between the groups with and without disabilities in terms of the percentage of students who completed 90 percent of the test items or on the total number of items attempted. The conclusion was that students with physical and learning disabilities should not be denied access to large-scale assessment opportunities.

In the Perlman and colleagues (1996) study, the students in the eighth-grade extended time group outperformed those in the eighth-grade standard time group. Additionally, posttest scores were found to be more reliable in the extended time condition. Interestingly, fourth graders in the nonstandard time condition scored higher than fourth graders in the standard time condition even though both groups on average took about the same amount of time for test completion. The authors considered the possibility that reduced stress and anxiety about time, rather than the time extension variable itself, may have resulted in this score pattern. Thurlow, Hurley, Spicuzza, & El Sawaf (1996) commented that the generalization of these findings may be limited due to the nonrandom assignment of participants to treatment conditions.

Presentation and Response Modifications

Mick (1989) studied the effects of test format modifications on the performance of students with learning disabilities and mild to moderate mental retardation taking the Instructional Objectives Exchange (IOX) Basic Skill Test.

The three format modifications were (1) using moderately enlarged print, (2) using unjustified lines for right-hand margins, and (3) responding in the test booklet rather than on a separate answer sheet. All students received all of the versions of the test in a repeated replication methodology. The researcher found that all of the students performed significantly better on the unmodified version of the test. Mick hypothesized that these students had a good deal of exposure to standardized tests and were test wise at this point. Thurlow, Hurley, Spicuzza, & El Sawaf (1996) put forth a cautionary note as to this interpretation of these findings. They observe that in terms of practical significance, it is important to note that less than one-half of the students with learning disabilities and only two of the students with mild–moderate mental disabilities passed either version of the exam.

Grise, Beattie, and Algozzine (1982) conducted two studies that examined the effect of test format modifications on the minimum competency outcomes of third- and fifth-grade students with learning disabilities on a version of the Florida State Student Assessment Test. The most significant finding was that 30 percent more of the students attained mastery level performance on the enlarged print version than on the regular print version of the test. Tolfa-Veit and Scruggs (1986) included nineteen students with learning disabilities among a sample of 101 fourth-grade students. They compared the performances of regular education and special education students using separate answer sheets for a standardized exam. The researchers noted a significant difference in the number of item responses on the answer sheets, yet there was no noted difference between the percentages of accurate responses provided by the groups (both groups attained about 97 percent accuracy).

An investigation by Tindal, Heath, Hollenbeck, Almond, & Harniss (1998), examined the effects of two major accommodations, one modifying test response and the other modifying test presentation, on reading and math scores. In the response modification condition, students were required to bubble in answers on a separate sheet for half of the test (standardized), and for the other half of the test, they responded directly in the test booklet (modified). For the presentation modification condition, the math test was read orally to a subgroup of the participants (modified). The researchers did not note significant differences between the groups in the response modification condition, yet there was a significant interaction effect for the modified test presentation condition. The researchers regard this finding as supportive documentation for the use of oral presentation with students determined to have learning disabilities.

Several researchers studied the effects of assistive devices, primarily computers and word processors, on the reading comprehension, essay writing, test scores, and motivation of students with learning disabilities. Keene and Davey (1987) examined the comparability of the reading comprehension performance of high school students when reading lengthy expository passages either in print format or from the computer screen. Prior to reading, the students were prompted to activate the use of different reading strategies that they had been taught. The findings suggested that the students performed equally well on both versions of the passage, yet they tended to look back at the passage in order to answer comprehension questions more often in the computerized format. The students asked to repeat the task more often in the computerized mode.

Horton and Lovitt (1994) studied the effects of computerized testing on the performance of adolescents with learning disabilities who took nine brief multiple-choice tests, each composed of factual and interpretive items. The students were given versions of the test in pencil-and-paper format and in a computerized edition. The findings indicate that only three of the students with learning disabilities demonstrated a significant difference in scores between versions, all favoring the pencil-and-paper mode, particularly when responding to interpretive items. Self-reports from the students indicated that 70 percent favored learning information on the computer rather than from a textbook. All of the teachers stated that they felt that the computer was a useful tool for evaluating the independent learning of students.

In a small-scale study, MacArthur and Graham (1987) examined the impact of expressive communication mode on the story production of fifth- and sixth-grade students classified as learning disabled. Using picture prompts, the students wrote three stories, one under each of three methods of text generation: dictation, word processing, and handwriting. The outcome measures included indices of language competency, quality and story structure, and quality and type of revisions. The researchers found that although handwriting a story took significantly less time than did word processing, no significant differences were found between handwriting and word processing on any of the dependent variables. The researchers found significant statistical and qualitative differences between the dictated stories and the other two modes of story production. They conclude that dictated stories were more grammatically accurate, lengthier, and of higher quality.

SOME CONCLUDING REMARKS AND RECOMMENDATIONS

The following general guidelines and recommendations should be considered when testing students with psychological disabilities.

- Students with learning, cognitive, and behavioral disabilities should not be excluded from large-scale assessment if accommodations can offer the opportunity for a valid measure of student knowledge and competence.

- The decision regarding the appropriateness or necessity for testing accommodations must be done on an individual basis. Not every student with a disability is in need of test accommodations. The decision should be made in consultation with the general or special educator, related school and medical professionals, and family members.
- The professionals conducting the evaluation should be knowledgeable about the unique characteristics of the particular disability as well as having background knowledge about the learning and affective characteristics of the student being assessed.
- It is especially important for these students that sufficient time is allowed to establish rapport between the professional and the student.
- The professionals conducting the evaluation should have a comprehensive knowledge of the underlying constructs and psychometric properties of a diversity of assessment measures.
- Under either standardized or accommodated testing conditions, students should have received prior exposure to, and practice with, test taking under similar conditions.

SUMMARY

Students with learning, cognitive, and behavioral disabilities represent a large percentage of the students receiving special education services in the nation's school system. The diagnosis and assessment of children with psychological disorders related to learning, attention, and behavior is more complex than that related to the sensory and physical disabilities addressed in the previous chapter. Whereas there is a consensus about the need for testing accommodations for a sector of students with sensory impairment, controversy surrounds the need for testing accommodations for students with learning, cognitive, and behavioral disabilities. This is due in part to the debate among mental health professionals and public policy makers regarding assessment methods, identification, appropriate educational placement, and funding allotment. No less significant are the perceptions and attitudes parents and teachers hold about labeling children, excluding them from mainstream practices, and special education options. Additionally, there are the factors of culture, developmental context, and comorbid diagnoses that make the initial diagnosis somewhat less reliable than those based on sensory and physiological criteria.

The specific diagnostic criteria for each of the learning, cognitive, behavioral disabilities discussed in this chapter derive from those developed by the American Psychiatric Association in *The Diagnostic and Statistical Manual of Mental Disorders—IV* (2000). The unique and overlapping characteristics among the disabilities are addressed. The most commonly offered testing accommodations are testing in a separate location, testing in an individualized setting or with a small group of students with similar testing needs, and time extension. Other accommodations may be offered with a consideration of the individual's current functional level and the nature of the disability.

Although a limited number of research studies have addressed the effect of testing accommodations on students with learning, cognitive, and behavioral disabilities, there has been a recent and positive trend in public policy, and increased federal funding for educational and vocational programs that have as their goals equal opportunity and access for individuals with disabilities.

CHAPTER SEVEN

USING ACCOMMODATIONS FOR ENGLISH LANGUAGE LEARNERS

In the previous two chapters the applications of testing accommodations to specific groups of students with disabilities were discussed. This chapter discusses the application of testing accommodations for English language learning students, or English language learners (ELLs). The problems of using standardized tests with ELLs and the need for accommodations in testing these students are reviewed. Accommodation methods that may be appropriate to enhance valid assessment of ELLs are discussed in a detailed manner. The topics covered in this chapter are ELLs in the public schools, need for testing accommodations for ELLs, steps in assessing ELLs with accommodations, assessing English language proficiency, exempting or deferring ELLs from testing, modifying standard test administration, using translated or adapted tests, using bilingual interpreters in testing, common guidelines are needed for providing testing accommodations to ELLs, and some concluding remarks and recommendations.

ELLs IN THE PUBLIC SCHOOLS

ELLs As an Increasing Student Population

As indicated in Chapter 2, ELLs in this book refer to students who are defined as Limited English Proficient (LEP) in the federal legislation. The Improving America's Schools Act, P. L. 103-382, defines an LEP student as one (1) whose native language is a language other than English and comes from an environment in which a language other than English is dominant; and (2) who has sufficient difficulty speaking, reading, writing, or understanding the English language and whose difficulties may deny such student the opportunity to learn successfully under English instruction in the classrooms. Using these two major considerations as a basis, states and school districts have developed their own definitions of this population of students. In a review of the terms and definitions used by the fifty states and the District of Columbia, Goh, Zupnik, and Mendez (2001) found a variety of terms were used in state regulations with regard to the education of ELLs with different language backgrounds. These terms include *limited English proficient students, non-English/ limited English proficient students, children of limited English speaking ability, students with limited proficiency in English, students whose dominant language is not English, eligible children for bilingual and bicultural program, students where the spoken language in the house is not English, non-English dominant students, students eligible for bilingual education, students eligible for multicultural education,* and *English language learners.*

Similarly, states also vary considerably in their definitions of these terms, as well as in the criteria and procedures they used in identifying ELLs. Whereas some states define ELLs in a rather vague manner, others use very specific definitions that specify the criteria and measurement of English language proficiency. For example, in California an ELL is defined as someone with a home language other than English. In addition, the student must have been assessed in English comprehension, speaking, reading, and writing, and must have a score less than fluent according to the norms on a state-authorized test of English proficiency. The different definitions used by states in identifying ELLs lead to the possibility that a student may be classified as ELL in one state but not in another.

A common message is conveyed, however, in the different terms and definitions used by the states in describing this particular population of students. That is, these students are limited in their usage of the English language and are learning English as a second language. Based on this common characteristic, it is appropriate to view ELLs as a broad term referring to all students whose native language is not English, who are in the process of learning English, and who demonstrate limited ability in communicating and performing academic work in English.

The number of ELLs has increased dramatically in the past three decades. In the late 1980s there were over 2.5 million school-age children in the United States who were not native English speakers. This number grew to 3.5 million in the late 1990s (Shaul, 1999) and to more than 4.5 million in the early 2000s, which is equivalent to 9.6 percent of the total student enrollment (Kindler, 2002). Since the 1990–1991 school year the ELL population has increased by approximately 105 percent in the public school system, while the general school population has grown by only 12 percent (Kindler, 2002). It is estimated that by the year of 2026, nearly a quarter of the U.S. student population will be comprised of ELLs from a myriad of different cultural and ethnic groups (Scribner, 2002). With the number of ELLs on the rise, states and school districts continue to face the challenge of meeting the educational needs of these students.

As indicated in Chapter 2, the readers are reminded that there is immense amount of within-group variability in this population of English language learning students. Although sharing a common thread in that they are learning English as a second language, ELLs differ widely in many other ways: language, ethnicity, cultural background, educational orientation, social-economic status, family history, custom, and other variables (LaCelle-Peterson & Rivera, 1994). For example, for a group of students whose primary language is Spanish, there may be wide differences in the linguistic, cultural, and educational backgrounds of these students. The majority of ELLs are those who have come from a wide variety of countries around the world and grown up speaking a language other than English at home. There are also ELLs who were born in the United States and have grown up in a multilingual and multicultural home with immigrant parents, in which no one is English fluent (Garcia, 2000). According to Feinberg (2002), in 1990 more than 70 percent of immigrant children lived with one or both parents who did not speak English. Given this scenario, one may find in any classroom ELLs with linguistic competency levels ranging anywhere from monolingual in a native language to varying degrees of bilingualism (Scribner, 2002).

Educational Risks of ELLs

Unique linguistic and cultural characteristics and insufficient English language skills of the ELLs often make successful participation in educational programs difficult. Research has shown that ELLs not proficient enough in English when they come to school to participate fully in mainstream all-English classrooms are at the highest risk for academic failure and school dropout (Garcia, 2000). It has been reported that language minority K–12 students score lower than majority population students on national tests assessing reading, math, and science (U.S. Department of Commerce Bureau of Census, 1993). Further evidence of an educational disparity between the majority population and certain language minority groups can be seen in the demographic makeup of those students receiving special services. For example, Kretschmer (1991) provides a series of statistics indicating the misdiagnosis of certain groups of ELLs who are inappropriately placed in special education programs throughout the United States. These educational disparities in large part reflect a lack of effective assessment and instructional programs for students whose native language is not English. Providing appropriate educational services for ELLs is a complex practice. The complexity is further exacerbated by the lack of universally established procedures for assessing these students.

NEED FOR TESTING ACCOMMODATIONS FOR ELLs

Historically, there are some concerns about whether standardized tests can be used fairly and accurately in assessing ELLs (Darling-Hammond, 1994a; Supovitz & Brennan, 1997). Standardized tests are based on English and a "mainstream" perspective, and they are intended for use with the English-speaking population. LaCelle-Peterson and Rivera (1994) posit that the values of standardized tests are not identical for monolingual English-speaking students and language minority students whose native language is not English. Lam (1993) identifies several assumptions about test takers of standardized tests: (1) the test takers have no linguistic barriers that inhibit their performance on the test; (2) the test content is suitable for the test takers; and (3) the test takers have the test sophistication for taking standardized tests, are motivated to do well on the test, and do not have strong negative psychological reactions to testing. Whereas these assumptions are generally true for monolingual English-speaking students, they are not commonly met when the examinees are ELLs from language minority groups.

Standardized tests have been criticized for their inability to accurately measure ELLs' abilities and competencies for several reasons. First, ELLs have limited skills in speaking, reading, writing, and understanding the English language. These language barriers often prevent ELLs from understanding the test instruction and questions and impede their test performance. The language barriers may also slow ELLs down in processing the test information and make it difficult, if not impossible, for them to complete the test within the standard time allowed. As a result, standardized tests may become a literacy or language test, instead of a skills assessment test for some ELLs (AERA, APA, & NCME, 1999). Consequently, the test results become invalid and underestimate ELLs' true abilities or achievement. Second, some standardized tests may be culturally biased and can favor the mainstream experiences and values. Despite test publishers' efforts to de-bias such tests, there is no guarantee that all standardized tests are free of bias against ELLs (Zehler, Hopstock, Fleischman, & Grenick, 1994). In addition, standardized achievement tests may include content that is not suitable for ELLs, if the examinees were educated in their home countries and have not been exposed to the American curriculum. Due to the lack of opportunity to acquire the knowledge being measured, test results for these ELLs may be invalid. Third, besides language and content issues, ELLs may exhibit test behaviors and coping styles that tend to affect negatively on their performance on standardized tests. According to Lam (1993), many ELLs are unfamiliar about how to take standardized tests and may lack necessary test-taking skills. Also, they may not appreciate the achievement aspects of testing and lack motivation to do well. As a result of being unfamiliar with test content and format, ELLs may experience anxiety, tension, and other negative emotions, at a level higher than normally would be expected of mainstream students, during test-taking situations. In addition, some ELLs may also exhibit response styles that are not conducive to good test performance. For example, in individual testing children are often expected to produce elaborative responses to receive maximum scores on test items. However, in some cultures children are not encouraged to talk a lot or to volunteer information in front of adults. This cultural style may be reflected in test behaviors. ELLs from such a culture may respond to the examiner with only brief phrases, instead of the spontaneous elaborative responses that would give them maximum scores. All of these test behaviors and coping styles may introduce errors in measurement and adversely affect ELLs' performance on standardized tests.

During the past two decades, considerable research has been attempted to detect and reduce test bias against linguistic as well as ethnic minority students. In the meantime, test users are strongly advised to be cautious in interpreting standardized test results of ELLs. However, until recent years testing accommodations have not been used as a means to enhance accurate assessment of ELLs in large-scale testing. ELLs were either exempted from taking standardized tests or required to take the tests along with their native English-speaking peers, without any accommodations. In the former case, valuable assessment data on the exempted ELLs are lost. In the latter case, invalid test results may be obtained, which often lead to misjudgment about and misplacement of these students. In either case, the lack of valid assessment information hinders the education of the ELLs involved.

Recent federal legislations have spurred significant changes in the assessment of ELLs (see Chapter 2). In general, federal and state laws now mandate that tests should be administered to ELLs, to the extent practicable, in the language and form most likely to yield valid and reliable information on these students. This means that necessary tests may be administered to ELLs in their native language or dominant language. Also, tests may be administered to ELLs with appropriate accommodations to overcome the effects of their language barriers. Moreover, alternative assessments may be used with

ELLs, if it is deemed inappropriate to assess them using standardized tests. The use of these different assessment methods is determined by an ELL's level of English proficiency. For example, for ELLs with no or minimum English proficiency, these students may be tested in their native language or dominant language, or they may be assessed by alternative assessment methods. For students who have English proficiency but at a level less than satisfactory as demanded by the test, accommodations may be used to overcome the language barriers these students have in taking standardized or classroom tests. In addition, no testing accommodations are needed for ELLs who demonstrate excellent or satisfactory English language skills as required by the tests.

STEPS IN ASSESSING ELLs WITH ACCOMMODATIONS

According to Zehler, and colleagues (1994), there are multiple purposes for ELL assessment in different individual and group settings. In assessment focused on individual students, the purposes include identification (to determine whether a student is an ELL), placement (to assign a student to appropriate educational services), language assessment (to determine a student's language skills and weaknesses), and academic assessment (to determine a student's academic progress skills, and weakness relevant to the content curriculum). In assessment intended for groups of ELLs, the purposes include instructional assessment (to assess class progress relevant to the curriculum), program evaluation (to assess the effectiveness of particular intervention or instructional programs), and accountability (to assess student achievement levels within specific schools or districts).

In both individual and group assessments, testing accommodations may be useful in collecting assessment data on ELLs. For some students, accommodations should be considered in administering tests in order to obtain valid results. Generally, the following steps are considered in using testing accommodations in assessing ELLs for various purposes.

- *Determining language dominance.* The first step is to determine what is the student's dominant language and whether the native language is the primary language the student uses at home.
- *Assessing English language proficiency.* If the student speaks a language other than English at home, the second step is to determine the ELL's proficiency in English. If necessary, the student's proficiency in his or her home language may also be assessed.

- *Determining requisite skills of the test to be administered.* In individual assessment, the test user usually chooses the most appropriate tests for use based on the purpose of the testing and the need of a particular ELL. In group testing (e.g., state or district-wide achievement testing, classroom testing), ELLs are required to take the same test as all other students. It is important to determine whether the test under consideration is linguistically appropriate for a particular ELL.
- *Selecting appropriate testing accommodations.* If it is determined that an ELL does not have the requisite English language skills to perform adequately on the test, then testing accommodations should be considered. The test user should evaluate the situation and determine what specific accommodations would be most appropriate for the student. The test user also needs to make a plan to provide the necessary accommodations (e.g., a bilingual dictionary, extended time, an interpreter).
- *Administering the test.* The individual or group test is administered to the ELL with the use of accommodations.
- *Interpreting results from the nonstandard test administration.* After the test is administered with the use of accommodation procedures, the results should be reported and interpreted with due consideration given to the nonstandard conditions employed.

ASSESSING ENGLISH LANGUAGE PROFICIENCY

An important initial step in assessing ELLs is to determine the student's primary or dominant language and proficiency in English so that a decision can be made whether the student is capable of taking a test in English. According to Yansen and Shulman (1996), primary language refers to the language that is more developed and preferred by the student in appropriate situations. The primary language of ELLs is usually their native language. However, in some cases an ELL's primary language may be English in a certain domain of functioning (e.g., academic learning) and native language in other domains (e.g., home). Language proficiency, on the other hand, refers to the degree to which the student exhibits control over the use of a language. It is an indication of how well a student has mastered the skills of a language. Information on ELLs' English language proficiency is critical in designing the type of assessment and intervention that these students need in school.

If the primary language of an ELL is found to be a language other than English, then the student's level of English proficiency should be assessed. The results of this assessment can be used to determine whether the student has adequate English language skills to take various tests in English as well as the type of accommodations necessary. The results can also be used to determine whether poor performance of an ELL on a test is due to the lack of knowledge or weak English skills (Heubert & Hauser, 1999).

Methods of Assessing English Proficiency

Several methods can be used to assess an ELL's level of English proficiency. These include standardized language tests, interviews, observations, evaluation of language samples, and school and parent information. The most common method in assessing the level of a student's English acquisition is the use of standardized language measures. According to Zehler and colleagues (1994), 83 percent of school districts with ELLs use this method, either alone or in conjunction with other techniques. In a more recent study, Kindler (2002) found that fifty-one of the fifty-four state education agencies surveyed reported they utilize some type of language proficiency test. Although there are many standardized language instruments, they vary considerably in the general construct of language proficiency and the methodology used to measure it. Some most frequently used English proficiency tests include the Language Assessment Scales (LAS), the Language Assessment Battery (LAB), the IDEA Language Proficiency Test (IPT), the Woodcock-Munoz Language Survey (Woodcock-Munoz), the Basic Inventory of Natural Language (BINL), the Bilingual Syntax Measure (BSM), and the Maculaitis Assessment Program. Locally developed tests are also used; for example, some states have developed their own English proficiency tests. From these measures, quantitative and qualitative results may be derived to assign or classify ELLs into different levels of English language proficiency (e.g., beginning, intermediate, advanced). For example, the Lau language category system classifies English proficiency into five levels: category A—monolingual speaker of a language other than English; category B—speaker of a language other than English predominantly; category C—bilingual speaker; category D—speaker of English predominantly; and category E—monolingual speaker of English (Lam, 1993).

Using standardized tests to measure language proficiency has several limitations. Current measures of English proficiency have been criticized for their lack of adequate reliability, validity, as well as the limited populations on which test norms are based. Most available language measures are standardized on monolingual samples and are inappropriate for ELLs with varying degrees of bilingual development (Li, Walton, & Nuttall, 1999). Another limitation is that these tests often give only a brief assessment of the students' receptive and productive language skills and do not assess academic language proficiency (Yansen & Shulman, 1996). Therefore, improved measures of English language proficiency suitable for use with ELLs are needed. In addition, it should be noted that a language proficiency measure alone is an insufficient method for determining the level of English proficiency. This method should be used in conjunction with other procedures of data collection, including observing students' speech in naturalistic situations, evaluating language samples taken in school and home environments (e.g., oral interview, writing sample, story retelling), and home language information.

Based on the assessment of English language proficiency, an ELL may be judged to have insufficient English language skills in taking individual, classroom, or large-scale tests. In this situation, several options are available in assessment of the ELL, depending on the student's level of English language usage. These options include exempting or deferring ELLs from testing, modifying standard testing conditions, using translated or adapted tests, and using interpreters in testing. All of these options are designed to accommodate the ELLs due to their limited use of English. These options are discussed in the following sections.

EXEMPTING OR DEFERRING ELLs FROM TESTING

If an ELL were judged to have minimum or no English language skills, it would be impossible and impractical for the student to take tests in English. In this situation, it will be appropriate to exempt or defer the student from testing in English until he or she has acquired certain proficiency in the English language. In the meantime, the ELL may be assessed in his or her native or primary language or using alternative assessment procedures. Some states exempt students with minimum English proficiency from participating in state mandated testing, if the students have been in the United States for a few years or less. However, once they have resided in the States for a longer period of time, they will be required to take part in the tests. For example, in Florida ELLs are exempted from high school graduation exams during the first two years in a school; but the students must pass the exams in order to receive a diploma. Similarly, Michigan exempts ELLs who have lived in the United States for less than two years from competency exams (Geisinger, 1992). In Louisiana, language minority students are exempted from the high school graduation test and receive a diploma if they began school during their junior or senior year (Rivera & Vincent, 1997).

ELLs in the lower grades who recently immigrated to the United States also may be exempted from taking state and district-wide tests. The decision is made usually based on different methods, including the ELL's level of English proficiency, length of time spent in an ESL or bilingual program, or language status classification (Goertz, Duffy, & Le Floch, 2001). For example, if a student has been placed in an ESL or bilingual program for a limited amount of time, he or she may be exempted from mandated state or district-wide testing. In the second method, an English language proficiency measure is administered to an ELL. If the student scores below a cutoff point, he or she is exempted from participating in mandated testing programs. For example, New York uses 30th percentile on the Language Assessment Battery (LAB) as a cutoff score in determining whether an ELL should participate in fourth- and eighth-grade language arts and mathematics exams. Students who score at or below the thirtieth percentile are exempted from testing for two years. Those who score above the thirtieth percentile on the LAB are required to participate in the assessments (Perez-Hogan & DeMauro, 1999). The third method uses school recommendation in making exemptions or deferring decisions. For example, ELLs who fall into the A, B, and C categories in the Lau language classification system (see earlier section) may be exempted from state-mandated testing, with teacher or principal recommendation (Lam, 1993).

States and school districts differ considerably on the practice of exempting or deferring ELLs from standardized testing. No universally accepted criteria and guidelines exist in making such decisions. Lam (1993) points out several problems in using language tests in making exemptions or deferring decisions. One difficulty lies in the lack of consistency of different language measures in classifying ELLs into different categories of English proficiency. A student may be classified as English proficient by one language test but as nonproficient by another test. The second problem involves the use of cutoff scores on the English proficiency tests. States or school districts usually select the cutoff scores they use on an arbitrary basis. Little empirical evidence supports the validity of the cutoff scores for deciding who should be exempted. As a result, states vary not only in the language proficiency tests they use but also in the cutoff scores they select on these tests. This raises concerns about the reliability and validity of the exemption or deferring decisions made on ELLs. For example, the same student with certain level of English proficiency may be treated quite differently in two different states. While a student may be exempted in one state, he or she may be required to participate in mandated testing in another state. These inconsistencies need to be reduced to enhance consistent assessment and educational decisions concerning ELLs.

MODIFYING STANDARD TEST ADMINISTRATION

ELLs with more than a minimum degree of English proficiency may be assessed on individual, classroom, or large-scale tests if certain accommodations are made to allow them to adequately demonstrate their knowledge and abilities. The accommodations usually involve the modification of some aspect of the standard test administration. The types of appropriate accommodations include modifying the setting in which tests are administered, modifying the time and scheduling requirements of the test, modifying the test instruction and presentation format, and modifying the way by which the student is required to respond to test items. The purpose for modifying different aspects of test administration is, of course, to reduce or eliminate the effect of language barriers that ELLs have in taking tests. The following material includes testing accommodations for ELLs that have been often reported in the professional literature (e.g., Liu, Anderson, Swierzbin, & Thurlow, 1999; Perez-Hogan & DeMauro, 1999; Rivera & Stansfield, 2000; Rivera & Vincent, 1997; Thurlow, Liu, Erickson, Spicuzza, & El Sawaf, 1996).

SETTING MODIFICATIONS
Permitting the use of dictionaries, bilingual glossaries, or word lists in the students' primary language; providing clarifying information (e.g., definitions of words) at the end of test booklet; administering test in small groups; administering test in a separate location; allowing a person to give the test who is familiar with the student (e.g., bilingual education teacher), allowing preferential seating (at the front of the room or in a study carrel).

TIMING AND SCHEDULING MODIFICATIONS
Extending test-taking time limits, allowing extra time to complete test; allowing rest breaks between subtests, administering test in multiple sessions; allowing flexible testing schedule.

PRESENTATION MODIFICATIONS
Allowing test directions to be repeated, clarified, or simplified; if necessary, translating test directions into the student's dominant language; allowing examiners to answer specific questions about the exam in the students' dominant language; reading the directions and/or questions aloud in English and in the student's dominant language; using audiocassettes in English for students having difficulty with printed words; replacing unfamiliar vocabulary with material more directly relevant to student's cultural backgrounds and education.

RESPONSE MODIFICATIONS
Permitting students to write or mark answers directly in the test booklet; using simplified test booklet; allowing dictation of answers to a scribe.

As indicated in Chapter 3, testing accommodations should be selected to meet the individual need of the examinee. This is also true for ELLs. Because each English language learning student is different from any other ELL, the decision on which accommodations to use should be individually determined based on the student's specific needs. For example, while some ELLs may need to use a bilingual dictionary and have the directions explained by a bilingual examiner, others may require only extra time. Liu, Thurlow, Erickson, Spicuzza, and Heinze (1997) recommend that a range of allowable test accommodations for students with differing language needs be specified. Then test users may choose from these accommodations the appropriate ones for use with a particular ELL under consideration. Level of English proficiency, degree of acculturation, and examinee's preference and past experience in using a specific accommodation are factors to consider in selecting testing accommodations.

Most Commonly Used Testing Accommodations

Testing accommodations for ELLs are permitted in many states and school districts, especially those with a high proportion of ELLs. A number of surveys at the national and state levels have investigated the most common types of testing accommodations used with ELLs. These surveys have generally found that (1) not all states have established guidelines on the use of testing accommodations for ELLs, and (2) there is a lack of consistency across states and school districts in the types of accommodations allowed for ELLs.

In a survey examining state guidelines on the use of testing accommodations for ELLs, Rivera and Vincent (1997) reported only twenty-seven states allow for testing accommodations for these students. The most commonly used accommodation was giving the student extra time to complete the test. Some states also translate standardized tests into various languages that are given to ELLs who are more competent in their native language as opposed to English. Thurlow, Liu, Erickson, Spicuzza, & El Sawaf (1996) reviewed written policies for assessment of ELLs from eighteen states. They found scheduling or setting modifications were the two major types of accommodations provided to ELLs. The most frequently used scheduling accommodation was allowing extra time to complete a test, and the most frequently allowed setting modifications were the use of a bilingual dictionary and administering the test in a separate location.

In a survey of twenty-two school districts in Minnesota conducted by Liu, Spicuzza, Erickson, Thurlow, and Ruhland (1997), the respondents reported that the most regularly used testing accommodation for ELLs on both reading and math tests was to extend the time allowed to complete the assessment. Other accommodations that were also used in various districts were to have the test directions clarified or translated, and to have the test administered in a small group or individually. In some instances, an oral or written translation of the entire test was provided. Additionally, the respondents who worked with ELLs listed accommodations that were not currently being used, but that they felt would be beneficial. These suggested modifications included having an examiner who is familiar to the students administer the test, allowing the use of a bilingual dictionary, allowing shorter versions of the tests, simplifying the English used, using an examiner who is the same ethnic background as the students, dictating the answers to a scribe, and using a computer to take the reading or math tests (Liu, Spicuzza, Erickson, Thurlow, & Ruhland, 1997).

Most Effective Testing Accommodations

After having reported on the most commonly used testing accommodations for ELLs, an important question to ask is "Are the most commonly used accommodations also the most effective testing accommodations for ELLs?" Menken (2000) indicates that although timing/scheduling and setting accommodations are the most commonly used procedures, they do not specifically address the linguistic needs of ELLs. Interestingly, presentation and response accommodations can address the linguistic needs of ELLs but are less commonly allowed. She suggests accommodations that would make test content more accessible to ELLs should be used. Currently, there is a general lack of empirical data on the effectiveness of the various types of testing accommodations for ELLs. The studies surveying the use of testing accommodations in various states did not discuss which accommodations had a positive or negative influence on ELLs' test performance. Although extra time has been reported the most frequently used accommodation in most settings, the effects of using extra time are not clearly understood (Liu, Spicuzza, Erickson, Thurlow, & Ruhland 1997).

Only two experimental studies are available in this area. Abedi (1999a, 1999b) investigated the effectiveness of testing accommodations on the National Assessment of Educational Progress (NAEP) math examination. The participants were 900 Spanish-speaking ELLs in eighth-grade math classes, pre-algebra courses, and algebra courses. The studies examined the effects of four different accommodations: the use of modified English (simplified English) on the exam directions, the use of an English glossary with definitions of nonmathematical terms, being given extra time, and the use of an English glossary plus extra time. The first study (Abedi, 1999a) focused solely on what testing accommodations were the most effective, while the second study

(Abedi, 1999b) concentrated on what the most effective accommodations were for students with different background characteristics. These characteristics included the level of math class, the language of the instructor, and the students' attitudes toward the subject of math.

The results of both studies found that the most effective accommodation of the four was the use of an English glossary plus extra time. The use of both methods combined produced a significant increase in test performance even when compared across various background characteristics. However, there was some variability with the effects of different accommodation types based on level of math class, language the class was taught in, and attitude toward math. An example of this is that students in the eighth-grade math class performed lower when given the extra time, while students in pre-algebra classes performed lowest when the directions were given in modified English. It was also found that students taught in Spanish performed lower when given modified English than those taught in English. There were many other combinations of the effectiveness of certain testing accommodations when paired with particular background characteristics (Abedi, 1999b). The author cautioned no conclusions could be drawn regarding what types of testing accommodations are most effective or should be used. Obviously, more empirical research is needed to investigate the effectiveness of various accommodations on the test performance of ELLs with different language needs.

USING TRANSLATED OR ADAPTED TESTS

As mentioned earlier, one accommodation for ELLs who have no or only minimum English proficiency is to test the students in their native or dominant language. In using this accommodation, it is assumed that the students are literate in their native language, have the opportunity to master the content covered in the test, and are unable to display their knowledge on an English test (Heubert & Hauser, 1999; Rivera and Vincent, 1997). Testing ELLs in their native language may take place in two different forms: to use a translated or adapted version of the original test or to use an interpreter during testing to assist in the administration of the test.

Test translation or adaptation is a form of accommodation often used in schools that have high proportions of ELLs. When there is a large student population of a specific type of language, it might be easier to provide an equivalent test in that language rather than having to provide many different types of accommodations for each student. For example, New York provides translated competency tests in thirty-five languages, and New Jersey has its high school proficiency test for graduation available in thirteen languages (O'Malley & Valdez-Pierce, 1994). However, in both New York and New Jersey, a passing score on a test in the student's native language is insufficient to receive a high school diploma, so the student must also obtain a minimum score on an English language proficiency test.

Equivalence between Translated/Adapted Test and the Original Test

Test translation involves translating a test from its original language to a target language in written form. In test translation, the focus is placed on the translation with regard to language; not much attention is paid to the cultural differences between the translated test and the original test. Test adaptation, on the other hand, involves more than a simple language translation. It also attends to cultural difference and includes additional changes in test wording and content that is made to better adapt the translated instrument to the target culture. Test adaptations are usually required when there are significant differences in life experiences and culture between the target population and the original test population (Geisinger, 1994b).

In using a translated/adapted test, an assumption is made that the translated/adapted test is equivalent to the original test in certain aspects of measurement. Four types of equivalence are considered critical: translation equivalence, functional equivalence, metric equivalence, and construct equivalence (Hui & Triandis, 1985). Translation equivalence means that the translated/adapted test should be comparable to the original test in linguistic meaning and content. Functional equivalence addresses the issue whether similar activities or behaviors have the same functions between the translated/adapted test and the original test. Metric equivalence requires the original test and the translated/adapted test to yield equal or comparable scores. Construct equivalence indicates that the translated/adapted test should measure the same construct as does the original test. Ideally, evidence documenting these equivalencies should be produced before a translated/adapted test is established for operational use. When the assumptions are met, one can be certain that the translated/adapted instrument is comparable to the original test and that valid inferences can be drawn from test scores of the translated/adapted instrument.

Phases of Translating or Adapting Tests

Research in cross-cultural measurement (e.g., Bracken & Barona, 1991; Geisinger, 1994b; Hansen, 1987) has discussed procedures necessary in translating or adapting a new measure to ensure its validity and usefulness.

These procedures can be organized into five sequential phases. In the initial phase, the original test in English is first translated into the target language. This is known as *forward translation*. During this process appropriate adaptations on some test items may be made to minimize linguistic and cultural differences between the original and translated tests. The second step is *back translation*—to back translate the translated test in the target language to English. The back-translated version (in English) is then compared to the original test in English to detect any discrepancies. The forward translation and the back translation should be done independently and by different translators. All translations should be made by qualified individuals. Qualified translators need to be fluent in both English and the target language, knowledgeable about both cultures, and familiar with the subject matter covered by the test. On completion of the translation/adaptation, a team of expert judges reviews and provides feedback on the quality of the translations. The feedback is then used to make improvements on the translated/adapted version of the test.

The second phase involves field testing of the translated/adapted test. The translated/adapted instrument is administered to different samples of the target population. Data from the field testing are analyzed to provide descriptive statistics and internal reliability estimates of the translated/adapted test. In addition, both the original and the translated/adapted tests should be administered to a sample of bilingual students who are fluent on both English and the target language. Data collected from the bilingual sample are then analyzed and compared to determine metric equivalence between the original and the translated/adapted tests.

In the third phase, validation research on the translated/adapted instrument is conducted. The primary purpose of this research is to determine whether the translated/adapted test measures the same construct as does the original test. Additional research may also be conducted to provide evidence on content validation and/or criterion-related validation of the translated/adapted test.

The fourth phase is to conduct standardization of the translated/adapted test on the target population and develop new norms. It would be inappropriate to use norms from the original test. The standardization of the translated/adapted test will require a sufficient and representative sample drawn from the target population.

Finally, a test manual and other documents should be developed to facilitate the use of the translated/adapted instrument. It is the test developer's responsibility to provide test users sufficient information on the development, standardization, administration, scoring, interpretation, reliability, and validity of the translated/adapted test (Geisinger, 1994b).

Using translated/adapted tests would allow ELLs to be tested in their native language. It is important to note, however, that whenever this method is used, the translated/adapted test should represent a clear and accurate translation/adaptation of the original test. The translated/adapted test must also show metric and construct equivalence to the original test to ensure that valid inference can be drawn from test scores. One cannot assume that a translated/adapted test is automatically equivalent in content, difficulty level, reliability, and validity to the original test (AERA, APA, & NCME, 1999). A limitation of most translated/adapted tests is that they are seldom subjected to fielding testing, validation, and new standardization (Goh & Yu, 2001; Hambleton & Kanjee, 1994). It is imperative that when translated or adapted tests are used in testing ELLs, they are of satisfactory psychometric qualities to ensure valid interpretation of the results. Local schools and individual professionals without such expertise should not make test translations on their own.

USING BILINGUAL INTERPRETERS IN TESTING

Using interpreters in testing ELLs is also a form of assessment accommodation. This section discusses the procedures and considerations in using interpreters in testing ELLs. Much of the basic information presented in this section also applies to using interpreters in testing students with hearing impairments. This method of accommodation is often used with ELL students who speak a low incidence language. When schools do not have trained personnel who speak an ELL's native language, it may become necessary to obtain an interpreter to assist in the assessment process. Interpreters can translate test instructions and items orally from English to the student's native language. They can also provide school personnel with important information in understanding ELLs and their families.

However, there are a number of inherent difficulties in using interpreters to conduct testing. These difficulties may pose threats to the validity of the test results. For example, the interpreter's oral translation may not be equivalent to the original test. There may be linguistic or dialectical differences between the interpreter's translation and the original test. Also, the use of an interpreter to administer tests to an ELL changes not only the language of testing but also the testing condition. The presence of an interpreter during testing is likely to introduce extraneous factors that may affect the test results. The standard testing procedures may not be followed closely and the interpreter may make errors in translating or give away answers or clues. Furthermore, testing with the assistance of an interpreter may preclude the use of the original test norms (Goh, 1989).

Qualifications and Training of an Interpreter

The most critical consideration in the use of interpreters in testing is the qualification and training of the interpreter. Lopez and Rooney (1997) and Ochoa, Gonzalez, Galarza, and Guillemard (1996) report that many interpreters used in the schools have little or no training in translation and assessment. Lopez (1994) indicates that untrained and inexperienced interpreters often make errors in the process of translating. Such errors may change the content and meaning of test questions, leading to wrong interpretation of the assessment data. The literature (e.g., Cokely, 1986; Fradd & Wilen, 1990) generally agrees that a qualified interpreter must possess a number of competencies. First, the interpreter should demonstrate bilingual and bicultural competence. Specifically, the interpreter should be fluent in both English and the ELL's native language or dialect, including spoken, reading, and written language abilities. The interpreter also needs to be familiar with the U.S. culture as well as the culture of the ELL. Second, the interpreter should have basic understanding of the process of translating and, preferably, prior experience in serving as an interpreter. Third, the interpreter must have some general understanding about the nature of school testing, the uses of test scores in making educational decisions, and the expectation of his or her role as an interpreter during testing.

In the current practice, untrained volunteers from local communities often are recruited to serve as interpreters in testing. As a consequence, both the quality of translation and the accuracy of assessment are compromised. To avoid this problem, professionally trained interpreters should be employed to help in administering tests to ELLs. With adequate preparation about the purpose and nature of testing, professionally trained interpreters can serve effectively in the role of an interpreter during testing. When professionally trained interpreters are not available, bilingual school personnel (e.g., bilingual education teachers, social workers, and teacher's aides) and bilingual college graduates with some background in education or psychology are good candidates to serve as potential interpreters. However, these individuals should receive adequate training to prepare themselves as interpreters during assessment. Such training must include knowledge about the process of translation, the concept of standard test administration, the role and responsibilities of the interpreter during testing, as well as some basic professional and ethical requirements (e.g., maintaining privacy and confidentiality).

The Roles of the Interpreter before, during, and after Testing

Once a qualified person has been selected as an interpreter, he or she should meet with the examiner prior to the testing. This allows the opportunity for the examiner to explain to the interpreter the purpose of testing as well as background information about the ELL examinee. The interpreter must be given time to review all test materials and to read and translate part or all of the test items before testing. On-the-spot translations of standardized tests are not recommended (Lopez, 2002; Wilen & Sweeting, 1986). In clinical testing, it is often desirable for the examiner to demonstrate for the interpreter how certain test items are administered and explain what to expect during testing. In addition, the examiner and the interpreter should use pretesting preparation to become familiar with each other's style of speaking and discuss the role of each during testing (Goh, 1989).

During the assessment, it is essential that the interpreter observe his or her role as assisting the examiner who conducts the testing. The interpreter should make every effort to accurately translate the test questions to the ELL and translate the examinee's responses to the examiner. The interpreter must hold a professional attitude and maintain neutrality throughout the testing. Untrained interpreters often have difficulty in meeting this requirement. For example, some interpreters may unintentionally coach or give cues to examinees on test items while translating. It is important to avoid such and other similar problems related to role confusion on the part of the interpreter.

After the testing, the examiner and the interpreter need to meet to review the examinee's responses and any difficulties encountered during the session. This allows the interpreter to share his or her own observations and insights that could help explain testing results (Paredes-Scribner, 1993). Responses that are difficult to interpret, nontest behaviors that might have special meanings, as well as language and cultural factors that might have an effect on test results should be discussed. All of this information may have bearing on and should be considered in interpreting test results.

Conducting testing with interpreter assistance needs to be done with great caution. Too many factors may affect the validity of test results. It should be clear by now that unqualified and untrained individuals must not be used as interpreters in school testing. Also, the use of parents, relatives, and siblings of the ELL examinee as interpreters during testing should be avoided. At the present time, there is a lack of established procedures on the selection, use, and credentialing of interpreters in school testing. The development of best practice guidelines in these areas is needed.

COMMON GUIDELINES ARE NEEDED FOR PROVIDING ACCOMMODATIONS TO ELLs

A problem in the current practice of using test accommodations with ELLs is the lack of general consensus in addressing important issues (Rivera, Vincent,

Hafner, & LaCelle-Peterson, 1997; Spicuzza, Erickson, Thurlow, Liu, & Ruhland, 1996). The problem begins with the lack of a uniformly accepted operational definition of English language learning students. States and school districts often vary in their definitions and labels in describing these students. Sometimes even definitions of these students within the same state may vary depending on the purpose of assessment. For example, a state may have an ELL definition for identifying students in need of ESL or bilingual services and another ELL definition for the purpose of determining accessibility on large-scale testing. If there were a standard definition of ELL, all states and districts would have a common reference point, and policies across states could be compared (Thurlow, Liu, Erickson, Spicuzza, & El Sawaf, 1996).

Another difficulty lies in the inconsistent criteria used in determining an ELL's eligibility for receiving testing accommodations. For example, there is a lack of consistent guidelines among states on the level of English proficiency to use in deciding whether an ELL should be provided accommodations in taking standardized tests. Likewise, common guidelines on exempting and deferring ELLs from testing do not exist. The U.S. Department of Education has developed a method that attempts to alleviate this problem. This method proposes a three-year goal for ELLs to reach English proficiency. In other words, ELLs who have been in U.S. schools for three or more years should take state or district-wide tests in English without any accommodations (Weise & Garcia, 1998). However, many educators question whether a new immigrant ELL can reach sufficient English proficiency within three years.

A further problem is the limited guidelines available on what and how testing accommodations are to be used with ELLs. States vary considerably on whether they provide accommodations to ELLs in taking standardized tests and the types of accommodations they allow (Homles, Hedlund, & Nickerson, 2000). States are also inconsistent on who makes the decision on what type of accommodations are to be offered to an ELL and on what basis such a decision is to be made. This inconsistency inevitably raises concerns about the reliability of the testing accommodation decisions made for ELLs. The problem is further complicated by the lack of empirical research on the effectiveness of testing accommodations used with this population of students. Currently, only minimum research is available on the effects of specific testing accommodations on ELLs' test performance. More research is needed to determine whether specific testing accommodations are helpful to ELLs, or whether some of the commonly recommended testing accommodations do have the expected effects on these students' performance. It would be beneficial if general guidelines could be developed to specify the types of accommodations that are useful for ELLs, when should they be used, and who should be involved in making accommodation decisions (Thurlow, Liu, Erickson, Spicuzza, El Sawaf, 1996).

SOME CONCLUDING REMARKS AND RECOMMENDATIONS

Finally, it is reiterated here that assessing ELLs is a complex matter. Special attention needs to be given to language- as well as cultural-related issues in using tests with these students. Such issues should be considered in administering, scoring, and interpreting tests and making decisions based on test results. The following recommendations are made for using standardized tests in assessing ELLs.

- Tests selected for use with ELLs should be appropriate for the specific purpose intended. It is important that the test results provide a valid indication of the students' abilities and achievement, not their language limitation.
- In assessing achievement, ELLs should have been given adequate opportunity to learn the content materials being assessed prior to testing. The test must contain no or minimum cultural or content biases against these students.
- In planning for assessment of ELLs, the students' linguistic and cultural backgrounds should be considered. This may include country of origin, academic history, amount of time living in the United States, exposure to English, and language of instruction (Yansen & Shulman, 1996).
- ELLs must be provided motivational strategies and appropriate test-taking skills in taking standardized tests. These tests should be given in an environment that is comfortable and familiar to the students.
- In administering a test to an ELL, it is important to ensure that the student has the level of English proficiency required by the test. If an ELL has insufficient English proficiency in taking the test, appropriate testing accommodations should be used in administering the test to the student.
- When testing accommodations are used in administering tests to ELLs, it is important to ensure that the use of accommodations does not change the construct the test purports to measure.
- When tests are translated into the student's native language or when an interpreter is involved in testing an ELL, the most qualified translators or interpreters should be used.
- In interpreting test results from ELLs, norms of standardized tests should be used with caution. The inclusion of token representation of

various groups of ELLs in the standardization sample is insufficient to assure a test's validity for use with such students. Valid inference cannot be drawn from test scores unless they are obtained from appropriate norms. In addition, test results should be interpreted as reflecting in part the student's current level of English proficiency.

- Tests that are intended for use with particular groups of ELLs should be developed with such students in mind. The linguistic and cultural backgrounds of the students should be reflected in examinee samples used throughout the processes of test design, item development, validation, and norming. At each of these stages of test development and standardization, these distinct groups must receive some specific attention (AERA, APA, & NCME, 1999).

SUMMARY

The number of ELLs has been on the rise over the past three decades. As of the early 2000s, about 9.6 percent of the total student population in the United States is nonnative English speakers. The unique linguistic and cultural characteristics and insufficient English language skills of these students often make successful participation in educational programs difficult. Standardized tests, which are commonly used in education, have been criticized for their inability to accurately measure ELLs' abilities and competencies. The language barriers and other related characteristics of ELLs often adversely affect their performance on tests administered in the standard form. Recent legislation mandates that ELLs be assessed in their native language, with testing accommodations, or using alternative assessment procedures.

A number of steps should be followed in assessing ELLs with accommodations. These include determining language dominance, assessing English proficiency, determining requisite skills of the test to be administered in English, selecting appropriate testing accommodations, administering the test, and interpreting results from nonstandard test administration.

Standardized language measures are the most commonly used method in assessing an ELL's English proficiency. However, due to the limitations of these measures, they should be utilized in conjunction with other information gathering procedures. If an ELL has minimum or no English language skills, the student may be exempted or deferred from testing in English, or assessed in his or her native language. However, state and school districts differ on the practice of exempting or deferring ELLs from standardized testing.

Modifying standard test administration constitutes a major type of accommodations for ELLs. These may include setting modifications, timing and scheduling modifications, presentation modifications, and response modifications. States differ in the testing accommodations they allow for ELLs. The use of extended time, a bilingual dictionary, or a separate room in testing are the most commonly allowed accommodations.

Test translation or adaptation can also be used as a testing accommodation. In translating or adapting a test, assumptions about four types of equivalence are made between the original test and the translated/adapted test: translation equivalence, functional equivalence, metric equivalence, and construct equivalence. There are several phases in translating or adapting a test: forward and backward translation, field testing, validation of the translated/adapted measure, standardization of the translated/adapted measure, and preparation of test manual and supplementary documents.

Using bilingual interpreters during testing is another testing accommodation. Schools often use interpreters to assist in administering tests to ELLs. Qualified interpreters need to be fluent in both English and the student's native language. They should also have some basic understanding about the translation process, as well as knowledge about school testing. Once an interpreter has been selected, he or she should meet with the examiner prior to testing to make adequate preparations. On-the-spot translation of tests is not recommended. The interpreter must also carefully observe his or her role during testing to ensure valid test results.

The lack of uniform standards and guidelines continues to affect the assessment and education of ELLs. Some common policies are needed at the national, state, and district levels to guide the use of testing accommodations with ELLs.

CHAPTER EIGHT

ALTERNATIVE ASSESSMENT

In addition to testing accommodations discussed in the previous chapters, the past two decades have witnessed an increasing interest in alternative assessment. A number of factors have contributed to this development. The educational reform movement (see Chapter 1) advocates educational excellence and sets high standards for all students and schools. As part of this effort, Goals 2000, IDEA, NCLB, and state legislations mandate all students should be included in educational accountability systems. Typically, students are evaluated by standardized achievement tests in state and district-wide assessment programs. However, the limitations of standardized tests have forced the re-examination of the traditional assessment practices and changes in the way schools evaluate students. In addition, as indicated in Chapter 3, standardized tests cannot be administered to some diverse learners even with testing accommodations, due to their severe disabilities or limited English proficiency. These students need to be assessed by other procedures. As part of the educational reform efforts, a different form of assessment, known as alternative or authentic assessment, has emerged and been used as a complement to traditional standardized tests. This approach to assessment differs significantly from standardized tests and is closely aligned with current curriculum theories and cognitive research. This chapter provides an overview of alternative assessment. The topics covered include what is alternative assessment, alternative assessment and diverse learners, types of alternative assessment, specific alternative assessment strategies, scoring and interpretation, technical considerations, and merits and limitations.

WHAT IS ALTERNATIVE ASSESSMENT?

Alternative assessment has become a popular term in education, although there has been a lack of widespread understanding of what it is. In a broad sense, alternative assessment refers to any method of finding out what a given student knows or can do, which is intended to show student growth, that is not a traditionally used standardized test (Hughes, 1993). It is important to know that alternative assessment is not a specific type of assessment, but rather an umbrella term that covers a number of assessments that have both commonalities and differences. Authentic assessment, performance assessment, and portfolio assessment are all included under the rubric of alternative assessment (Bintz & Harste, 1994).

The goal of alternative assessment is to provide a more direct and authentic measure of student learning and progress than do standardized tests. Bennett (1993) view alternative assessment as a different paradigm of assessment than standardized testing. Instead of giving an objective test that consists of a number of items believed to constitute a sample of some underlying knowledge or skills, alternative assessment attempts to directly assess student performance and measure demonstrated competencies. Many educators—including some advocates of alternative assessment—erroneously view this type of direct assessment of student performance as a newcomer to the educational scene. In fact, some of the assessment procedures used in alternative assessment, such as oral examinations and observations, have been in existence since the beginning of the history of education. Other time-honored examples of direct assessment of performance include judging performance in music and athletics; language proficiency testing in speaking and writing; competency testing for pilots and dentists; hands-on assessment in carpentry and mechanics; and the use of art portfolios—to name only a few. Likewise, teachers have long used many of these types of direct assessment in evaluating student performance in the classroom. For example, elementary school teachers were keeping anecdotal records and folders of student work long before such records were legitimized and refined by recent attention on better ways of using portfolios to assess student learning.

Although there are different types of alternative assessment, they share some common characteristics. Four such characteristics are explained next.

■ *Alternative assessment is based on direct assessment of student performance.* A major characteristic of alternative assessment is its emphasis on direct assessment of student performance or products that are valued in their own right. Whereas standardized testing requires students to select responses on objective test items (e.g., multiple-choice, true–false), alternative assessment seeks to evaluate students' actual performance on relevant and meaningful tasks. It may require students to engage in some cognitive activity or produce some learning product. By performing actual tasks or producing products, the students demonstrate what they know and what they can do with their knowledge (Worthen, 1993). Because of this reason, alternative assessment is said to be authentic or "performance based."

■ *Alternative assessment measures high-order thinking skills.* One of the limitations of standardized tests is that they focus on the end results of learning rather than on the process of learning (Henning-Stout, 1994; Rudner & Boston, 1994). For example, scores on a multiple-choice achievement or aptitude test indicate whether students know the correct answers, but they do not directly reflect the thinking skills students use to arrive at their answers. Alternative assessment, on the other hand, is designed to measure complex cognitive skills and other skills important to functioning in school or work settings. It requires the students to demonstrate their knowledge and skills in applied, procedural, and open-ended settings. Alternative assessment evaluates not only what the students know but also how they utilize and integrate their knowledge and skills to solve problems (Falk, 1994). By emphasizing the process of problem solving, this form of assessment reveals student high-order cognitive skills (e.g., reasoning, evaluation, analysis, hypothesis testing, etc.) that are important to future success (Herman, 1997; Supovitz & Brennan, 1997).

■ *Alternative assessment informs teaching and instruction.* The rich information that results from alternative assessment may be used to change curriculum and instruction to enhance student learning, and results in greater student achievement. This is because tasks used in alternative assessment are closely aligned with instructional activities in the classroom. Many such tasks are developed directly out of local curriculum objectives and student performance standards (Valdez-Pierce & O'Malley, 1992). Therefore, results from alternative assessment yield useful information about what the students know and can do as well as their strengths and weaknesses with reference to the learning objectives. Unlike scores on standardized tests that indicate only a student's standing relative to other students, results on alternative assessment give teachers, students, and parents meaningful feedback about the teaching–learning process. Teachers can use this information to modify curriculum and instruction to improve student achievement (Adams, 1998).

■ *Alternative assessment allows for self-assessment of students.* Another characteristic of alternative assessment is self-assessment. According to Darling-Hammond (1994b), self-assessment plays a big role in alternative assessment. Students are given the opportunity to provide input in developing evaluation criteria as well as to evaluate their own performance or work product. Through self-assessment, students develop the ability to evaluate their own work against a given standard or the work of others. It also enables the students to develop an understanding of their learning activities, accomplishments, as well as strengths and weaknesses. In addition, by placing some control of the assessment process in the hands of the students themselves, alternative assessment increases the students' sense of shared responsibility, which may enhance their motivation for learning (Travis, 1996). Students may use information from self-assessment to make plans to address areas in need of improvement. Students may also discuss their plans with their teachers to obtain feedback and suggestions.

ALTERNATIVE ASSESSMENT AND DIVERSE LEARNERS

Alternative assessment has been developed and used as an assessment technology in general education settings. Classroom teachers have used it widely in evaluating student learning. Some states also have included alternative assessment (i.e., portfolios, performance assessment) in their state and district-wide assessment programs. Moya and O'Malley (1994) indicate the following uses of information from alternative assessment:

- Diagnosing student strengths and needs with regard to curriculum objectives
- Monitoring student progress over the course of learning
- Placing student at the appropriate instructional level
- Assigning grades for evaluation purpose
- Designing instructional interventions
- Providing feedback on instructional effectiveness
- Communicating with teachers and parents about student performance
- Determining when it is appropriate to phase the student out of special instructional programs

Alternative assessment also has special utility in assessing diverse learners. Hughes (1993) describes ways that alternative assessment can be used for students with disabilities in classroom settings. In the same vein, Solomon and Rhodes (1995) also discuss the many uses of alternative assessment for ELLs. Moreover, Bernstein (1989) and Shaul (1999) pointed out that schools often encounter difficulties in deciding what types of testing accommodations are appropriate and effective for students with special needs. The use of alternative assessment is one solution to alleviate such difficulties in assessing students with disabilities.

A particular merit of alternative assessment is that it can be used to assess students with severe disabilities or students with very limited English proficiency. As indicated earlier, these students cannot be assessed by standardized tests, even with the provision of testing accommodations. Alternative assessment affords these students an opportunity to demonstrate their competence in nontraditional forms. Thurlow, Olsen, Elliott, Ysseldyke, Erickson, and Ahearn (1996) discuss the use of alternative assessment for students with severe disabilities in large-scale assessment programs. Participation in state or district-wide assessment is deemed inappropriate for these students. Also, students with severe disabilities are most likely to have curriculum (e.g., communication and functional living skills) that differs significantly from the content normally covered by state or district-wide standardized achievement tests. Thurlow, Olsen, Elliott, Ysseldyke, Erickson, & Ahearn (1996) suggested that state assessment programs should include a broad set of standards that encompasses the curriculum of students with very significant disabilities and assesses the curriculum using a subset of the broad standards with alternative assessment methods. They reported that a small number of states have begun to do this as part of their state assessment programs. Scores on the alternative assessment are used to derive accountability indexes just as do scores on the general standardized assessment.

Alternative assessment is equally useful in evaluating ELLs. Damico (1992) indicates that a good assessment technique should be designed to match the developmental and language proficiency levels of students. When used with ELLs, alternative assessment can be conducted in the students' language of instruction. The goal is to reduce the English language load and provide a more accurate measure of the students' knowledge and skills. Therefore, depending on the level of English proficiency of the student, alternative assessment can be conducted in the student's native language or a combination of English and the student's native language. Furthermore, alternative assessment can be adapted to different situations and forms to assess ELLs' learning and achievement. The findings can then be used to draw inferences about the students' ability to apply their knowledge and skills in solving complex problems, something that cannot be achieved with standardized tests (Lacelle-Peterson & Rivera, 1994).

TYPES OF ALTERNATIVE ASSESSMENT

From the literature, three terms have been most commonly associated with alternative assessment: *performance assessment, authentic assessment,* and *portfolio assessment.* These assessments share the common characteristics just cited.

Sometimes, the terms *performance assessment* and *authentic assessment* are used interchangeably. Certain authors also view portfolio assessment as a subcategory of performance assessment. Nevertheless, conceptually some differences make each assessment distinct. The three types of assessment are described next.

Performance Assessment

According to Khattri and Sweet (1996), "Performance assessment refers to a type of assessment that requires students to actually perform, demonstrate, construct, develop a product or a solution under defined conditions and standards" (p. 3). Valdez-Pierce and O'Malley (1992) define performance assessment as an exercise in which a student demonstrates specific skills and competencies relating to a continuum of agreed-upon standards of proficiency or excellence. Typically, the student is required to perform a task that is designed to allow him or her to demonstrate or apply knowledge about the subject material learned. The student is also required to explain his or her performance or the process by which he or she arrived at the solutions or answers. The task may involve a behavior or activity to be performed by the student or something that results in a tangible product (Bachor, 1990). The teacher or assessment professional observes and makes judgment about the student's ability in carrying out the task or producing a product (Arter & Stiggins, 1992). The evaluation is done based on scoring criteria and performance standards developed prior to the implementation of the assessment. Generally, the following steps are recommended in designing and carrying out performance assessments (Chase, 1999; Kubiszyn & Borich, 2003; Worthen, White, Fan, & Sudweeks, 1999). (1) Decide the performance (e.g., skills, behaviors, proficiencies) to be measured and clearly define each. (2) Create the performance tasks or exercises, and make sure each task or exercise matches closely the learning outcome to be assessed. (3) Define the criteria and performance standards to be used to judge the quality of student performance. (4) Specify test constraints under which the students take the test (e.g., time limits, availability of dictionaries, textbook, or other reference materials or equipment, etc.). (5) Observe and record the results of the observation. (6) Score and interpret the results.

In addition, Elliott and Fuchs (1997) identify several important elements of performance assessment. These include the following: (1) linking assessment tasks to what has been taught to the students, (2) sharing with students scoring criteria for assessment task, (3) sharing with students standards and model of acceptable and exemplary performance prior to assessment, (4) encouraging students to conduct self-assessment of their performance, and

(5) comparing students' performance to predetermined standards as well as to the performances of other students.

Performance assessment can be used in local classroom or school settings as well as in large-scale assessment. When used in the local classroom or school settings, active involvement of teachers is critical in all phases of the design and implementation of the assessment. When used in large-scale assessment, educational experts outside of the school usually develop the tasks and evaluation criteria. Typically, the tasks used in the assessment should reflect what is taught in the schools.

Authentic Assessment

Authentic assessment is a term sometimes used interchangeably with alternative assessment. Some educators view performance assessment as a subset of authentic assessment. Authentic assessment, like performance assessment, focuses on the direct examination of student performance or work product. However, authentic assessment places an additional requirement on the measurement of behaviors and skills that are relevant to the real world (Hamayan, 1995). It is believed that basing evaluation on real-world experience makes learning more relevant, and hopefully more meaningful to students. For example, it makes more sense to assess students on their ability to make change by setting up a classroom store than by having them complete a worksheet of addition and subtraction problems. Often, the abilities demanded on a simple task such as basic computation do not translate well to a practical situation. According to Travis (1996), an assessment measure is considered to be authentic if the test questions or problems are designed to take place in a real-life setting outside the classroom. Under this requirement, not all performance assessments are authentic in nature. Meyer (1992) described an example in which students participated in a standardized series of activities for four days to produce a writing sample. This is an example of performance assessment, but it is not an authentic assessment, because performance was assessed in a contrived rather than a real-life setting. The tasks that students are required to do on authentic assessment must closely resemble what a student may be called on to do in the real world (Hughes, 1993).

Portfolio Assessment

Generally, portfolio assessment involves the evaluation of student knowledge, skills, and achievement based on a collection of student work. Moya & O'Malley (1994) defined portfolio assessment as the procedure used to plan, collect, and analyze the multiple sources of data that reflect a student's accomplishments. The aim is to provide accurate and meaningful information about the student. The contents of a portfolio may include a multitude of student work samples, performance, experiences, exhibitions, and so on. The portfolio may also contain information such as narrative descriptions of work completed, rationale for the inclusion of the selected items, teacher ratings, quizzes, student self-assessment, and summary of learning experiences and insights developed during the course of learning. Together, these data reflect a systematic, cumulative record of a student's learning relative to specific instructional objectives. The type and amount of material to be included in a portfolio are determined by the purpose of the assessment. Some portfolios seek to highlight a student's completed efforts on a particular learning objective, whereas others are more comprehensive and designed to provide evidence of student progress in a content area over an extended period of time.

A portfolio should not be a random collection of student work. Many considerations enter in the design of an effective portfolio. For example, Adams (1998) emphasized that a portfolio should be a well-planned documentation of student performance systematically collected based on the purpose of assessment. The contents of the portfolio should usually be varied and furnish multiple perspectives of the student's academic work or development. Other researchers maintain that portfolio assessment should encourage students to take responsibility for their learning. To this end, students need to be given the opportunity to provide input regarding portfolio contents and be allowed to select the work samples to be included in the portfolio, based on the criteria given by the teacher or school (Solomon & Rhodes, 1995). This enables students to display their best work and allow others to see the quality of their thinking as well as their interpretation of their work (Darling-Hammond, 1994b). In addition, a good portfolio assessment takes into account the special characteristics and backgrounds of diverse learners and is tailored to the assessment needs of these students.

According to Moya and O'Malley (1994) and Valdez-Pierce & O'Malley (1992), a model portfolio assessment procedure must include the following five elements. (1) Identify the purpose and focus of the portfolio; (2) design the portfolio (e.g., contents, data collection procedures, criteria for evaluation of the portfolio); (3) collect and analyze portfolio content; (4) use analysis of results to make educational (e.g., high school graduation) or instructional decisions (e.g., improve instruction to meet the need of the student); and (5) examine reliability and validity of the procedure. From a slightly different perspective, Popham (1999) identifies the following key ingredients in classroom portfolio assessment. (1) Make sure the students perceive portfolios to be collections of their own work; (2) decide on what kinds of work samples to collect; (3) collect and store work samples; (4) select criteria by which to evaluate work samples; (5) require students to continually evaluate their own portfolio products; (6) schedule and conduct portfolio conferences between teachers and students; and (7) involve parents in the portfolio assessment process.

Portfolio assessment has both classroom and large-scale applications. Portfolios can be used effectively as a tool to assess academic achievement of individual students or groups of students. Some schools use portfolios on a periodic, ongoing basis to monitor students' progress and to document their growth toward specific learning goals (French, 1992; Liebars, 1999; Solomon & Rhodes, 1995; Valdez-Pierce & O'Malley, 1992).

SPECIFIC ALTERNATIVE ASSESSMENT STRATEGIES

Alternative assessment involves a variety of strategies and procedures that can be used to collect data about a student. These range from a teacher's record of various assessments generated in the classroom to more structured performance tasks or student portfolios used in large-scale assessments. Some of the strategies and procedures focus on the performance of the student (e.g., oral responses or presentations, demonstrations, hands-on execution of experiments, dramatic or musical performances), others focus on the end product of learning (e.g., writing samples, essay examinations, drawings, exhibits), and still others focus on the process by which learning takes place (e.g., observations, learning journals, interviews, student self-reports, and self-assessment). The purpose of assessment and the nature of the competencies or skills to be measured determine the selection of the particular assessment strategy or procedure to be used. Often, it is appropriate to use a combination of different procedures. A variety of alternative assessment procedures have been reported for use with diverse learners. For example, Hughes (1993) described a number of alternative assessment strategies that are appropriate for students with disabilities, including portfolios, observations, read and retell, journals, group work, and class presentations. Similarly, Solomon and Rhodes (1995) found portfolios, physical demonstration, oral performances, pictorial products, oral and written products, and teacher-made measures were useful alternative assessment strategies with ELLs. The following describes some frequently used procedures for diverse learners.

Performance Tasks

Performance tasks are often used in alternative assessment to assess a student's acquisition of knowledge and skills. In this procedure, the student is required to perform on tasks that are designed to measure specific learning outcomes. In contrast to standardized tests which include closed-ended items, on which students must select the correct answers, performance tasks employ an open-ended format and require students to construct their responses on actual tasks. The tasks may require students to demonstrate knowledge, organize information, evaluate solutions, or justify their answers. For example, a student may be asked to answer open-ended questions in mathematics and explain his or her responses. Through performing or completing tasks, the students display their knowledge, abilities, and skills. The more complex performance tasks require the students to demonstrate high-order cognitive skills in problem-solving situations. Performance tasks should be carefully designed, administered, and scored to ensure reliability and validity of the results

Demonstration

Demonstration of mastery is a formal, public performance of skills that permits an assessment of a student's achievement. It also may be used as an ongoing, informal assessment procedure in everyday practice. Experiments in science provide ideal hands-on opportunities for students to demonstrate understanding of learned materials. For example, the teacher can ask students studying electric circuits to build circuits or to solve circuit design problems (Solomon & Rhodes, 1995). Demonstration as an assessment strategy can be adapted to meet the specific needs of students with disabilities or ELLs by allowing them to show their knowledge using their preferred mode of presentation. For example, physical demonstration is a nonverbal means of expressing academic concepts and knowledge. Students with language and speech disabilities can use gestures and motions, or other nonverbal signs to demonstrate their knowledge and skills. Kelner (1993) encourages the use of dramatization with ELLs to demonstrate their understanding of content subjects, because little language is required in the procedure. Likewise, Farnham-Doggory (1992) points out that some students with learning disabilities have difficulty in spatial representation and are unable to solve math problems on paper. But these students may successfully solve the problems if allowed to invoke motor functions (e.g., physical grouping).

Oral Assessment

Oral assessment is an evaluation of what a student tells about what he or she knows. The student may be asked to make oral reports, role-play, describe, explain, summarize, or retell stories or text material (Soloman & Rhodes, 1995). The teacher or assessment professional listens and probes for evidence of the student's knowledge or competency on certain subject matters. The teacher may also ask the student to explain why certain answers were given or how the student derived the answers. In the oral responses the teacher would evaluate the student's accuracy and comprehensiveness of his or her knowledge. The tasks or material used in oral assessment should be meaningful to the student. The results of oral assessment may offer insightful information about not only the student's knowledge but also his or her thinking processes and problem-solving abilities. When used with ELLs, oral assessment may be conducted in the student's native language, with the assistance of an interpreter when necessary.

Learning Products

Learning products are work products completed by students. They can be used to assess content knowledge as well as high-order thinking skills. Learning products of various types are widely used in assessing students' learning across curriculum in different disciplines. Written products may include samples of students' writing, essays, and papers. Oral products may include audio or videotapes of student oral reading, presentations, and dramatics. Pictorial products may include drawings, dioramas, models, graphs, and charts. Learning products can be kept in portfolios and used as evidence of student learning and growth.

Group Work

Group work or activity can be used as an assessment technique with general education students as well as students with disabilities (Hughes, 1993). It provides an opportunity for students to interact with the teacher, materials, and each other. In a group activity (small or whole group learning situation), students may work together to write a dialogue, find a solution to a math problem, or prepare a project paper. The teacher may question the students about their work and ask them to justify their answers or clarify their ideas. In addition, the teacher may generate other semicontrolled or controlled discussion to collect assessment data about the students. Observations of the entire process of evaluation may be recorded and later analyzed.

Observations

A historically important assessment strategy, observations have taken on renewed emphasis in alternative assessment. Students can be observed while engaging in learning tasks or activities. From observation, the teacher or assessment professional may make a record of the learning event and describe what the student did. The student is also given opportunity to explain the reasoning behind his or her actions. By observing what the student did, the teacher may gain insight into the processes the student used while performing the learning tasks. This procedure is useful for identifying particular difficulties students have that cannot be revealed by written tests. Assessing student learning on subject matters (e.g., reading and math) by observation is beneficial to students with disabilities (Hughes, 1993).

Observations as an assessment technique should be used with predefined tasks and specific recording and scoring procedures. Anecdotal record and systematic observation are two frequently used types of observation in classroom settings (Gronlund, 1993). Anecdotal record is a less structured approach to obtain a brief description of some significant learning event. It includes the observed behavior of a student, the setting in which the behavior occurred, and a separate interpretation of the event. In systematic observation, some quantified record of the observation is made. These are often done with the use of checklists or rating scales. Checklists usually include a list of measurable dimensions of a performance, with a place to record a "yes" or "no" judgment. Alternately, rating scales provide a means to mark the degree to which a performance is presented. The scale for rating can be based on the frequency with which a behavior is performed, the quality of a performance, or a set of descriptive phrases that indicates degrees of acceptable performance. These quantified observational data are useful in arriving at more objective evaluation of students.

Journals

Journals or learning logs offer a useful way to understand and evaluate student learning and accomplishments. The purpose of using journals is to allow the student to communicate directly with the teacher regarding individual learning, progress, reflections, concerns, and attitudes on the learning process. Adams (1998) suggested the following key ideas for journals. (1) Develop a purpose for journals in the classroom and share this purpose with the students; (2) have the students keep a notebook for their journal entries; (3) create opportunities for dialogue and add value to the experience for the students by responding to their journal entries; (4) allow the students to share their journal entries with each other; and (5) encourage the students to review and reflect on their own journal entries to support further monitoring of their learning experiences.

Journals may vary in their format and serve different purposes (Liebars, 1999; Solomon & Rhodes, 1995). Teachers use *content area journals* to assess and monitor student learning in a particular content areas on an ongoing basis. In *response journals,* the teacher provides carefully designed questions or prompts after each learning activity or task, to which the students must respond. Some prompts are related to content materials; others explore student strategies of problem solving, attitudes, and ideas. *Open-ended reflection* journals allow the students to write about what they have learned in class and their reactions to and feelings about the learning activities. *Dialogue journals* offer interactive, ongoing correspondence between teachers and students. They provide students with disabilities an opportunity to demonstrate their knowledge and concerns when the teacher responds to what the students have written (Hughes, 1993).

According to Hatfield and Price (1992), although some diverse learners have limited writing ability, they should be encouraged to write journals and allowed to participate at their level of language proficiency. Students with writing difficulties may be encouraged also to communicate learning through drawings or illustrations. For example, in studying plants a student with a writing disability may be allowed to keep a pictorial journal of a plant's need, care, and observable changes. In a subsequent oral assessment of the topic, the student can point to the correct illustration in his or her pictorial journal in response to the teacher's questions (Solomon & Rhodes, 1995).

Interviewing

Interviewing is another technique that can be used as an alternative assessment procedure. It involves direct personal communication between teachers and students. When both teacher and student are open and honest, an interview can provide valuable information about student knowledge and thinking. Structured as well as nonstructured interviews may be used to assess a student's mastery and achievement. However, successful interviewing should focus on specific themes and content (Staggins, 1994). Interviewing can be less time-consuming through the application of a qualitative paradigm, which allows for limited but purposeful sampling (Travis, 1996). Not bound by standardization, each interview may be specifically tailored to the particular student's need. In conducting interviews with ELLs or students with speech or language difficulties, the teacher or assessment professional may use visual cues to compensate for the language barriers of these students.

Portfolios

A valuable strategy in alternative assessment is the use of portfolios. As mentioned earlier in the chapter, a portfolio is a collection of student work used to

evaluate student performance and learning outcomes. The content of a portfolio may include in-class work, prescribed exercises, home assignments,
writing samples, journal entries, and audio and/or videotapes of presentations
(Arter & Stiggins, 1992; Tannenbaum, 1996). It may also include other evidence
of student achievement (e.g., teacher ratings, student self-assessment, etc.).
Hughes (1993) stresses the value of portfolios in assessing the skills and growth
of students with disabilities and suggests the collection of multiple samples of
student work in the portfolio. Likewise, Solomon and Rhodes (1995) recommend the use of portfolios in assessing ELLs. They suggest that portfolios for
ELLs may contain any of the following in English, the student's native language, or a combination of both: writing samples/computer printouts, dialog
journal entries, books reports, writing assignments, reading log entries, projects, pictures or drawings, graphs and charts, conference or interview notes,
anecdotal records, evaluations or checklists (by teacher, peer, or student),
tests/quiz samples, lists of books read, audio and video recordings of read-
ings or oral presentations.

Teacher-Made Classroom Measures

Teacher-made measures of various types are a major source of information
about student learning. They can be used as alternative assessment procedures to standardized tests. However, special considerations should be made
to make teacher-made classroom tests more suitable to diverse learners. For
example, Solomon and Rhodes (1995) point out that teachers working with
ELLs need to design or modify tests to match the English proficiency of their
students. It would be desirable to simplify the language and grammar while
keeping the concept and content at the appropriate grade level. Short (1991)
made the following suggestions about modifying classroom measures to increase their suitability to ELLs. (1) Use short sentences with simple grammatical structures; (2) use the simpler verb tense (such as present, simple past, and
simple future); (3) write in the active voice, not the passive; (4) use pronouns
judiciously, only when their antecedents are obvious; (5) be careful with in-
definite words such as *it, there,* and *that* at the beginning of sentences; (6) eliminate relative clauses with *who, which,* and *whom* wherever possible; and
(7) minimize the use of negatives.

SCORING AND INTERPRETATION

Alternative assessment can be scored and interpreted in a variety of ways depending on the nature of the particular assessment strategies or procedures

used (e.g., performance tasks, portfolios, etc.). Although many alternative assessment procedures are evaluated qualitatively, some can be scored quantitatively. A most important—and perhaps most difficult as well—element in conducting an alternative assessment is designing scoring rubrics. A scoring rubric is a set of well-defined rules or guidelines that can be used to evaluate the quality of student performance or product. Clear scoring criteria and standards of performance must be established in a rubric for evaluating the degree to which a student has demonstrated the learning outcomes that the assessment procedure is designed to measure. Designing a scoring rubric begins from precisely defining behavior objectives and contents or skills to be assessed. Specific procedures and criteria are then developed to rate or judge the quality of a student's performance. Scoring may be done with the aid of checklists or rating scales. The criteria should include well-articulated quality standards at different levels of performance (e.g., excellent, good, average, poor, or unacceptable). It is important for the criteria to offer clear descriptions of each level of performance in terms of what the students are able to do and assign values to these levels (Pate, Homestead, & McGinnis, 1993). In addition, ample examples of performance need to be provided at each level of performance to guide the evaluation of student performance or work product.

A scoring rubric may contain a single evaluative criterion or multiple evaluative criteria. When using multiple evaluative criteria, the student performance or work product can be rated using either a holistic or an analytic scoring approach (Popham, 1999). In the holistic approach, all of the criteria are used collectively to arrive at a single, overall judgment about a student's performance. On the other hand, the analytic scoring approach allows awarding of response points on a criterion-by-criterion basis. The student's performance is rated on each criterion.

Because alternative assessments may not be subjected to standardized testing conditions, it is critical that assessment contents (e.g., performance tasks), scoring criteria, and quality standards are precisely defined and apply to all students to ensure objective and accurate measurement. The goal is to make the evaluation process as reliable as possible to produce useful and interpretable results. In addition, the evaluation criteria and quality standards should be made known to the students prior to assessment to let them know how their work will be scored or rated (Darling-Hammond, 1994b; Elliott & Fuchs, 1997). Compared to traditional standardized tests, the scoring of alternative assessments is far more complex and involved. Persons who are responsible for scoring or judging student performance or work product must be adequately trained to use the scoring rubric of a particular alternative assessment procedure. In addition, it helps to use multiple judges or raters, if possible, to score alternative assessment results to ensure their accuracy.

Moya and O'Malley (1994) indicate that three complementary points of reference can be used to interpret alternative assessment results: mastery of skills, relative group standing, and individual performance across time. When mastery of skills is used as a point of reference, the assessment results are interpreted using a criterion-referenced framework. Student performance is rated in terms of mastery of the content being assessed. The results yield qualitative descriptions of what the student can or cannot do based on predetermined evaluation criteria. On the other hand, alternative assessment results can be interpreted by indicating the relative standing of a student's performance in comparison to a group of students or a particular norm, following the norm-referenced model. Finally, interpretation of a diverse learner's performance across time enables the teacher or assessment professional to collect multiple sets of alternative assessment data over a period of time. These data then can be used as points of comparison in interpreting assessment results and gauging the student's progress.

TECHNICAL CONSIDERATIONS

Like any other type of assessments, alternative assessment needs to be valid and reliable in order to ensure meaningful and useful results. However, evidence of reliability and validity of alternative assessment has not been encouraging so far. This problem is exacerbated by the wide variety of alternative assessment procedures available, as well as disagreement over which procedures are best used with particular students. The available research in validity and reliability of major types of alternative assessment has been primarily on general education students; very little information is available regarding diverse learners (Elliott & Fuchs, 1997). Some researchers maintain that the traditional psychometric methods of evaluating objective, standardized tests may not apply to alternative assessment strategies, and it may be necessary to rethink the issues of reliability and validity with these new forms of assessment. Nevertheless, others believe that if alternative assessments are to be used as an assessment method, the notion of reliable and valid score interpretation remains critical (Miller & Legg, 1993).

Reliability

Reliability refers to the consistency of assessment results. Two types of reliability are of particular importance to alternative assessment: content or task reliability and interrater reliability. Alternative assessments have been reported to have low reliability across tasks (Shavelson, Baxter, & Pine, 1991).

Performance assessment, for example, is limited in the degree of sampling and generalizability across tasks. Linn (1993) describes performance assessment as "highly task specific" and a student's performance on one task may have a weak relationship to his or her performance on another similar task. One method to overcome this problem and improve generalizability across tasks is to increase the number of tasks used on the assessment. However, this would require a large amount of time for the administration of multiple tasks in order to achieve a reasonable level of generalizability.

The second type of reliability that is important to alternative assessment is interrater reliability. Scoring of alternate assessment results are done by various raters or judges. The scoring can be influenced by extraneous factors such as rater bias, generosity error, and halo effect. Due to these reasons, scoring reliability on alternative assessments is generally lower than that on traditional standardized tests (Bachor, 1990; Worthen, 1993). In order to minimize error variance due to rating, raters should be trained with the use of the scoring procedure and adhere to the specific criteria in evaluating student performance or product. In addition, multiple raters or judges are necessary to establish interrater reliability, before the scoring rubric is put to use. Finally, it should be noted that both task reliability and interrater reliability are influenced by the complexity of the assessment task or contents to be assessed. As the task and scoring criteria increase in their complexity, it becomes more difficult to establish high reliability of alternative assessments (Miller & Legg, 1993).

Validity

Validity refers to the degree to which test scores can be used to serve the proposed use of an alternative assessment. Little information is currently available about the technical validity of alternative assessments. It has been said that alternative assessments have relatively high face validity. However, face validity—an assessment's appearance of tapping the construct (e.g., contents, skills) to be measured—is not sufficient to assure accurate measurement and test interpretation (Herman, 1997). Abundant research is needed to provide other forms of validity evidence. For example, the usefulness of alternative assessment data in making instructional decisions or educational placement decisions must be established with empirical data rather than simply theorized. The assumption that alternative assessment measures high-order thinking skills also needs to be validated with empirical evidence. These validity evidences may be gathered through traditional procedures of test validation. In addition, Linn, Baker, and Dunbar (1991) offered the following expanded criteria for the validation of alternative assessments. Again, much research is needed to examine whether alternative assessments meet these criteria, using existing or new methods of validation.

- *Consequence of test use:* Does the assessment have positive consequences or are there unintended adverse effects on disadvantaged students?
- *Fairness:* Is the assessment fair to students from racial/ethnic, disability, or gender subpopulations?
- *Transfer and generalizability:* Can the assessment results be used to draw accurate generalizations about the student's ability or knowledge?
- *Cognitive complexity:* Does the assessment measure more complex, higher-level thinking skills?
- *Content quality:* Does the assessment reflect important contents that are worthy of the time and efforts of students?
- *Content coverage:* Does the assessment reflect an adequate content coverage of the curriculum to be assessed?
- *Meaningfulness:* Does the assessment assure that the students are engaged in meaningful problems?
- *Cost and efficiency:* Does the assessment involve efficient data collection designs and scoring procedures?

MERITS AND LIMITATIONS

Alternative assessment has many advantages. As mentioned at the beginning of the chapter, it provides direct examination of a student's performance or work product on significant and relevant tasks. The information obtained from the assessment not only describes what the student knows or can do but also reveals the student's higher-order thinking skills. Teachers may use this assessment information to improve instruction and student achievement. In addition, alternative assessment places an emphasis on the self-assessment of students by involving the students in the assessment process, which has an effect of enhancing the students' learning skills and motivation. Another important merit of alternative assessment is its emphasis on the developmental and functional appropriateness of the assessment. Specifically, assessment content and procedure must be appropriate in terms of the students' abilities, disabilities, language proficiencies, and cultural backgrounds. This emphasis on contextual significance is particularly relevant with regard to diverse learners (Tannenbaum, 1996). It has the potential to decrease biases and inequities in measurement and produce more accurate estimates of the ability and achievement of students with disabilities and ELLs (Supovitz & Brennan, 1997). Moreover, alternative assessment provides a useful method of assessing the learning of those diverse learners who are unable to participate in standardized testing. This allows these students to be assessed and included in the educational accountability systems. Overall, alternative assessment constitutes a viable and useful method of assessing diverse learners in classroom settings as well as large-scale assessment programs.

Despite the advantages indicated above, alternative assessment is not without its problems and critics. A number of obstacles remain to be overcome before alternative assessment achieves popularity in its use. One problem is the limited empirical evidence available to support the reliability and validity of alternative assessment, as pointed out earlier. Another issue that poses a serious concern about alternative assessments is the lack of standardization. Research has shown that student performance is very sensitive to changes in assessment format and condition. The context in which students are asked to perform can greatly influence the assessment results (Worthen, 1993). It is more difficult to ensure standardized assessment conditions with performance tasks or portfolios than with traditional standardized tests. The very nature of some alternative assessment procedures makes it difficult to establish standardized assessment conditions, because student performance and work samples are developed in various ways. For example, there are differences in the amount of time students spend on work samples, the amount of support teachers provide to students, and the level of support students receive from other sources such as peers, tutors, and parents. Some recent efforts have attempted to standardize alternative assessments so students' scores on these assessments can be compared. For example, Vermont has developed standardized assessment conditions in its statewide writing portfolio program. Fourth- and eighth-grade students are administered the writing prompt at the same time across the state, and teachers receive training about the testing accommodations they are permitted to use (Gomez, 1999). Developing standardized assessment conditions remains a key issue in alternative assessment. This issue is likely to influence the future popularity of alternative assessment as a useful accountability tool in large-scale assessment.

Other limitations of alternative assessment are that it is time-consuming and costly. A substantial amount of time is needed to develop, administer, and score alternative assessments. Many alternative assessment procedures are administered individually rather than in groups. Performance tests are much more time-consuming to administer than are standardized tests. Also, a great amount of time is needed to develop scoring criteria, checklists, and rating scales for alternative assessments, as well as actually to score the results. In addition to being labor intensive, alternative assessments are costly. Arter and Stiggiens (1992) reported some performance tests in the science area were three to ten times more costly than multiple-choice tests in large-scale assessments. Herman (1997) indicated that alternative assessment may cost four to five times as much to score when compared to standardized multiple-choice tests. The schools need to receive appropriate support and resources to use alternative assessments in a valid and reliable manner for diverse learners as well as for general education students (Navarrete & Gustke, 1996).

SUMMARY

The goal of educational assessment is to gather useful information about students. Alternative assessment incorporates this goal by focusing on direct examination of students' learning performance and products. It seeks to measure students' abilities and competencies that traditional standardized tests are not able to assess.

Alternative assessment has several major features. It is based on direct assessment of student performance; it measures higher-order thinking skills; it informs teaching and instruction; and it allows for self-assessment of students. This alternative form of assessment to standardized testing affords diverse learners an opportunity to give their answers, present their knowledge, and demonstrate their skills in ways that are developmentally and functionally appropriate for them. It also offers a mechanism for these students to participate in large-scale assessment and be included in the accountability system.

There are three major types of alternative assessment: performance assessment, authentic assessment, and portfolio assessment. These three types of assessment share some common characteristics, but differ in other ways. Sometimes, they are used in combination in assessing students for different purposes. There is a variety of specific strategies and procedures of alternative assessment. Some frequently used ones for diverse learners include performance tasks, demonstration, oral assessment, learning products, group work, observations, journals, interviewing, portfolios, and teacher-made classroom measures. A critical element in designing and implementing alternative assessment procedures is the development of objective scoring criteria and procedures to ensure objective and accuracte scoring and interpretation.

At the present time, only limited evidence is available on the reliability and validity of alternative assessments, so more research is needed in this area. There are many merits as well as limitations of alternative assessment. Compared to traditional standardized tests, alternative assessments are more likely to yield less biased estimates of the abilities and achievements of students with disabilities and ELLs. The current trend suggests more states and school districts are developing alternative assessment programs. However, a number of technical and practical concerns remain, such as reliability, validity, standardization, cost, and efficiency. These issues must be resolved before alternative assessment can be legitimately and fully incorporated into the practice of school assessment.

REFERENCES

Abedi, J. (1999a). *NAEP math test accommodations for students with limited English proficiency.* Los Angeles, CA: National Center for Research Evaluation, Standards, and Student Testing. (ERIC Document Reproduction Service No. ED 431787).

Abedi, J. (1999b). *The impact of student's background characteristics on accommodation results for students with limited English proficiency.* Los Angeles, CA: National Center for Research Evaluation, Standards, and Student Testing. (ERIC Document Reproduction Service No. ED 431786).

Adams, T. L. (1998). Alternative assessment in elementary school mathematics. *Childhood Education, 74,* 220–224.

AERA (2000). *AERA position statement concerning high-stakes testing in preK–12 education.* Washington, DC: American Educational Research Association.

AERA, APA, & NCME (1999). *Standards for educational and psychological testing.* Washington, DC: American Educational Research Association.

Alster, E. H. (1997). The effects of extended time on algebra test scores for college students with and without learning disabilities. *Journal of Learning Disabilities, 30*(2), 222–227.

Amendments to Individuals with Disabilities Education Act of 1997, 20 U.S.C.A. § 1412 et seq.

American Association on Mental Retardation (1992). *Mental retardation: Definition, classification, and systems of supports* (9th ed.). Washington, DC: Author.

American Printing House for the Blind (1996). *Annual report of the American Printing House for the Blind, Inc.: July, 1995 to June 30, 1996.* Louisville, KY: American Printing House for the Blind

American Psychiatric Association (2000). *Diagnostic and statistical manual of mental disorders: Text revision* (4th ed.). Washington, DC: Author.

Americans with Disabilities Act of 1990, 42 U.S.C.A. § 12101 et seq.

Anastasi, A., & Urbina, S. (1997). *Psychological testing* (7th ed.). Upper Saddle River, NJ: Prentice Hall.

Aronofsky, D. (1992). ADD: A brief summary of school district legal obligations and children's education rights. In M. Fowler (Ed.), *C.H.A.D.D. Educators' manual.* Plantation, FL: C.H.A.D.D.

Arter, J. A., & Stiggins, R. J. (1992, April). Performance assessment in education. Paper presented at the annual meeting of the American Educational Research Association, San Francisco, CA.

Association of Learning Disabilities (1993). Position paper on full inclusion of all students with learning disabilities in the regular classroom. *Journal of Learning Disabilities, 26,* 594–598.

August, D., Hakuta, K., Olgum, F., & Pomps, D. (1995). LEP students and Title 1: A guidebook for educators. *National Clearinghouse for Bilingual Education Resource Collection Resources.* Washington, DC: George Washington University Center for Excellence and Equity in Education.

August, D., & McArthur, E. (1996). Proceedings on the Conference on Guidelines and Accommodations for Limited English Proficient Students in the National Assessment of Educational Progress. (Report No. NCES 96-861). Washington, DC: National Center for Educational Statistics.

Bachor, D. G. (1990). Toward improving assessments of students with special needs: Expanding the database to include classroom performance. *The Alberta Journal of Educational Research, 36,* 65–77.

Baldwin, R. S., Murfin, P., Ross, G., Seidel, D., Clements, N., & Morris, C. (1989). Effects of extending administration time on standardized reading achievement tests. *Reading Research and Instruction, 29*(1), 33–38.

Beattie, S., Grise, P., & Algozzine, B. (1983). Effects of test modifications on the minimum competency performance of learning disabled students. *Learning Disability Quarterly, 6,* 75–77.

Beninghof, A. M. (1997). *Modifications for inclusion of students with disabilities: A handout for teachers.* Bethesda, MD: National Association of School Psychologists.

Bennett, R. E. (1993). On the meaning of constructed response. In R. E. Bennett & W. C. Ward (Eds.), *Construction versus choice in cognitive measurement: Issues in constructed response, performance testing, and portfolio assessment* (pp. 1–27). Hillsdale, NJ: Erlbaum.

Bennett, R. E., Rock, D. A., & Kaplan, B. A. (1987). SAT differential item performance for nine handicapped groups. *Journal of Educational Measurement, 24,* 41–55.

Bennett, R. E., Rock, D. A., & Kaplan, B. A. (1985). *The psychometric characteristics of the SAT for three handicapped groups* (ETS Research Report 85–49). Princeton, NJ: Educational Testing Service.

Bennett, R. E., Rock, D. A., Kaplan, B. A., & Jirele, T. (1988). Psychometric characteristics. In W. W. Willingham, M. Ragosta, R. E. Bennett, H. Braun, D. A. Rock, & D. E. Powers (Eds.), *Testing handicapped people.* Boston: Allyn & Bacon.

Bennett, R. A., Rock, D. A., & Novatkoski, I. (1989). Differential item functioning on the SAT-M Braille Edition. *Journal of Educational Measurement, 26,* 67–79.

Bernstein, D. K. (1989). Assessing children with limited English proficiency: Current perspectives. *Topics in Language Disorders, 9*(3), 15–20.

Bilingual Education Act of 1968, 20 U.S.C.A. § 7401 et seq.

Bintz, W., & Harste, J. (1994). Where are we going with alternative assessment and is it really worth our time? *Contemporary Education, 66,* 7–12.

Bracken, B. A., & Barona, A. (1991). State of the art procedures for translating, validating and using psychoeducational tests in cross-cultural assessment. *School Psychology International, 12,* 119–132.

Braden, J. P. (2002). Best practices for school psychologists in educational accountability: High-stakes testing and educational reform. In A. Thomas & J. Grimes (Eds.), *Best practices in school psychology IV* (Vol. 1 pp. 301–336). Bethesda, MD: National Association of School Psychologists.

Bradley-Johnson, S. (1995). Best practices in planning instruction for students who are visually impaired or blind. In A. Thomas & J. Grimes (Eds.), *Best practices in school psychology III* (pp. 1133–1140). Washington, DC: National Association of School Psychologists.

Bradley-Johnson, S., & Harris, S. (1990). Best practices in working with students with a visual loss. In A. Thomas & J. Grimes (Eds.), *Best practices in school psychology II* (pp. 871–885). Washington, DC: National Association of School Psychologists.

Braun, H.., Ragosta, M., & Kaplan, B. (1988). Predictive validity. In W. Willingham (Ed.), *Testing handicapped people* (pp. 109–132). Boston: Allyn & Bacon.

Braun, H., Ragosta, M., & Kaplan, B. (1986). *The predictive validity of the GRE General Test for disabled students* (ETS Research Report 86-42). Princeton, NJ: Educational Testing Service.

Buills, M., & Reiman, J. (1992). Development and preliminary psychometric properties of a transition competence battery for deaf adolescents and young adults. *Exceptional Children, 59*(1), 12–26.

Burns, E. (1998). *Test accommodations for students with disabilities.* Springfield, IL: Charles C. Thomas.

Camara, W. F. (1998). *Effects of extended time on score growth for students with learning disabilities.* New York: College Board.

Centra, J. A. (1986). Handicapped student performance on the Scholastic Aptitude Test. *Journal of Learning Disabilities, 19,* 324–327.

Chase, C. I. (1999). *Contemporary assessment for educators.* New York: Longman.

Christensen, B. (1990). Best practices in working with children with motor impairments. In A. Thomas & J. Grimes (Eds.), *Best practices in school psychology II* (pp. 799–810). Washington, DC: National Association of School Psychologists.

Civil Rights Act of 1964, 42 U.S.C.A. § 1983 et seq.

Cohen, L. G., & Spenciner, L. J. (1998). *Assessment of children and youth.* New York: Longman.

Cokely, D. R. (1986). Towards a sociolinguistic model of the interpreting process: Focus on ASL and English. *Dissertation Abstracts International, 46*(12A), 3704.

Coleman, M. (1996). *Educational and behavioral disorders: Theory and practice* (3rd ed.). Boston: Allyn & Bacon.

Cronbach, L. J. (1984). *Essentials of psychological testing* (4th ed.). New York: Harper & Row.

Culbertson, L. D., & Jalongo, M. R. (1999). "But what's wrong with letter grades?" Responding to parents' questions about alternative assessment. *Childhood Education, 75,* 130–135.

Damico, J. S. (1992, September). Focus on evaluation and measurement. *Performance assessment of language minority students.* Symposium conducted at the National Research Symposium on Limited English Proficient Student Issues, Washington, DC.

Darling-Hammond, L. (2002). What's at stake in high-stakes testing. *The Brown University Child and Adolescent Behavior Letter, 18,* 1–3.

Darling-Hammond, L. (1994a). Performance-based assessment and educational equity. *Harvard Educational Review, 64,* 5–30.

Darling-Hammond, L. (1994b). Setting standards for students: The case for authentic assessment. *The Educational Forum, 59*(1), 14–21.

Education for All Handicapped Children Act of 1975, 20 U.S.C.A. § 1400 et seq.

Educational Testing Service (1998a). *Policy statement for documentation of attention-deficit/hyperactivity disorder in adolescents and adults.* Princeton, NJ: Educational Testing Service.

Educational Testing Service (1998b). *Policy statement for documentation of a learning disability in adolescents and adults.* Princeton, NJ: Educational Testing Service.

Elementary and Secondary Education Act of 1965, 20 U.S.C.A. § 2701 et seq.

Elliott, S. N., & Fuchs, L. S. (1997). The utility of curriculum-based measurement and performance assessment as alternatives to traditional intelligence and achievement tests. *School Psychology Review, 26*(2), 224–233.

Elliott, S., Kratochwill, T. R., & McKevitt, B. C. (2001). Experimental analysis of the effects of testing accommodations on the scores of students with and without disabilities. *Journal of School Psychology, 39*(1), 3–24.

Engel, B. S. (1994). Portfolio assessment and the new paradigm: New instruments and new places. *The Educational Forum, 59*, 22–27.

Erickson, R., Ysseldyke, J. E., Thurlow, M. L., & Elliott, J. (1998). Inclusive assessments and accountability systems: Tools of the trade in educational reform. *Teaching Exceptional Children, 31*(2), 4–9.

Evans, F. R. (1980). A study of the relationships among speed and power aptitude test scores, and ethnic identity (College Board Report RDR 80-81, No. 2, and ETS RR 80-22). Princeton, NJ: Educational Testing Scores.

Falk, B. (1994). How assessment supports teaching and learning. *The Educational Forum, 9*(1), 30–38.

Farnham-Doggory, S. (1992). *The learning disabled child.* Cambridge, MA: Harvard University Press.

Federal Registrar (1992, September 29), *57*(189), 44794–44852. Washington, DC: U.S. Government Printing Office.

Feinberg, R. C. (2002). *Bilingual education: A reference handbook.* Santa Barbara: ABC-CLIO.

Fitzsimmons, M. K. (1998). *Including students with disabilities in large-scale testing: Emerging practices* (ERIC/OSEP Digest E564). Reston, VA: ERIC Clearinghouse on Disabilities and Gifted Education.

Foote, W. E. (2000). A model for psychological consultation in cases involving the Americans with Disabilities Act. *Professional Psychology: Research and Practice, 31*(2), 190–196.

Fradd, S. H., & Wilen, D. K. (1990, Summer). Using interpreters and translators to meet the needs of handicapped language minority students and their families. *NCBE Program Information Guide Series,* (4), 1–19.

Freeman, S. T. (1989). Cultural and linguistic bias in mental health evaluations of deaf people. *Rehabilitation Psychology, 34*(1), 54–63.

French, R. L. (1992, September). Focus on evaluation and measurement. *Portfolio assessment and LEP students.* Symposium conducted at the National Research Symposium on Limited English Proficient Student Issues, Washington, DC.

Fuchs, L., Fuchs, D., Eaton, S., Hamlett, C., & Karns, K. (2000). Supplementing teacher judgment of mathematics test accommodations with objective data sources. *School Psychology Review, 29*(1), 65–85.

Gajria, M., Salend, S. J., & Hemrick, M. A. (1994). Teacher acceptability of testing modifications for mainstreaming students. *Learning Disabilities Research and Practice, 9*, 236–243.

Garcia, G. E. (1994). Equity challenge in authentically assessing students from diverse backgrounds. *The Educational Forum, 59*, 64–72.

Garcia, G. N. (2000). Lesson from research: What is the length of time it takes limited English proficient students to acquire English and succeed in an all-English classroom? *National Clearinghouse for Bilingual Education,* (5). Washington, DC.

Gardner, H. (1991). *The unschooled mind.* New York: Basic Books.

Geisinger, K. F. (1994a). Psychometric issues in testing students with disabilities. *Applied Measurement in Education, 7*(2), 121–140.

Geisinger, K. F. (1994b). Cross-cultural normative assessment: Translation and adaptation issues influencing the normative interpretation of assessment instruments. *Psychological Assessment, 6*(4), 304–312.

Geisinger, K. F. (1992, September). Focus on evaluation and measurement. *Testing limited English proficient students for minimum competency and high school graduation.* Symposium conducted at the National Research Symposium on Limited English Proficient Student Issues, Washington, DC.

Geisinger, K. F., & Carlson, J. F. (1995). *Testing students with disabilities* (ERIC Digest Ed 391984). Greensboro, NC: ERIC Clearinghouse on Counseling and Student Services.

Goals 2000: Educate America Act of 1994, 20 U.S.C.A. § 5801 et seq.

Goertz, M. E., Duffy, M. C., & Le Floch, K. C. (2001). *Assessment and accountability systems in the 50 states: 1999–2000* (CPRE Research Report Series). University of Pennsylvania, Graduate School of Education, Consortium for Policy Research in Education. Retrieved December 1, 2002, from www.cpre.org/publications/publications-accountability.htm.

Goh, D. S. (1989, August). *The use of interpreters in the psychological assessment of Asian American children.* Paper presented at the Asian American Psychological Association National Convention III, New Orleans, LA.

Goh, D. S., & Yu, J. Y. (2001). Translation and empirical validation of the Chinese form of the Strong Interest Inventory. *Applied Psychology: An International Review, 50,* 252–268.

Goh, D. S., Zupnik, S., & Mendez, Y. (2001). *A national survey of state regulations for servicing limited English proficient students.* Flushing, NY: Queens College of the City University of New York.

Gomez, E. L. (1999). *Creating large-scale assessment portfolios that include English language learners.* Providence, RI: Northeast and Islands Regional Research Laboratory.

Gomez, J. (1997). *High stakes assessment: A research agenda for English language learners.* Washington, DC: National Clearinghouse for Bilingual Education. (ERIC Document Reproduction Service No. ED 417589).

Gordon, R. P., Stump, K., & Glaser, S. (1996). Assessment of individuals with hearing impairments: Equity in testing procedures and accommodations. *Measurement and Evaluation in Counseling and Development, 29,* 111–118.

Gredler, M. E. (1999). *Classroom assessment and learning.* New York: Longman.

Gregory, R. J. (1996). *Psychological testing: History, principles, and applications* (2nd ed.). Boston: Allyn & Bacon.

Grise, P., Beattie, S., & Algozzine, B. (1982). Assessment of minimum competency in fifth grade learning disabled students: Test modifications make a difference. *Journal of Educational Research, 76,* 35–40.

Gronlund, N. E. (1993). *How to make achievement tests and assessments* (5th ed.). Boston: Allyn & Bacon.

Hamayan, E. V. (1995). Approaches to alternative assessment. *Annual Review of Applied Linguistics, 15,* 212–226.

Hambleton, R. K., & Kanjee, A. (1994). Enhancing the validity of cross-cultural studies: Improvements in instrument translation methods. In T. Husen & T. N. Prostlethwaite (Eds.), *International Encyclopedia of Education* (2nd ed.). Oxford, UK: Pergamon Press.

Hanley, T. V. (1995). The need for technological advances in assessment related to national educational reform. *Exceptional Children, 61*(3), 222–229.

Hansen, J-I. C. (1987). Cross-cultural research on vocational interests. *Measurement and Evaluation in Counseling and Development, 19,* 163–176.

Harrington, A. M., & Morrison, R. A. (1981). Modifying classroom exams for secondary LD students. *Academic Therapy, 16,* 571–577.

Hatfield, M. M., & Price, J. (1992). Promoting local change: Models for implementing NCTM's curriculum and evaluation standards. *Arithmetic Teacher, 39,* 34–37.

Henning-Stout, M. (1994). *Responsive assessment: A new way of thinking about learning.* San Francisco: Jossey-Bass.

Herman, J. L. (1997). Assessing new assessments: How do they measure up? *Theory into Practice, 36,* 196–204.

Heubert, J. P., & Hauser, R. M. (Eds.). (1999). *High stakes: Testing for tracking, promotion, and graduation.* Washington, DC: National Academy Press.

Hishinuma, E. S. (1995). WISC-III accommodations: The need for practitioner guidelines. *Journal of Learning Disabilities, 28*(3), 130–135.

Homles, D., Hedlund, P., & Nickerson, B. (2000). *Accommodating English language learners in state and local assessments.* Washington, DC: National Clearinghouse for Bilingual Education.

Horton, S. W., & Lovitt, T. C. (1994). A comparison of two methods of administering group reading inventories to diverse learners. *Remedial and Special Education, 15,* 378–390.

Hughes, S. (1993). What is alternative/authentic assessment and how does it impact special education? *Educational Horizons, 72,* 28–35.

Hui, C. H., & Triandis, H. C. (1985). Measurement in cross-cultural psychology: A review and comparison of strategies. *Journal of Cross Cultural Psychology, 16,* 131–152.

Improving America's Schools Act of 1994, 20 U.S.C.A. § 6301 et seq.

Inclusion: As the trend mushrooms, what have we learned? (1997, April). *New York Teacher,* 13–15.

Individuals with Disabilities Education Act of 1990, 20 U.S.C.A. § 1400 et seq.

Jayanthi, M., Bursuck, W. D., Havekost, D. M., Epstein, M. H., & Polloway, E. A. (1994). School district policies and students with disabilities: A national survey. *School Psychology Review, 23*(4), 694–703.

Jayanthi, M., Epstein, M. H., Polloway, E. A., & Bursuck, W. D. (1996). A national survey of general education teachers' perceptions of testing adaptations. *Journal of Special Education, 30*(1), 99–115.

Johnson, C. M., Bradley-Johnson, S., McCarthy, R., & Jamie, M. (1984). Token reinforcement during WISC-R administration II. Effects of mildly retarded black students. *Applied Research in Mental Retardation, 5,* 43–53.

Johnston, R. C. (1998). Court frees California from ban on publishing LEP test results. *Education Week, 17*(43), 29.

Jorgenson, O., and Vanosdall, R. (2002). High-stakes testing: The death of science? What we risk in our rush towards standardized testing and the three r's. *Phi Delta Kappan, 83,* 601–606.

Kauffman, J. (2001). *Characteristics of emotional and behavioral disorders of children and youth* (5th ed.). Columbus, OH: Merrill/Macmillan.

Keene, S., & Davey, B. (1987). Effect of computer presented text on LD adolescents' reading behaviors. *Learning Disabilities Quarterly, 10,* 23–39.

Keith, T. Z., Reimers, T. M., Fehrmann, P. G., Pottebaum, S. M., & Aubey, L. W. (1986). Parental involvement, homework, and TV time: Direct and indirect effects on high school achievement. *Journal of Educational Psychology, 78*(5), 373–380.

Kelner, L. B. (1993). *The creative classroom: A guide for using creative drama in the classroom, preK–6.* Portsmouth, NH: Heinemann.

Khathi, N. & Sweet, D. (1966). Assessment reform: Promises and challenges. In M. B. Kane & R. Mitchell (eds.), *Implementing performance assessment: Promises, problems, and challenges* (pp. 1–21). Mahwah, NJ: Elrbaum.

Kindler, A. L. (2002). *Survey of the states' limited English proficiency students and available educational programs and services 2000–2001 summary report.* Retrieved December 1, 2002, from http://www.ncela.gwu.edu.

Kirk, S., Gallagher, J., & Anastasiow, N. (2003). *Educating exceptional children.* New York: Houghton Mifflin.

Kleinert, H., Kennedy, S., & Kearns, J. (1999). The impact of alternate assessments: A statewide teacher survey. *The Journal of Special Education, 33*(2), 93–102.

Klotz, M. B., & Canter, A. (2002). IDEA in practice. *Communique, 31*(4), 24.

Kretschmer, R. E. (1991). Exceptionality and the limited English proficient student: Historical and practical contexts. In E. V. Hamayan & J. S. Damico (Eds.), *Limiting bias in the assessment of bilingual students* (pp. 1–38). Austin, TX: Pro-Ed.

Kubiszyn, T., & Borich, G. (2003). *Educational testing and measurement: Classroom application and practice.* New York: John Wiley.

LaCelle-Peterson, M. W., & Rivera, C. (1994). Is it real for all kids? A framework for equitable assessment policies for English language learners. *Harvard Educational Review, 64,* 55–75.

Lachat, M. A. (1999). *Standards, equity, and cultural diversity.* Providence, RI: Northeast and Islands Regional Research Laboratory.

Lagurada, K. G., Breckenridge, J. S., Hightower, M. M., & Adelman, N. E. (1994). *Assessment program in the statewide system initiatives (SSI) states: Using student achievement data to evaluate the SSI.* Washington, DC: Policy Study Associates.

Lam, T. C. M. (1993). Testability: A critical issue in testing language minority students with standardized achievement tests. *Measurement in Counseling and Evaluation, 26,* 179–191.

Lashway, L. (1999). *Holding Schools Accountable for Achievement.* Eugene, OR: University of Oregon. (ERIC Digests No. ED 434381).

Li, C., Walton, J. R., & Nuttall, E. (1999). Preschool evaluation of culturally and linguistically diverse children. In E. Nuttall, I. Romero, & J. Kalesnik (Eds.), *Assessing and screening preschoolers: Psychological and educational dimensions (rev. ed.)* (pp. 216–317). Boston: Allyn & Bacon.

Liebars, C. S. (1999). Alternative assessment for pre-service teachers. *Teaching Children Mathematics, 6,* 164–169.

Linn, R. L. (1993). Educational assessment: Expanded expectations and challenges. *Educational Evaluation and Policy Analysis, 15,* 1–16.

Linn, R. L., Baker, E. L., & Dunbar, S. B. (1991). Complex, performance-based assessment: Expectations and validation criteria. *Educational Researcher, 20,* 15–21.

Liu, K., Albus, D., & Thurlow, M. (2000). *Data on LEP students in state education reports* (Synthesis Report No. 26). Minneapolis, MN: University of Minnesota, National Center on Educational Outcomes.

Liu, K., Anderson, M., Swierzbin, B., & Thurlow, M. (1999). *Bilingual accommodations for limited English proficient students on statewide reading tests: Phase 1* (Synthesis Report No. 20). Minneapolis, MN: University of Minnesota, National Center on Educational Outcomes.

Liu, K., Spicuzza, R., Erickson, R., Thurlow, M., & Ruhland, A. (1997). *Educators' responses to LEP students' participation in the 1997 basic standards testing* (Synthesis Report No. 15). Minneapolis, MN: University of Minnesota, National Center on Educational Outcomes.

Liu, K., Thurlow, M., Erickson, R., Spicuzza, R., & Heinze, K. (1997). *A review of the literature on students with limited English proficiency and assessment* (Synthesis Report No. 11). Minneapolis, MN: University of Minnesota, National Center on Educational Outcomes.

Liu, K., Thurlow, M., Vieburg, K., El Sawaf, H., & Ruhland, A. (1996). *Resources: Limited English proficient students in national and statewide assessments* (Synthesis Report No. 8). Minneapolis, MN: University of Minnesota, National Center on Educational Outcomes.

Lopez, E. C. (2002). Best practices in working with school interpreters to deliver psychological services to children and families. In A. Thomas & J. Grimes (Eds.), *Best practices in school psychology IV* (Vol. 2, pp. 1419–1432). Bethesda, MD: National Association of School Psychologists.

Lopez, E. C. (1994). Best practices in working with bilingual children. In A. Thomas & J. Grimes (Eds.), *Best practices in school psychology III* (pp. 1111–1121). Washington, DC: National Association of School Psychologists.

Lopez, E. C., & Rooney, M. E. (1997). A preliminary investigation of the roles and backgrounds of school interpreters: Implications for training and recruiting. *Journal of Social Distress & the Homeless, 6*(2), 161–174.

Lucio, E., Reyes-Lagunes, I., & Scott, R. L. (1994). MMPI-2 for Mexico: Translation and adaptation. *Journal of Personality Assessment, 63,* 105–116.

MacArthur, C. A., & Graham, S. (1987). Learning disabled students' composing under three methods of text production: Handwriting, word processing, and dictation. *The Journal of Special Education, 21,* 22–42.

Malarz, L. (1996). Using staff development to create inclusive schools. *Journal of Staff Development, 17*(3), 8–11.

Martino, J. (1999, January). The specificity of norms. *BetaWaves.* Retrieved 6/14/00 from www.nybetacom/newsletter/jan_3.html.

McGrew, K. S., Thurlow, M. L., Shriner, J. G., & Spiegel, A. N. (1992). *Inclusion of students with disabilities in national and state data collection programs* (Brief Report 1). Minneapolis, MN: University of Minnesota, National Center on Educational Outcomes.

Mehrens, W. A. (1997). *Flagging test scores: Policy, practice and research.* East Lansing, MI: Michigan State University.

Mehrens, W. A., & Lehman, I. J. (1988). *Using standardized tests in education* (4th ed.). New York: Longman.

Menken, K. (2000). What are the critical issues in wide-scale assessment of English language learners? *NCSB Issues & Briefs, 6,* 1–4. Washington, DC: National Clearinghouse for Bilingual Education.

Messick, S. (1980). Test validity and the ethics of assessment. *American Psychologist, 35,* 1012–1017.

Meyer, C. (1992). What is the difference between authentic and performance assessment? *Educational Leadership, 49,* 39–40.

Mick, L. B. (1989). Measurement effects of modifications in minimum competency test formats for exceptional students. *Measurement and Evaluation in Counseling and Development, 22,* 31–36.

Miller, D. M., & Legg, S. M. (1993). Alternative assessment in a high-stakes environment. *Educational Measurement: Issues and Practice, 12,* 9–15.

Moya, S. S., & O'Malley, J. M. (1994). A portfolio assessment model for ESL. *The Journal of Educational Issues of Language Minority Students. 13,* 13–36.

Munger, G. F., & Lloyd, B. H. (1991). Effect of speededness on test performance of handicapped and non-handicapped examinees. *Journal of Educational Research, 85,* 53–57.

Munson, M. M. (1987). Regular education teacher modifications for mainstreamed mildly handicapped students. *The Journal of Special Education, 20*(4), 489–499.

National Association of School Psychologists (2002). *Large scale assessments and high stakes decisions: Facts, cautions, and guidelines.* Bethesda, MD: Author.

National Association of School Psychologists (1995). *Solve your child's school-related problems.* Bethesda, MD: Author.

National Center for Education Statistics (2000). *The digest of education statistics* (Online). Available: www.nces.ed.gov.

National Center for Health Statistics (2000). *Fast stats A to Z/disabilities* (Online). Available: www.cdc.gov/nchs.

National Center for Learning Disabilities. (1999). *The early warning signs of learning disabilities.* New York: Author.

National Commission on Excellence in Education (1983). *A nation at risk: The imperative for educational reform.* Washington, DC: U.S. Government Printing Office.

National Council of Teachers of Mathematics (2001). NCMT: High-stakes testing gets low grades. *Curriculum Administrator, 37,* 22.

National Urban League (1999). *Educational accountability: First school systems, then the students.* New York: Author.

Navarrete, C., & Gustke, C. (1996). *A guide to performance assessment for linguistically diverse students.* Albuquerque, NM: Evaluation Assistance Center West.

New York State Education Department. (2000). *New York State Part 200 Amendments: An overview.* Albany, NY: Author.

New York State Education Department (1998). *Guidance on the implementation of the reauthorization of Individuals with Disabilities Education Act.* Albany, NY: Author.

New York State Education Department (1995). *Test access and modification for individuals with disabilities.* Albany, NY: Author.

No Child Left Behind Act of 2001, 20 U.S.C.A. § 6301 et seq.

Ochoa, S. H., Gonzalez, D., Galarza, A., & Guillemard, L. (1996). The training and use of interpreters in bilingual psycho-educational assessment: An alternative in need of study. *Diagnostique, 21*(3), 19–40.

Ochoa, S. H., Powell, M. P., & Robles-Pina, R. (1996). School psychologists' assessment practices with bilingual and limited-English-proficient students. *Journal of Psychoeducational Assessment, 14,* 250–275.

O'Keeffe, J. (1994). Disability, discrimination, and the Americans with Disabilities Act. In S. M. Bruyere, J. O'Keeffe, et al. (Eds.), *Implications of the Americans with Disabilities Act for psychology* (pp. 1–14). Washington, DC: American Psychological Association.

Olsen, K. (1998). *Alternative assessment issues and practices* (pp. 1–34). Lexington, KY: Mid-South Regional Resource Center, Interdisciplinary Human Development Institute.

Olsen, L. (1999). "Shining a spotlight on results." Quality counts '99. *Education Week, 18*(17), 8–10.

Olson, J., & Goldstein, A. (1997). *The inclusion of students with disabilities and limited English proficient students in large scale assessments: A summary of recent progress.* Research and Development Report. Washington, DC: National Center for Education Statistics.

O'Malley, J. M., & Valdez-Pierce, L. (1994). State assessment policies, practices, and language minority students. *Educational Assessment, 2,* 213–255.

Orfield, G., & Ward, J. (2000). The high-stakes testing mania hurts poor and minority students the most: Testing, testing. *The Nation, 270,* 38–41.

Paredes-Scribner, A. (1993). The use of interpreters in the assessment of language minority students. *The Bilingual Education Perspective, 12*(2), 1–6.

Passman, R. (2001). Experiences with student-centered teaching and learning in high-stakes assessment environments. *Education, 22,* 189–200.

Pate, P. E., Homestead, E., & McGinnis, K. (1993). Designing rubrics for authentic assessment. *Middle School Journal, 3,* 25–27.

Perez-Hogan, C. A., & DeMauro, G. (1999). *Testing procedures for limited English proficient students.* Albany, NY: New York State Office of Bilingual Education. Available: www.nysben.org/documents/memo010499.html.

Perlman, C., Borger, J., Collins, C., Elenbogen, J., & Wood, J. (1996). The effect of extended time limits on learning disabled students' scores on standardized reading tests. Paper presented at the annual meeting of the National Council on Measurement in Education, New York.

Phillips, S. E. (1994). High stakes testing accommodations: Validity versus disabled rights. *Applied Measurement in Education, 7*(2), 93–120.

Pitoniak, M. J., & Royer, J. M. (2001). Testing accommodations for examinees with disabilities: A review of psychometric, legal, and social policy issues. *Review of Educational Research, 71*(1), 53–104.

Popham, W. J. (1999). *Classroom assessment: What teachers need to know.* Boston: Allyn & Bacon.

Putnam, M. L. (1992). The testing practices of mainstream secondary classroom teachers. *Remedial and Special Education, 13*(5), 11–21.

Ragosta, M., & Wendler, C. (1992). *Eligibility issues and comparable time limits for disabled and nondisabled SAT examinees* (Report No. 925). New York: College Entrance Examination Board. (ERIC Document Reproduction Service No. ED 349337).

Ranseen, J. D. (1998). Lawyers with ADHD: The special test accommodation controversy. *Professional Psychology: Research and Practice, 29*(5), 450–459.

Rehabilitation Act of 1973, 29 U.S.C.A § 701 et seq.

Reschly, D. J. (1993). Consequences and incentives: Implications for inclusion/exclusion decisions regarding students with disabilities in state and national assessment programs. In J. E. Ysseldyke & M. L. Thurlow (Eds.), *Views on inclusion and testing accommodations for students with disabilities.* Minneapolis, MN: University of Minnesota, National Center on Educational Outcomes.

Reschly, D. J., & Ysseldyke, J. E. (1995). School psychology paradigm shift. In A. Thomas & J. Grimes (Eds.), *Best practices in school psychology III* (pp. 17–31). Washington, DC: National Association of School Psychologists.

Rivera, C., & LaCelle-Paterson, M. (1993). *Will the national education goals improve the progress of English language learners?* Washington, DC: ERIC Clearinghouse on Language and Linguistics.

Rivera, C., & Stansfield, C. (2000). *An analysis of state policies for the inclusion and accommodation of English language learners in state assessment programs during*

1998–1999 (Executive summary). Washington, DC: George Washington University, Center for Equity and Excellence in Education.

Rivera, C., & Vincent, C. (1997). High school graduation testing: Policies and practices in the assessment of English language learners. *Educational Assessment, 4,* 335–355.

Rivera, C., Vincent, C., Hafner, A., & LaCelle-Paterson, M. (1997). *Statewide assessment programs: Policies and practices for the inclusion of limited English proficient students* (Report No. TM 026831). Washington, DC: ERIC Clearinghouse on Assessment and Evaluation. (ERIC Document Reproduction Service No. ED 421484).

Robison, L. M., Sclar, D. A., Skaer, T. L., & Galin, R. S. (1999). National trends in the prevalence of attention-deficit/hyperactivity disorder and the prescription of methylphenidate among school-age children. *Clinical Pediatrics, 38*(4), 209–219.

Rock, D. A., Bennett, R. E., & Jirele, T. (1988). Factor structure of the Graduate Record Examination general test in handicapped and nonhandicapped groups. *Journal of Applied Psychology, 73*(3), 383–392.

Rudner, L. M., & Boston, C. (1994). Performance assessment. *ERIC Review, 3,* 2–12.

Runyan, M. K. (1991). The effect of extra time on reading comprehension scores for university students with and without learning disabilities. *Journal of Learning Disabilities, 24*(2), 104–108.

Saigh, P. A., & Payne, D. A. (1979). The effect of type of reinforcer and reinforcement schedule on performances of EMR students on four selected subtests of the WISC-R. *Psychology in the Schools, 16,* 106–110.

Salend, S., & Salend, S. J. (1985). Adapting teacher-made tests for mainstreamed students. *Journal of Learning Disabilities, 18,* 373–375.

Salvia, J., & Ysseldyke, J. E. (2001). *Assessment* (8th ed.). Boston: Houghton Mifflin.

Salvia, J., & Ysseldyke, J. E. (1995). Adapting tests to accommodate students with disabilities. In J. Salvia, & J. E. Ysseldyke *Assessment* (6th ed., pp. 176–195). Boston: Houghton Mifflin.

Sattler, J. (2001). *Assessment of children: Cognitive applications* (4th ed.). San Diego, CA: Jerome M. Sattler.

Sauter, D. L., & McPeek, D. (1993). Dyslexia in the workplace: Implications of the Americans with Disabilities Act. *Annals of Dyslexia, 43,* 271–278.

Sax, G. (1989). *Principles of educational and psychological measurement and evaluation* (3rd ed.). Belmont, CA: Wadsworth.

Schildroth, A. N., & Hotto, S. A. (1994). Inclusion of exclusion: Deaf students and the inclusion movement. *American Annals of the Deaf, 139,* 239–243.

Schmidt, J. J. (1999). *Counseling in schools essential services and comprehensive programs* (3rd ed.) Boston: Allyn & Bacon.

Schrag, P. (2000). High stakes are for tomatoes. *The Atlanta Monthly, 286*(2), 19–21.

Schulte, A. C., Villwock, D. N., Wichard, S. M., & Stallings, C. F. (2001). High-stakes testing and expected progress standards for students with learning disabilities: A five year study of one district. *School Psychology Review, 30,* 487–507.

Scribner, A. P. (2002). Best assessment and intervention practices with second language learners. In A. Thomas & J. Grimes (Eds.), *Best practices in school psychology IV.* Washington, DC: National Association of School Psychologists.

Scruggs, T. E., Bennion, K., & Lifson, S. (1985). Learning disabled students' spontaneous use of test-taking skills on reading achievement tests. *Learning Disability Quarterly, 8,* 205–210.

Shaul, M. S. (1999). *Public education: Title I services provided to students with limited English proficiency* (Report No. HEHS-00-25). Washington, DC: U.S. General Accounting Office.

Shavelson, R. J., Baxter, G. P., & Gao, X. (1993). Sampling variability of performance assessments. *Journal of Educational Measurement, 30,* 215–232.

Shavelson, R. J., Baxter, G. P., & Pine, J. (1991). Performance assessments in science. *Applied Measurement in Education, 4,* 347–362.

Short, D. (1991). *How to integrate language and content instruction.* Washington, DC: Center for Applied Linguistics.

Siskind, T. G. (1993). Teachers' knowledge about test modifications for students with disabilities. *Diagnostique, 18*(2), 145–157.

Sleek, S. (1998). Psychology's cultural competence, once simplistic now broadening. *APA Monitor, 29,* 1, 27.

Smith, M. L., & Frey, P. (2000). Validity and accountability in high-stakes testing. *Journal of Teacher Education, 51,* 334–347.

Solomon, J., & Rhodes, N. (1995). *Assessing academic language of English language learners: Final report* (Report No. FL 023 531). Washington, DC: National Center for Research on Cultural Diversity and Second Language Learning. (ERIC Document Reproduction Service No. ED 391375).

Southern Regional Education Board. (1998). *Getting results: A fresh look at school accountability.* Atlanta: Southern Regional Education Board. (ERIC Document Reproduction Service No. ED 426510).

Spicuzza, R., Erickson, R., Thurlow, M., Liu, K., & Ruhland, A. (1996). *Input from the field on assessing students with Limited English Proficiency in Minnesota's Basic Requirements Exams* (Synthesis Report No. 2). Minneapolis, MN: University of Minnesota, National Center on Educational Outcomes.

Spicuzza, R., Erickson, R., Thurlow, M., & Ruhland, A. (1996). *Input from the field on the participation of students with Limited English Proficiency and students with disabilities in meeting the high standards of Minnesota's Profile of Learning* (Synthesis Report No. 10). Minneapolis, MN: University of Minnesota, National Center on Educational Outcomes.

Spinelli, C. (1997). Accommodating the adolescent with attention deficit disorder: The role of the resource center teacher. *Journal of Attention Disorders, 1,* 209–220.

Steinberg, R. (1987, April 25). Why Japan's students outdo ours. *New York Times,* 31.

Stevenson, H. W., Lee, S., & Stigler, J. W. (1986). Mathematics achievement of Chinese, Japanese, and American children, *Science, 231,* 693–699.

Stiggins, R. (1987). Design and development of performance assessment. *Educational Measurement: Issues and Practices, 6,* 33–42.

Stiggins, R. J. (1994). *Student-centered classroom assessment.* New York: Merrill.

Stigler, J. W., Lee, S., Lucker, G. W., & Stevenson, H. W. (1982). Curriculum and achievement in mathematics: A study of elementary school children in Japan, Taiwan, and the United States. *Journal of Educational Psychology, 74*(3), 315–322.

Sullivan, P. M. (1982). Administration modifications on the WISC-R Performance scale with different categories of deaf children. *American Annals of the Deaf, 127,* 780–788.

Supovitz, J. A., & Brennan, R. T. (1997). Mirror, mirror on the wall, which is the fairest test of all? An examination of the equitability of portfolio assessment relative to standardized tests. *Harvard Educational Review, 67,* 472–506.

Tannenbaum, J. E. (1996). *Practical ideas on alternative assessment for ESL students* (Report No. ED0 FL 96 07). Washington, DC: ERIC Clearinghouse on Language and Linguistics. (ERIC Document Reproduction Service No. ED 395500).

Tapper, R. (1997). *The problem of high stakes assessment in public education.* Washington, DC: ERIC Clearinghouse for Tests, Measurement and Evaluation. (ERIC Document Reproduction Service No. ED 430021).

Terrell, F., Terrell, S. L., & Taylor, J. (1981). Effects of type of reinforcement on the intelligence test performance of retarded black children. *Psychology in the Schools, 18,* 225–227.

Thurlow, M., Hurley, C., Spicuzza, T., & El Sawaf, H. (1996). *A review of the literature on testing accommodations for students with disabilities* (Synthesis Report No. 9). Minneapolis, MN: University of Minnesota, National Center on Educational Outcomes.

Thurlow, M. L., & Johnson, D. R. (2002). High-stakes testing of students with disabilities. *Journal of Teacher Education, 51,* 305–318.

Thurlow, M. L., Liu, K., Erickson, R., Spicuzza, R., & El Sawaf, H. (1996). *Accommodations for students with Limited English Proficiency: Analysis of guidelines from states with graduation exams* (Synthesis Report No. 6). Minneapolis, MN: University of Minnesota, National Center on Educational Outcomes.

Thurlow, M. L., Olsen, K., Elliot, J., Ysseldyke, J., Erickson, R., & Ahearn, E. (1996). Alternate assessments for students with disabilities. *NCEO Policy Directions, 5,* 1–6.

Thurlow, M. L., Scott, D. L., & Ysseldyke, J. E. (1995). *A compilation of states' guidelines for accommodations in assessment for students with disabilities* (Synthesis Report No. 18). Minneapolis, MN: University of Minnesota, National Center on Educational Outcomes.

Thurlow, M. L., Ysseldyke, J. E., & Silverstein, B. (1995). Testing accommodations for students with disabilities. *Journal of Remedial and Special Education, 16,* 260–270

Thurlow, M. L., Ysseldyke, J. E., & Silverstein, B. (1993). *Testing accommodations for students with disabilities: A review of the literature* (Synthesis Report No. 4). Minneapolis, MN: University of Minnesota, National Center on Educational Outcomes.

Tindal, G., & Fuchs, L. (1999). A summary of research on test changes: An empirical basis for defining accommodations. Lexington, KY: Mid-South Regional Resource Center.

Tindal, G., Heath, B., Hollenbeck, K., Almond, P., & Harniss, M. (1998). Accommodating students with disabilities on large scale tests: An empirical study. *Exceptional Children, 64*(4), 439–450

Tirozzi, G. N., & Uro, G. (1997). Education reform in the United States: National policy in support of local efforts for school improvement. *American Psychologist, 52*(3), 241–249.

Tolfa-Veit, D., & Scruggs, T. E. (1986). Can learning disabled students effectively use separate answer sheets? *Perceptual and Motor Skills, 63,* 155–160.

Travis, J. E. (1996). Meaningful assessment. *The Clearing House, 69,* 308–312.

Turnbull, R., Turnbull, A., Shank, M., Smith, S., & Leal, D. (2002). *Exceptional lives: Special education in today's schools.* Upper Saddle River, NJ: Merrill/Prentice Hall.

U.S. Department of Commerce, Bureau of Census (1993). *Statistical abstract of the United States: The national data book* (115th ed). Washington, DC: U.S. Government Printing Office.

U.S. Department of Education (1999). *Annual report to Congress on the implementation of the Individuals with Disabilities Education Act, 1988–1998.* Washington, DC: Author. Available: http://nces.ed.gov/pubs99/condition99/indicator-20.html.

Valdez-Pierce, L., & O'Malley, J. M. (1992). *Performance and portfolio assessment for language minority students* (Report No. 9). Washington, DC: National Clearing House for Bilingual Education.

Vaughn, S., Bos, C., & Schumm, J. (2000). *Teaching exceptional, diverse, and at-risk students.* Boston: Allyn & Bacon.

Vaughn, S., Schumm, J. S., & Kouzekanani, K. (1993). What do students with learning disabilities think when their general teachers make adaptations? *Journal of Learning Disabilities, 26*(8), 545–555.

Weise, A.-M., & Garcia, E. (1998). The Bilingual Education Act: Language minority students and educational opportunity. *Bilingual Research Journal, 22*(1), 1–16.

Werts, M. G., Wolery, M., Snyder, E. D., Caldwell, N. K., & Salisbury, C. L. (1996). Supports and resources associated with inclusive schooling: Perceptions of elementary school teachers about need and availability. *The Journal of Special Education, 30*(2), 187–203.

Wild, C. L., Durso, R., & Rubin, D. B. (1982). Effect of increased test taking time on test scores by ethnic group, years out of school, and sex. *Journal of Educational Measurement, 19*(1), 19–28.

Wilen, D. K., & Sweeting, C. M. (1986). Assessment of limited English proficiency Hispanic students. *School Psychology Review, 15,* 59–75.

Will, M. (1986). Educating children with learning problems: A shared responsibility. *Exceptional Children, 51*(1), 411–416.

Willingham, W. W. (1988). Testing handicapped children—The validity issue. In H. Wainer & H. I. Braun (Eds.), *Test validity* (pp. 89–103). Hillsdale, NJ: Erlbaum.

Willingham, W. W., Ragosta, M., Bennett, R. E., Braun, H., Rock, D. A., & Powers D. E. (Eds.). (1988). *Testing handicapped people.* Boston: Allyn & Bacon.

Wilson, B. L., & Dickson, C. H. (1991). *Two state minimum competency testing programs and their effects on curriculum and instruction.* Washington, DC: ERIC Clearinghouse for Tests, Measurement and Evaluation. (ERIC Document Reproduction Service No. ED 377251).

Worthen, B. R. (1993). Critical issues that will determine the future of alternative assessment. *Phi Delta Kappan, 23,* 444–453.

Worthen, B. R., White, K. R., Fan, X., & Sudweeks, R. R. (1999). *Measurement and assessment in schools.* New York: Longman.

Yansen, E. A., & Shulman, E. L. (1996). Language assessment: Multicultural considerations. In L. A. Suzuki, P. J. Meller, & J. G. Ponterotto (Eds.), *Handbook of multicultural assessment.* San Francisco: Jossey-Bass.

Young, R. M., Bradley-Johnson, S., & Johnson, C. M. (1982). Immediate and delayed reinforcement on WISC-R performance for mentally retarded students. *Applied Research in Mental Retardation, 3,* 13–20.

Ysseldyke, J. E., Thurlow M. L., McGrew, K., & Vanderwood, M. (1994). *Making decisions about the inclusion of students with disabilities in large scale assessments* (Synthesis Report No. 13). Minneapolis, MN: University of Minnesota, National Center on Educational Outcomes.

Zehler, A. M., Hopstock, P. J., Fleischman, H. L., & Grenick, C. (1994). *An examination of assessment of limited English proficient students.* (Task Order Report D070). Arlington, VA: Special Issues Analysis Center.

Abedi, J., 131–132
Accommodations for diverse
    learners, 1, 15, 27–33
    attention-deficit/
        hyperactivity disorder
        (ADHD), 41–42, 49,
        106–108
    avoiding use of, 40
    behavioral and emotional
        disturbance, 110–112
    blindness and visual
        impairment, 21, 83–86
    in classroom testing, 55–59
    considerations in using,
        39–40
    deafness and hard of
        hearing, 20, 87–89
    effects on test performance,
        71–78
    English language learners
        (ELLs), 122–141
    flagging scores in, 78–79
    granting, 46–49
    interpreting results from,
        49–51
    learning disability, 21,
        58–59, 73–78, 99–102
    legal bases for, 30–33
    mental retardation, 21,
        103–105
    nature of, 28–29
    physical disabilities, 21, 89–93
    psychometric soundness of,
        61–62
    purpose of using, 37–38
    reasons for using, 27–28
    reliability and, 63–64, 69–71
    reporting assessment data
        for, 51–52, 54–55, 78–79
    requesting, 46–49
    research on use of, 52–59,
        93–94, 112–115

    selecting, 44–46
    standardization and, 62–63
    types of, 40–44
    validity and, 64–71
Accountability, 6–7
Achievement tests, 16
Adams, T. L., 145, 150, 154
Adapted tests, 132–135
Adelman, N. E., 9
AERA. See American
    Educational Research
    Association (AERA)
Ahearn, E., 147
Albus, D., 52
Algozzine, B., 72, 114
Almond, P., 72, 114
Alster, E. H., 77
Alternative assessment, 1,
    143–163
    diverse learners and,
        146–147
    interpretation in, 156–158
    limitations, 160–162
    merits, 160–162
    nature of, 143–146
    scoring in, 156–158
    specific strategies in, 151–156
    technical considerations,
        158–160
    types of, 147–151
American Association of
    Mental Retardation
    (AAMR), 103
American College Testing
    Program (ACT), 93–94
American Educational
    Research Association
    (AERA), 2–3, 8, 10, 14, 24,
    25, 29, 38, 40, 44, 46, 50,
    65–69, 78–79, 122, 135, 140
American Printing House for
    the Blind, 81–82

American Psychiatric
    Association, 98, 99, 102,
    103, 105, 106, 109–110
American Psychological
    Association (APA), 2–3,
    14, 24, 25, 29, 38, 40, 44,
    46, 50, 65–69, 78–79, 122,
    135, 140
Americans with Disabilities
    Act (ADA) of 1990, 20,
    29–31, 65, 79
Anastasi, A., 25, 62, 100, 103, 107
Anderson, M., 39, 129
APA. See American
    Psychological Association
    (APA)
Appropriate
    accommodations, 39
Aronofsky, D., 105
Arter, J. A., 148, 156, 161
Assessment. See also
    Accommodations for
    diverse learners;
    Alternative assessment
    contemporary
        developments affecting,
        5–12
    defined, 2
    emphasizing, 15–16
    general requirements of, 23
    linking to intervention, 16
    recent trends in, 13–16
    reducing bias in, 14–15
    standards-based education
        reform and, 5–10
    testing versus, 2–3
Association of Learning
    Disabilities, 10
Attention-deficit/
    hyperactivity disorder
    (ADHD), 41–42, 49,
    105–108

Aubey, L. W., 5–6
August, D., 52
Authentic assessment, 144, 149
Autism, 20
Average/high achieving
    (A/HA) students, 58–59

Bachor, D. G., 148, 159
Back translation, 134
Baker, E. L., 159
Baldwin, R. S., 76
Barona, A., 133
Basic Inventory of Natural
    Language (BINL), 126
Baxter, G. P., 16, 158
Beattie, S., 72, 114
Behavioral and emotional
    disturbance, 109–112
Behavioral rating scales, 14
Bennett, R. E., 40, 67, 70, 71,
    93–94, 144
Bennion, K., 28
Bernstein, D. K., 40, 146
Bilingual Education Act
    (1968), 31, 32
Bilingual interpreters,
    135–137
Bilingual students. See
    English language
    learners (ELLs)
Bilingual Syntax Measure
    (BSM), 126
Bintz, W., 144
Blindness and visual
    impairment, 21, 81–86
Borger, J., 100, 113
Borich, G., 6, 26, 148
Bos, C., 103, 104, 108, 111, 112
Boston, C., 145
Bracken, B. A., 133
Braden, J. P., 7–9
Bradley-Johnson, S., 84, 85,
    104, 105
Braun, H., 70, 71, 93–94
Breckenridge, J. S., 9
Brennan, R. T., 14, 122, 145, 160
Buills, M., 89
Bureau of the Census, 121
Burns, E., 47, 48
Bursuck, W. D., 53, 54, 57

Caldwell, N. K., 12
Camara, W. F., 75–76

Canter, A., 33
Centra, J. A., 75, 100, 113
Certification decisions, 5
Chase, C. I., 8, 15, 148
Christensen, B., 90, 92
Civil Rights Act (1964), 31–32
Classification decisions, 3–4
Classroom assessment
    accommodations in testing,
    55–59
    alternative assessment, 156
Clements, N., 76
Cognitive tests, 16
Cohen, L. G., 23
Cokely, D. R., 136
Coleman, M., 109–111
College Board, 69–71
Collins, C., 100, 113
Component–test correlations,
    68
Conduct disorder (CD), 105,
    109–110
Consequences of testing,
    validity based on, 69
Construct equivalence, 133
Construct validity, 64
Content area journals,
    154–155
Content reliability, 158–159
Content standards, 6, 7
Content validity, 66
Criterion-referenced tests
    (CRT), 14, 26–27
Cronbach, L. J., 24
Cross-cultural assessment, 29
Culbertson, L. D., 28
Curriculum-based
    measurement, 73–74

Damico, J. S., 147
Darling-Hammond, L., 9, 10,
    14, 122, 145, 150, 157
Deaf-blindness, 20
Deafness and hard of hearing,
    20, 86–89
DeMauro, G., 128, 129
Demonstration, 152
Diagnostic and Statistical
    Manual of Mental
    Disorders (DSM-IV), 99
Diagnostic decisions, 4
Dialogue journals, 155
Dickson, C. H., 10

Differential item functioning
    (DIF), 68
Diverse learners. See also
    Accommodations for
    diverse learners
    alternative assessment and,
    146–147
    defined, 19–24
    in large-scale assessment,
    12–13
    standards-based reform
    and, 8–10, 12–13
Duffy, M. C., 127
Dunbar, S. B., 159
Durso, R., 75

Eaton, S., 73, 76
Educable mental retardation
    (EMR), 73
Educational Testing Service
    (ETS), 69–71, 84, 93–94,
    99–100, 107
Education for All
    Handicapped Children
    Act (1975), 10, 30–31
Elementary and Secondary
    Education Act (1965), 32
Elenbogen, J., 100, 113
Elliott, J., 7, 8, 12, 13, 51, 147
Elliott, S. N., 74, 78, 148, 157,
    158
El Sawaf, H., 41, 46, 53,
    54, 55, 84, 88, 92, 94,
    112, 113, 114, 129, 130,
    138–139
Emotional disturbance, 20
Engel, B. S., 16
English language learners
    (ELLs), 119–141. See also
    Accommodations for
    diverse learners; Diverse
    learners
    assessing English language
    proficiency, 125–127
    defined, 21–23
    educational risks of,
    121–122
    exemption or deferral from
    testing, 127–128
    as growing student
    population, 119–121
    legislation pertaining to,
    31–32

English Speakers of Other Languages. *See* English language learners (ELLs)
Epstein, M. H., 53, 54, 57
Erickson, R., 7, 8, 12, 13, 41, 46, 51, 53, 54, 55, 129, 130, 131, 137–138, 138–139, 147
Evaluation decisions, 3
Evans, F. R., 75

Factor analysis, 67
Fair accommodations, 39–40
Falk, B., 14, 145
Fan, X., 4, 148
Farnham-Doggory, S., 152
Fehrmann, P. G., 5–6
Feinberg, R. C., 121
Fleischman, H. L., 64, 122, 124, 126
Florida, 127
Florida State Student Assessment Test (SSAT), 72, 114
Foote, W. E., 20
Forward translation, 134
Fourteenth Amendment, 30
Fradd, S. H., 136
Freeman, S. T., 87, 88
French, R. L., 64, 151
Frey, P., 9
Fuchs, D., 73, 76
Fuchs, L. S., 73, 76, 84, 88, 92, 148, 157, 158
Functional equivalence, 133

Gajria, M., 56
Galarza, A., 136
Galin, R. S., 105
Gallagher, J., 100, 103, 107
Gao, X., 16
Garcia, E., 138
Garcia, G. E., 14
Garcia, G. N., 121
Gardner, H., 4–5
Geisinger, K. F., 5–6, 37, 45, 49–50, 63, 127, 133, 134
Glaser, S., 30, 87, 88
Goals 2000: Educate America Act (1994), 6, 8, 32–33, 143
Goertz, M. E., 127
Goh, D. S., 22, 120, 135, 137

Goldstein, A., 52
Gomez, E. L., 161
Gomez, J., 32
Gonzalez, D., 136
Gordon, R. P., 30, 87, 88
Graduate Record Examination (GRE), 69–72, 75–78, 93–94
Graham, S., 101, 102, 108, 115
Gredler, M. E., 13
Gregory, R. J., 63
Grenick, C., 64, 122, 124, 126
Grise, P., 72, 114
Gronlund, N. E., 154
Group tests, 25–26
Group work, 153
Guillemard, L., 136
Gustke, C., 162

Hafner, A., 7
Hakuta, K., 52
Hamayan, E. V., 149
Hambleton, R. K., 135
Hamlett, C., 73, 76
Hanley, T. V., 8, 33
Hansen, J-I. C., 133
Harniss, M., 72, 114
Harris, S., 85
Harste, J., 144
Hatfield, M. M., 155
Hauser, R. M., 12, 40, 125–126, 132
Hearing impairment, 20, 86–89
Heath, B., 72, 114
Hedlund, P., 138
Heinze, K., 46, 54, 130
Hemrick, M. A., 56
Henning-Stout, M., 145
Herman, J. L., 145, 159, 162
Heubert, J. P., 12, 40, 125–126, 132
High-order thinking skills, 145
High-stakes testing, 7–8
Hightower, M. M., 9
Hishinuma, E. S., 40
Hollenbeck, K., 72, 114
Homestead, E., 157
Homles, D., 138
Hopstock, P. J., 64, 122, 124, 126
Horton, S. W., 101, 102, 108, 115
Hotto, S. A., 86

Hughes, S., 144, 146, 149, 151, 153–156
Hui, C. H., 133
Hurley, C., 84, 88, 92, 94, 112, 113, 114

IDEA Language Proficiency Test (IPT), 126
Improving America's Schools Act (1994), 6, 21–22, 31, 32, 119
Inclusive education reform, 10–12
Individual Education Program (IEP), 4, 47, 48, 74, 107
Individualized accommodations, 39
Individuals with Disabilities Education Act (IDEA) of 1990, 10, 20, 30, 31, 46, 61–62, 83, 87, 90, 109, 143
Amendments of 1997, 10, 12–13, 14, 30, 31, 55, 99, 102, 109
Individual tests, 25
Instructional decisions, 4
Instructional Objectives Exchange (IOX) Basic Skill Test: Reading, 73, 113–115
Internal structure, validity based on, 67–68
Interpreters, 135–137
Interrater reliability, 159
Interventional decisions, 4
Interviews, 14, 155
Iowa Test of Basic Skills (ITBS), 76, 94, 113
Item-test correlations, 68

Jalongo, M. R., 28
Jamie, M., 104, 105
Jayanthi, M., 53, 54, 57
Jirele, T., 70, 71
Johnson, C. M., 104, 105
Johnson, D. R., 10
Johnston, R. C., 51, 54
Jorgenson, O., 10
Journals, 154–155

Kanjee, A., 135
Kaplan, B. A., 70, 71, 94

Karns, K., 73
Kauffman, J., 109
Kearns, J., 13
Keith, T. Z., 5–6
Kelner, L. B., 152
Kennedy, S., 13
Khathi, N., 148
Kindler, A. L., 22, 120–121, 126
Kirk, S., 100, 103, 107
Kleinert, H., 13
Klotz, M. B., 33
Kouzekanani, K., 58–59
Kratochwill, T. R., 74, 78
Kretschmer, R. E., 121
Kubiszyn, T., 6, 26, 148

LaCelle-Peterson, M. W., 7, 9, 22–23, 64, 121, 122, 147
Lachat, M. A., 52
Lagurada, K. G., 9
Lam, T. C. M., 12, 14, 28, 38, 122, 123, 126, 128
Language Assessment Battery (LAB), 126, 128
Language Assessment Scales (LAS), 126
Language dominance, 124
Language impairment, 21
Large-scale testing programs, 7–8, 12–13. See also Accommodations for diverse learners
Lashway, L., 7
Leal, D., 85–86
Learning disability (LD), 21, 58–59, 73–78, 98–102
Learning logs, 154–155
Learning products, 153
Lee, S., 5–6
Le Floch, K. C., 127
Legg, S. M., 158, 159
Lehman, I. J., 66
Li, C., 126
Liebars, C. S., 151, 154–155
Lifson, S., 28
Limited English Proficient (LEP). See English language learners (ELLs)
Limits, testing of, 44
Linn, R. L., 159
Liu, K., 39, 41, 46, 52–55, 129–131, 137–139

Lloyd, B. H., 76, 91–92, 94, 100, 113
Loop, C., 21
Lopez, E. C., 136, 137
Louisiana, 127
Lovitt, T. C., 101, 102, 108, 115
Low achieving (LA) students, 58–59
Lucker, G. W., 5–6

MacArthur, C. A., 101, 102, 108, 115
Maculaitis Assessment Program, 126
Malarz, L., 11
Martino, J., 51
McCarthy, R., 104, 105
McGinnis, K., 157
McGrew, K. S., 38, 54
McKevitt, B. C., 74, 78
McPeek, D., 31
Mehrens, W. A., 30, 66
Mendez, Y., 22, 120
Menken, K., 9, 131
Mental retardation, 21, 102–105
Messick, S., 64
Metric equivalence, 133
Meyer, C., 149
Michigan, 127
Mick, L. B., 73, 113–114
Miller, D. M., 158, 159
Minimum competency test (MCT), 73
Minnesota, 130–131
Morris, C., 76
Moya, S. S., 146, 149–150, 158
Multiple-choice tests, 14
Multiple disabilities, 21, 90–91
Munger, G. F., 76, 91–92, 94, 100, 113
Murfin, P., 76

National Assessment of Educational Progress (NAEP), 54, 131–132
National Association of School Psychologists, 33, 98
National Center for Health Statistics, 86
National Center for Learning Disabilities, 98, 99

National Center on Educational Outcomes (NCEO), 112
National Commission on Excellence in Education, 6
National Council of Teachers of Mathematics (NCTM), 9
National Council on Measurement in Education (NCME), 2–3, 14, 24, 25, 29, 38, 40, 44, 46, 50, 65–69, 78–79, 122, 135, 140
National Urban League, 9
Nation at Risk, A, 6
Naturalistic observation, 14
Navarrette, C., 162
NCME. See National Council on Measurement in Education (NCME)
Nelson-Denny Reading Test (NDRT), 76–77
New Jersey, 132–133
New York, 132–133
New York State Education Department, 29, 47, 84, 88, 92, 100, 104, 107, 111
Nickerson, B., 138
No Child Left Behind Act (2001), 12–13, 22, 31–33, 55, 61–62
Norm-referenced tests (NRT), 14, 26–27, 28
North Central Regional Educational Laboratory, 54
Novatkoski, I., 67, 70
Nuttall, E., 126

Observations, 153–154
Ochoa, S. H., 136
O'Keeffe, J., 20
Olgum, F., 52
Olsen, K., 51, 147
Olsen, L., 7
Olson, J., 52
O'Malley, J. M., 9, 132–133, 145, 146, 148–151, 158
Open-ended reflection, 155
Oppositional defiant disorder (ODD), 105, 109–110

Oral assessment, 152–153
Orfield, G., 9–10
Orthopedic impairment, 21
Other health impairment, 21, 90, 105

Parades-Scribner, A., 137
Passman, R., 10
Pate, P. E., 157
Payne, D. A., 104, 105
Perez-Hogan, C. A., 128, 129
Performance assessment, 16, 144, 148–149, 159
Performance standards, 6
Performance tasks, 151–152
Perlman, C., 100, 113
Phillips, S. E., 100, 112
Physical disabilities, 21, 89–93
Pine, J., 158
Pitoniak, M. J., 68, 70
Placement decisions, 3–4
Policies and practices
  on reporting assessment results, 54–55
  on use of testing accommodations, 53–54
Polloway, E. A., 53, 54, 57
Pomps, D., 52
Popham, W. J., 2, 150, 157
Portfolio assessment, 16, 144, 149–151, 155–156
Portions of test, accommodations using, 43–44, 89
Pottebaum, S. M., 5–6
Powers, D. E., 93–94
Power tests, 26
Presentation format, modification of, 42, 85–86, 89, 92–93, 101, 105, 108, 111–112, 113–115, 129
Price, J., 155
Problem solving, 16
Program evaluation decisions, 4–5
Putnam, M. L., 57

Quality of education, 9

Ragosta, M., 70, 71, 84, 93–94
Ranseen, J. D., 31, 43, 48–49
Reasonable accommodations, 48–49

Rehabilitation Act (1973), 30, 62
  Section 504, 20, 47–48, 62, 92, 107
Reiman, J., 89
Reimers, T. M., 5–6
Reliability, 14, 25, 63–64, 69–71, 158–159
Reporting assessment data, 51–52, 54–55, 78–79
Requested accommodations, 48–49
Reschly, D. J., 9, 51
Research, on
  accommodations, 52–59, 93–94, 112–115
Response format, modification of, 42, 86, 89, 93, 101–102, 108, 113–115, 129
Response journals, 154–155
Response processes, validity based on, 66–67
Rhodes, N., 146, 150–156
Rivera, C., 7, 9, 22–23, 54, 64, 121, 122, 127, 129, 130, 132, 137–138, 147
Robison, L. M., 105
Rock, D. A., 67, 70, 71, 93–94
Rooney, M. E., 136
Ross, G., 76
Royer, J. M., 68, 70
Rubin, D. B., 75
Rudner, L. M., 145
Ruhland, A., 130, 131, 137–138
Runyan, M. K., 77

Saigh, P. A., 104, 105
Salend, S. J., 56
Salisbury, C. L., 12
Salvia, J., 8, 82, 86, 90–91
Sattler, J., 44, 82, 84, 86, 88, 89, 91–93, 104, 105, 110, 111
Sauter, D. L., 31
Sax, G., 63
Scheduling, modification of, 42–43, 85, 88–89, 92, 101, 104–105, 107–108, 111, 113, 129, 130–131
Schildroth, A. N., 86
Schmidt, J. J., 24–25

Scholastic Aptitude Test (SAT), 69–72, 75–78, 84, 93–94, 113
Schrag, P., 10
Schulte, A. C., 5
Schumm, J. S., 58–59, 103, 104, 108, 111, 112
Sclar, D. A., 105
Scott, D. L., 28, 53, 55
Scribner, A. P., 121
Scruggs, T. E., 28, 114
Second-language Learners. See English language learners (ELLs)
Section 504 Accommodation Plan (504 Plan), 20, 47–48, 62, 92, 107
Seidel, D., 76
Selection decisions, 5
Self-assessment of students, 145–146, 160
Setting, modification of, 41–42, 84–85, 88, 92, 100, 104, 107, 111, 129, 130–131
Shank, M., 85–86
Shaul, M. S., 7, 120, 146
Shavelson, R. J., 16, 158
Short, D., 156
Shriner, J. G., 54
Shulman, E. L., 125, 126, 139
Silverstein, B., 10–11, 29–31, 41, 55
Siskind, T. G., 41, 56
Skaer, T. L., 105
Smith, M. L., 9
Smith, S., 85–86
Snyder, E. D., 12
Solomon, J., 146, 150–156
Southern Regional Education Board, 7
Specific learning disability, 21
Speech impairment, 21
Speed tests, 26
Spenciner, L. J., 23
Spicuzza, R., 41, 46, 53–55, 129–131, 137–139
Spicuzza, T., 84, 88, 92, 94, 112–114
Spiegel, A. N., 54
Spinelli, C., 107
Stallings, C. F., 5

Standardized tests, 1. *See also* Accommodations for diverse learners; Tests and testing
  characteristics of, 24–25
  diverse learners and, 62–63
  types of, 25–27
Standards-based education reform, 5–10, 12–13
Standards for Educational and Psychological Testing (AERA, APA, & NCME), 2–3, 8, 10, 14, 24, 25, 29, 38, 40, 44–46, 50, 65–69, 78–79, 122, 135, 140
Stansfield, C., 129
Statewide assessments, 72–73. *See also names of specific states*
Steinberg, R., 5–6
Stevenson, H. W., 5–6
Stiggins, R. J., 148, 155, 156, 161
Stigler, J. W., 5–6
Students of diverse linguistic backgrounds. *See* English language learners (ELLs)
Students with disabilities. *See also* Accommodations for diverse learners; Diverse learners
  defined, 20–21
  legislation pertaining to, 30–31
Stump, K., 30, 87, 88
Substitute tests, accommodations using, 43–44
Sudweeks, R. R., 4, 148
Sullivan, P. M., 89
Supovitz, J. A., 14, 122, 145, 160
Sweet, D., 148
Sweeting, C. M., 137
Swierzbin, B., 39, 129

Tannenbaum, J. E., 156, 160
Tapper, R., 8, 10
Task reliability, 158–159
Taylor, J., 104

Teacher-made classroom measures, 156
Terrell, F., 104
Terrell, S. L., 104
Test adaptation, 29
Test content, validity based on, 66
Test of English as a Foreign Language (TOEFL), 76–77
Tests and testing. *See also* Standardized tests
  assessment versus, 2–3
  education uses of, 3–5
  reducing bias in, 14–15
  testing, defined, 2
Thorndike, E. L., 1
Thurlow, M. L., 7, 8, 10–13, 28–31, 38, 39, 41, 46, 51–55, 84, 88, 92, 94, 112–114, 129–131, 137–139, 147
Timing, modification of, 42–43, 75–78, 85, 88–89, 92, 101, 104–105, 107–108, 111, 113, 129, 130
Tindal, G., 72, 84, 88, 92, 114
Tirozzi, G. N., 6–8
Tolfa-Veit, D., 114
Translation, 130–131, 132–135
Translation equivalence, 133
Traumatic brain injury, 21
Travis, J. E., 146, 149, 155
Triandis, H. C., 133
Turnbull, A., 85–86
Turnbull, R., 85–86

U.S. Department of Commerce, 121
U.S. Department of Education, 11, 32, 82, 89, 109, 138
U.S. Department of Health, Education, and Welfare, 30
Urbina, S., 25, 62
Uro, G., 6–8

Valdez-Pierce, L., 9, 132–133, 145, 148, 150, 151
Validation research, 134

Validity, 14, 25, 28, 64–71, 159–160
Vanderwood, M., 38, 54
Vandosdall, R., 10
Vaughn, S., 58–59, 103, 104, 108, 111, 112
Vermont, 161
Villwock, D. N., 5
Vincent, C., 7, 54, 127, 129, 130, 132, 137–138, 147
Visual impairment. *See* Blindness and visual impairment

Walton, J. R., 126
Ward, J., 9–10
Wechsler Intelligence Scale for Children-Revised (WISC-R), 104
Weise, A-M., 138
Wendler, C., 84
Werts, M. G., 12
White, K. R., 4, 148
Wichard, S. M., 5
Wild, C. L., 75
Wilen, D. K., 136, 137
Will, M., 11–12
Willingham, W., 30, 93–94
Wilson, B. L., 10
Wolery, M., 12
Wood, J., 100, 113
Woodcock-Munoz Language Survey (Woodcock-Munoz), 126
Work samples, 161
Worthen, B. R., 4, 14, 144–145, 148, 159, 161
Writing samples, 14

Yansen, E. A., 125, 126, 139
Young, R. M., 104, 105
Ysseldyke, J. E., 7–13, 28–31, 38, 41, 51, 53–55, 82, 86, 90–91, 147
Yu, J. Y., 135

Zehler, A. M., 64, 122, 124, 126
Zupnik, S., 22, 120